How Schools Transform

Also available from Bloomsbury

Transforming Schools: Creativity, Critical Reflection, Communication, Collaboration, Miranda Jefferson and Michael Anderson

Transforming Education: Reimagining Learning, Pedagogy and Curriculum, Miranda Jefferson and Michael Anderson

Teacher Agency: An Ecological Approach, Mark Priestley, Gert Biesta and Sarah Robinson

Reflective Teaching in Secondary Schools, Andrew Pollard and Caroline Daly with Katharine Burn, Steve Higgins, Aileen Kennedy, Margaret Mulholland, Jo Fraser-Pearce, Mary Richardson, Dominic Wyse and John Yandell

How Schools Transform

Practices, Research and Actions that Change Schools

Edited by Michael Anderson and Miranda Jefferson

BLOOMSBURY ACADEMIC
LONDON • NEW YORK • OXFORD • NEW DELHI • SYDNEY

BLOOMSBURY ACADEMIC

Bloomsbury Publishing Plc

50 Bedford Square, London, WC1B 3DP, UK

1385 Broadway, New York, NY 10018, USA

29 Earlsfort Terrace, Dublin 2, Ireland

BLOOMSBURY, BLOOMSBURY ACADEMIC and the Diana logo are trademarks of Bloomsbury Publishing Plc

First published in Great Britain 2024

Copyright © Michael Anderson and Miranda Jefferson, 2024

Michael Anderson and Miranda Jefferson have asserted their right under the Copyright, Designs and Patents Act, 1988, to be identified as Editors of this work.

Cover image © shunli zhao via Getty Images

All rights reserved. No part of this publication may be reproduced or transmitted in any form or by any means, electronic or mechanical, including photocopying, recording, or any information storage or retrieval system, without prior permission in writing from the publishers.

Bloomsbury Publishing Plc does not have any control over, or responsibility for, any third-party websites referred to or in this book. All internet addresses given in this book were correct at the time of going to press. The author and publisher regret any inconvenience caused if addresses have changed or sites have ceased to exist, but can accept no responsibility for any such changes.

A catalogue record for this book is available from the British Library.

Library of Congress Control Number: 2024933916

ISBN: HB: 978-1-3502-9333-5
PB: 978-1-3502-9332-8
ePDF: 978-1-3502-9335-9
eBook: 978-1-3502-9334-2

Typeset by Deanta Global Publishing Services, Chennai, India
Printed and bound in Great Britain

To find out more about our authors and books visit www.bloomsbury.com and sign up for our newsletters.

Contents

List of Figures   vii
List of Tables   viii
List of Contributors   ix

Introduction Sleep Walking and Waking Up: How Schools Transform *Michael Anderson and Miranda Jefferson*   1

1. **Transforming Leading through Coherence** *Christine Grice and Susan Orlovich*   15
2. **Pedagogies and Politics** Drawing on the 4Cs and *Normal Pig* *Justine Bruyère and Noelle Yoo*   31
3. **Connection, Creative Chaos and Vulnerability** Reflections on Transformative Praxis *Moema Gregorzewski, Jean M Uasike Allen and Peter O'Connor*   53
4. **Transforming Pedagogy** How Do We Take the Jump? *Denise Lofts and Miranda Jefferson*   69
5. **Transforming Learning** Walking on Water *Mark Steed and Michael Anderson*   87
6. **How Schools Transform through Creative Disruption** *Mitch Ulacco and Michael Anderson*   103
7. **Time to Be Seen** Transforming Learning through Community Engagement for Children with Special Educational Needs Using Drama and Technology *Paul Sutton, Max Dean and Margaret Jones*   123

8 **Transforming Assessment** Assessing the
   'Unassessable' *Debbie Hunter and Miranda Jefferson* 139
9 **Transforming Teacher Education** The Power of Praxis and
   Inquiry *Alison Rourke and Kelly Freebody* 165
10 **Conclusion** The Threads of Transformation: Finding the
   Patterns *Miranda Jefferson and Michael Anderson* 181

Index 189

Figures

The following figures are the property of 4C Transformative Learning and are used with their kind permission 1.1, 1.2, 2.1, 4.2, 6.2, 6.4, 6.5, 6.6, 6.7 8.2, and 8.4

I.1	'Aerosol words' vanish when you try and get hold of them	4
I.2	The Learning Disposition Wheel synthesizes the capacities that develop a disposition or inherent qualities for learning and agency	6
1.1	The Leadership Wheel	22
2.1	'The Learning Prism'	33
4.1	Teaching can be compared to an extreme sport like skydiving	70
4.2	The Pedagogy Parachute (from Jefferson and Anderson's *Transforming Education*) is used by Ulladulla High School as a tool to explore and deepen their pedagogy	71
4.3	Developing pedagogic practice	74
5.1	Snowy McAlister with his iconic surfboard	88
6.1	Mountain biking is now popular in Derby, Tasmania	105
6.2	The Creativity Cascade	106
6.3	Meerkats are a metaphor in school transformation to engage the curious outsider	112
6.4	The Wonder Web	112
6.5	The Learning Disposition Wheel	114
6.6	Collaboration Circles	118
6.7	Communication Crystal	119
8.1	What motivates a child to fly a balsa wood aeroplane?	141
8.2	The Learning Disposition Wheel describes the dispositions for deeper learning	142
8.3	Grit is being determined in seeking out and persevering with challenges, and resilient when navigating setbacks or difficulties	148
8.4	The Wonder Web	149
8.5	In this diagram, D. I. Hill (1982) explains the curvilinear relationship between activation levels and the effectiveness of learning	159
9.1	The Spirals of Inquiry	170
10.1	The case studies in this book are like squares in a patchwork quilt, each story is unique but together they create patterns or threads for us to learn from	182

Tables

I.1	The 4Cs: How creativity, critical reflection, communication and collaboration drive transformation described in brief with coherence makers	7
6.1	Application of the creativity cascade to school transformation	107
8.1	An example of a teacher using the Wonder Web to frame a learning focused on grit and the building of a tower	150
8.2	Three students and their teacher reflect on the development of grit in a particular area of learning	151
10.1	A matrix for the innovation and transformation of processes and structures in schools adapted from Gary Pisanos *Creative Construction: The DNA of Sustained Innovation* (2019)	186

Contributors

Jean M. Uasike Allen is a lecturer in the Faculty of Education and Social Work at Waipapa Taumata Rau University of Auckland, New Zealand. She has a background in teaching in primary schools and universities and is passionate about education, justice and her community. Her research canvases a range of fields including health education, media representations, stereotyping, post-colonial theory, Indigenizing education, Pacific methodologies and arts-based methods. Jean is the author of numerous articles and book chapters and is a member of the Centre for Arts and Social Transformation (CAST).

Michael Anderson is a professor of education at The University of Sydney, Australia. His research and teaching focus on how leaders and organizations can transform through deep and direct engagement with creativity, critical reflection, collaboration and communication. Michael has designed and delivered MBA and EMBA and Interdisciplinary Education programmes in creativity and critical communication and presents international keynotes in these areas. Michael is co-founder and academic leader of 4C Transformative Learning.

Justine Bruyère has worked as an educator, researcher and curriculum writer for the past twenty years. As an elementary school teacher, Justine focused on engagement strategies that incorporated the arts into core curriculum subjects. Later, as a faculty member at Vanderbilt University's Peabody College, United States, Justine's research explored how critical discourse might influence authoring ideas and learner voice. More specifically, she employed arts-education teaching philosophies to breathe life into story, to engage learners in critical conversations and to foster author fluency. Today, Justine works globally as a curriculum writer and is best known for her creative approaches to learning design. Her work revolves around the intersection of simulated encounters, human-centred design and creativity in learning. These learning creations leverage the latest advancements in instructional technology while maintaining a keen focus on the unique needs of specific learners. Justine's commitment to blending research, innovation and creative practices continues to ensure that her curriculum designs are engaging, informative and transformational.

Max Dean is an applied theatre practitioner and researcher. Recent projects designed, developed and delivered by Max include *HydroSchool* (2021), a motion detection interface for Special Educational Needs and Disabled (SEND) young people to become facilitators of their own interactive sensory dramas; *Kardashev* (2022), a five player applied theatre constructivist game exploring AI and existentialism, facilitated entirely through participants mobile phones; and *Alama* (2022), which documented sacred rock art sites across Kenya in 360 video and immersive audio to form the basis of workshops with young people across Nairobi's slum districts, enabling participants to explore their own cultural heritage through drama practice. Max's research focus is in hybridizing the pedagogical approaches of participatory theatre practice with the methodologies of constructivist gaming. Max Dean is a recipient of a collaborative doctoral award from Warwick University for his research.

Kelly Freebody is a professor and Head of School at the University of Sydney, Australia. Her research focuses on drama, young people, education and social justice. Her work considers the history of ideas in the fields of drama education and theatre. Kelly was co-editor of the recent *Routledge Companion to Theatre and Young People* (2022) and is co-editor of the *Applied Theatre Research* journal. Her programme of research seeks to develop theoretical and practical understandings of the ways in which drama of/for/about social justice operates in a variety of institutional and educational settings.

Moema Gregorzewski is a research fellow at Te Rito Toi Centre for Arts and Social Transformation, Te Kura Akoranga me Te Tauwhiro Tangata Faculty of Education and Social Work, Waipapa Taumata Rau the University of Auckland, New Zealand. Her research focuses on exploring Drama Education as a catalyst for critical citizenship education and drama-based learning as a potent pedagogy for mental health education in Aotearoa New Zealand primary schools.

Christine Grice is an Australian educator. Christine's research seeks to understand what underpins pedagogical decisions in schools. Her key research interests are in leading learning, curriculum and pedagogy, using practice theory approaches. Christine has over twenty-five years of teaching and leadership experience in schools and universities. She enjoys supporting educators to connect theory and practice for purposeful leading in her research and practice. She coordinates the Master of Educational Leadership at the University of Sydney, Australia.

Debbie Hunter has been an educator for over forty years and is presently the principal of Oatley Public School, Australia. She has always had a passion for students being reflective in their learning and the authenticity of the learning. Involvement in an action research project implementing and evaluating changes in her pedagogy through a focus on student engagement enhanced her thinking. As a lead learner this passion was again ignited advocating student agency through the Transforming Schools research.

Miranda Jefferson is co-founder and director of 4C Transformative Learning. She has been involved in research and leading innovation in organizations and schools for over twenty years. Miranda works with leadership and organizations to facilitate transformation that is responsive to the challenges and opportunities of the twenty-first century. She is co-author of *Transforming Schools*, *Transforming Education* and *Transforming Organizaions*.

Margaret Jones began her career as a nursery nurse and was matron at a residential school in Worcestershire, UK. She then moved on to work part time with women and children who had experienced domestic violence. Margaret then went on to manage a UK charity Home Start in the Worcester area, offering support, friendship and practical help to families. She was the grants and fundraising manager at Fort Royal special needs primary school before retiring in 2022 and is now a school governor. She is a trustee of a number of Worcester charities supporting local residents experiencing financial hardship or homelessness by providing housing and educational opportunities as well as a board member of C&T, who she worked closely with on the Time To Be Seen project.

Denise Lofts has over twenty years experience in Australian education and has been the principal of Ulladulla High School in New South Wales, Australia, since 2013. In her role as principal Denise promotes authentic learning focused on real-world issues and helps develop students' lateral thinking and problem-solving skills. Before becoming principal, Denise worked as a teacher, head teacher and deputy principal. In 2013, Denise received the Department of Education Leadership Fellowship to research leadership skills and professional practices that support future global learning.

Peter O'Connor is an expert in applied theatre and Director of the Centre for Arts and Social Transformation (CAST), New Zealand. His work aims to create equitable societies using the arts. Peter has worked with diverse groups such as prisoners, psychiatric patients, earthquake victims and the homeless. He established the Teaspoon of Light Theatre Company, won the Arts Access Creative New Zealand Community Arts Award and developed Te Rito Toi, an online resource used in 120 countries during Covid-19. Peter leads the University of Auckland team for a mental health education programme in primary schools with the Sir John Kirwan Foundation.

Susan Orlovich is a researcher and sessional tutor at the University of Sydney, Australia, with a focus on the field of teacher practice and pedagogy. With over thirty years of experience as a teacher and Principal in diverse public schools across Sydney, New South Wales, Australia, she brings a practical knowledge and lived experience to her teaching and research. Susan holds a BEd (Primary), MEd (Curriculum Studies) and MEd (Literacy Education). Currently pursuing her PhD in teacher professional learning in the 4Cs (Communication, Collaboration, Creativity and Critical Reflection), at the University of Sydney, Susan is seeking to better understanding how the practices enacted in school settings lead to transformed teacher practice and improved student learning.

Alison Rourke is the foundation principal at Gregory Hills Public School in southwest Sydney, Australia. Having been the previous principal of Buxton Public School and Fairy Meadow Demonstration School in Wollongong, Alison brings a wealth of knowledge and twenty-nine years' experience as a teacher to lead this new school. Prior to being a principal, Alison was a deputy principal, instructional leader, highly accomplished teacher (lead accreditation) and assistant principal. Alison has been awarded a Schools Plus and Commonwealth Bank teaching fellowship in 2019 for her ability to provide expert professional learning for her staff and valuing teamwork, innovation and collaboration to improve student learning. She has also been awarded various network awards from the Department of Education. In 2020, Fairy Meadow Demonstration School was named Primary School of the Year at the Australian Education Awards.

Mark Steed has been working in education for the past thirty years and in over ten NSW public primary schools, most recently as principal of Hurstville Public School, Australia, since 2017. Mark's experience includes holding all leadership positions within primary schools over the span of his career. Holding the role of substantive principal since 2011, Mark has led five different school communities as either the long-term relieving or substantive principal during this time. From this deep experience in educational leadership, Mark has been able to establish a clear understanding of what different school communities need to be relevant, rigorous and respectful. Mark's ongoing passion and commitment to the education of young people is closely linked to the disposition of altruism, which is the profound responsibility we all hold to play a role in the betterment of society for all of its members, not just its most privileged or affluent.

Paul Sutton is the founder and artistic director of C&T. He has over thirty years experience working in the fields of educational drama, applied theatre and digital technology, working across schools, colleges, universities as well as in youth and community settings. He has worked with many arts, media and cultural organizations, including Arts Council England, the BBC, the Royal Central School of Speech and Drama and Roundabout Theater, on Broadway. For ten years he was Honorary Research Fellow at the University of Worcester. As an author he has contributed to multiple books on applied theatre and digital technology, including the Applied Theatre Reader and is Digital Editor of *Research in Drama Education: The Journal of Applied Performance*.

Mitch Ulacco is currently the P-12 Head (Middle/Senior Years) at St Eugene College in Burpengary Brisbane, Australia. Previously Mitch has work in NSW Education schools for fourteen years as English, History and Drama teacher. He held many positions of responsibility including head teacher – Creative Arts across a number of schools. In this time, he ran workshops for teacher for new syllabus programmes with a speciality in Boys Education initiatives. In 2007, he moved to Brisbane to begin his work as middle years coordinator with the primary role to introduce Year 7 to secondary. Southern Cross Catholic Scarborough was one of the first school to implement this initiative before the entire state moved Year 7 to secondary in 2015. Mitch as a passion for learning and is currently working in the space of student voice. The focus is how voice can move from voice to agency to advocacy.

Noelle Yoo is a senior analyst of the Digital and Cultural Consumer Insights at Nickelodeon dedicated to bringing joy and being a voice for children and families in the media space. Noelle's research and insights have contributed to content across the Nick, Nick Jr. And Noggin platforms. With a background in educational research and commitment to delivering culturally relevant experiences, Noelle can often be seen squeezing in some extra questions and sharing a laugh or heartfelt moment with families in research sessions. Prior to joining the Nick family, Noelle taught third grade at a Reggio Emilia School on the East Coast and served as an educational and cultural consultant at companies such as OK Play and OneFish TwoFish Consulting. In her free time, Noelle can be found looking up this week's Crumbl flavours, training jiu jitsu or spending time with her family and dogs.

Introduction
Sleep Walking and Waking Up: How Schools Transform

Michael Anderson and Miranda Jefferson

- **The 'how' of transformation** (p. 2)
- **The '99.6 per cent'** (p. 3)
- **What is the 4C approach?** (p. 3)
- **What are coherence makers?** (p. 4)
- **The 4Cs enable transformation** (p. 5)
- **What is the Learning Disposition Wheel and how is it used in education?** (p. 6)
- **How is the Learning Disposition Wheel used in schools?** (p. 10)
- **Some caveats and limitations** (p. 10)
- **Overview of chapters** (p. 11)
- **Conclusion** (p. 12)

Schools for the most part are meant to run on order and routine. The bells, the timetables and the weekly meetings all contribute to the orderly running of a complex organization and are designed to provide a sense of calm security for students, parents, teachers and leaders. In many ways, this is essential but it also comes with unintended consequences. One potential consequence is that schools can become kind of 'automatic'. The rules, routines and procedures are so ingrained and established that they become unquestioned and remain untransformed. Discussing this tendency to 'sleepwalk' through practice, psychologist Sheila Ryan encourages an 'interruption of practice' (in this case through reflective practice or as she calls it 'professional supervision'). She argues 'Supervision interrupts practice. It wakes us up to what we are doing. When we are alive to what we are doing, we wake up to what is, instead of falling asleep in the comfort stories of our routines and daily practice.'[1]

In essence this book was an invitation to contributors to pause and critically reflect on their practice, interrupt comfortable or automatic processes and attempt to describe how transformation can be made possible. For us this book was a necessary step in the explanation of what transformation looks like 'on the ground', at the chalk face, in the staff rooms and classrooms of real schools. Our intent in this book was to move beyond the 'why' and 'what' of *Transforming Schools*, *Transforming Organizations* and *Transforming Education* to the *how* of transformation in different settings, countries and contexts.

The 'how' of transformation

One of the lessons from the contributions in this book is that there is no one 'how'. The various case studies, narratives and approaches emphasize how critical context continues to be in school transformation processes. For us, case studies allow an understanding that there is no 'one size fits all' or 'silver bullet' solution for every school. Schools are variable and the chapters in this book reflect the different cultural and contextual features that make the shape, form and processes of transformation different. To explain this we often use the analogy of human DNA. We are as humans 99.6 per cent identical genetically. It is, however, the .4 per cent that differentiates us from each other.

In the same way as we might think people similar, it is tempting to think of schools as homogenous. Many of them look the same, have similar routines and approaches. They are probably substantially similar to each other. This of course allows us to speak to each other with a common understanding as educators. It is, however, the minor differences in staff, leadership, student population and many other contextual factors that make schools distinctive from each other, even within the same suburb. This is why we showcase many different schools and education contexts in this book to demonstrate that difference and illustrate that there are no silver bullets,[2] no one-size-fits-all and no roll-outs that are ever likely to be effective for the different schools in our communities.

The '99.6 per cent'

As we read over these contributions there are paradoxically perhaps some common features of transformation. The contributions here are explicitly or implicitly reliant on a foundation of collaboration, communication, critical reflection and creativity. The 4Cs remain as they have been through human development foundational to driving transformation and change in the world. There are some additional elements that are worth noticing in these chapters as well. In our view, there is a consistent focus on courageous leadership. To return to Sheila Ryan's analogy, waking up to the possibilities of transformation can be difficult. Of course, the initial imaginings can be exciting, but the real work (demonstrated in these contributions) is the grit required to change hearts and minds through persistent courageous leadership. The work of values, curriculum, pedagogy, learning, assessment transformation relies on vision, passion and skilled implementation. Our aspiration for this book was not a 'brochure for transformation' with the downsides minimized or hidden. Rather we wanted to hear and see the tangle of transformation in all its joy, difficulty and complexity. Looking over these chapters, we have achieved that in part. Perhaps more critically, what we do see here is a record of how transformation has been made possible in different places.

These stories of transformation are not intended to act as recipes. Their purpose is to inspire and suggest ways forward for others considering transforming their school, early childcare setting or organization. These are not exemplar or showcase schools but rather normal everyday places. And perhaps this is the real value of *How Schools Transform*. It dispels the persistent mythology that transformation requires special powers or special resources. Rather, it demonstrates transformation is possible in different schools at different times if the leadership, will and skills exist to make it possible. In short, transformation is possible where you teach or lead because it depends on very human capacities not superhuman powers. Transformation is an everyday occurrence. There are no heroes in these pages but there are wonderful educators who have their students thriving at the centre of their practice. People just like you. Before we preview the chapters, some discussion of the 4Cs approach may be useful.

What is the 4C approach?

Many (but not all) of the chapters in *How Schools Transform* refer explicitly or implicitly to the 4Cs or the 4C approach. Many of the schools that are engaged in these case studies have engaged with the 4Cs through the work of 4C Transformative Learning and the editors of this volume are co-founders of that organization.

The 4Cs approach uses coherence makers for the 4Cs and learning dispositions to generate an understanding of how learning, schools and organizations work. Perhaps more critically, these foundations can become the instruments of transformation for schools who have an interest in creating beneficial change for their students, teachers and leaders and everybody who engages with the school.

At the heart of the work we do with schools is the idea of transformation. The frameworks we use for this approach are called coherence makers. The coherence makers we begin with in schools (and are discussed in this book) are the Learning Disposition Wheel and the 4C coherence makers, one each for creativity, collaboration, critical reflection and communication. If you would like a comprehensive discussion of the 4Cs approach, these can be found in *Transforming Schools* and *Transforming Education*. The next section provides a selected precis of these coherence makers to contextualize some of the work in the remainder of this book.

What are coherence makers?

Coherence makers are designed to bring meaning and structure to critical concepts in education. They are schemas that organize knowledge. They are also metacognitive devices that help educators consider deeply the quality and effectiveness of their processes and strategies in learning, curriculum, pedagogy and leadership. Our coherence makers are schemas that organize knowledge, skills and understanding for educators.

Some of these words or concepts that the coherence makers are based on have become vague and undefined, becoming buzzwords or as we call them 'aerosol words' (see Figure I.1). For them to become useful and powerful again, we need to bring meaning and coherence to them so educators can understand them and put them into practice. For instance, the 4Cs creativity, critical reflection, communication and collaboration have become 'aerosol words'; they are sprayed around, they smell

Figure I.1 'Aerosol words' vanish when you try and get hold of them.

pleasant but quickly vaporize into nothing. Perhaps due to their overuse, the 4Cs as concepts have lost their meaning. Coherence makers bring structure to understanding the 4Cs to make them 'teachable' and 'learnable'.

Learning is complex, and coherence makers such as conceptual schemas provide order to complexity. The paradox of a coherence maker is that in its simplicity to make ideas clear, it also opens up ever-greater complexity. A coherence maker should not make thinking reductive, limited or procedural. For example, the simple and the complex are evident in the theorems and equations of mathematics. $E=mc^2$ (energy = mass × speed of light squared) is a seemingly simple algebraic formula that explains a profound relationship between energy and matter. While our coherence makers are not equations, nor as profound, they attempt to reveal and address the complexity of processes in education through simplicity. The 4Cs are foundational to learning and to transformation.

The 4Cs enable transformation

The 4Cs (Table I.1) are shorthand for developing the capacities for creativity, critical reflection, communication and collaboration. The 4Cs are somewhat of a paradox. They are inherent in each of us. Yet we need to develop and engage with them in our context to ensure we grow in our ability to apply them. Like a muscle, the 4Cs need exercise to strengthen. As humans, we are all capable of and depend upon creativity, critical reflection, communication and collaboration to navigate our lives whether we know it or not. Yet our ability to understand them and enact them individually and collectively determines the success or otherwise of our endeavours individually and in our communities.

The 4Cs are increasingly more critical in postnormal times of chaos, contradiction and complexity. In these times, they provide the foundational capacities that allow us as individuals and communities to respond with agility as challenges arise. In other words, rather than narrow skills, the 4Cs provide the core skills that can be adapted to any emergent or insoluble problem. How we respond to and transform out of crises will rely on our ability to communicate, collaborate, create and critically reflect.

When we work with schools their ability to collaborate, create, communicate and critically reflect determines their ability to imagine, enable and enact transformative change. Making coherence and meaning of these processes is vital and yet we expect our young people, our schools and our teachers to know what the 4Cs are and how they can be used almost by accident. An understanding and ability to enact the 4Cs can shape, unify and transform education through reimagined student and teacher learning, pedagogy, curriculum and leadership. In short, the better we understand the 4Cs, the more effective our transformative efforts will be.

Another foundational coherence maker helps educators conceptualize the dispositions required to be an effective learner. This coherence maker is called the Learning Disposition Wheel (see Figure I.2).

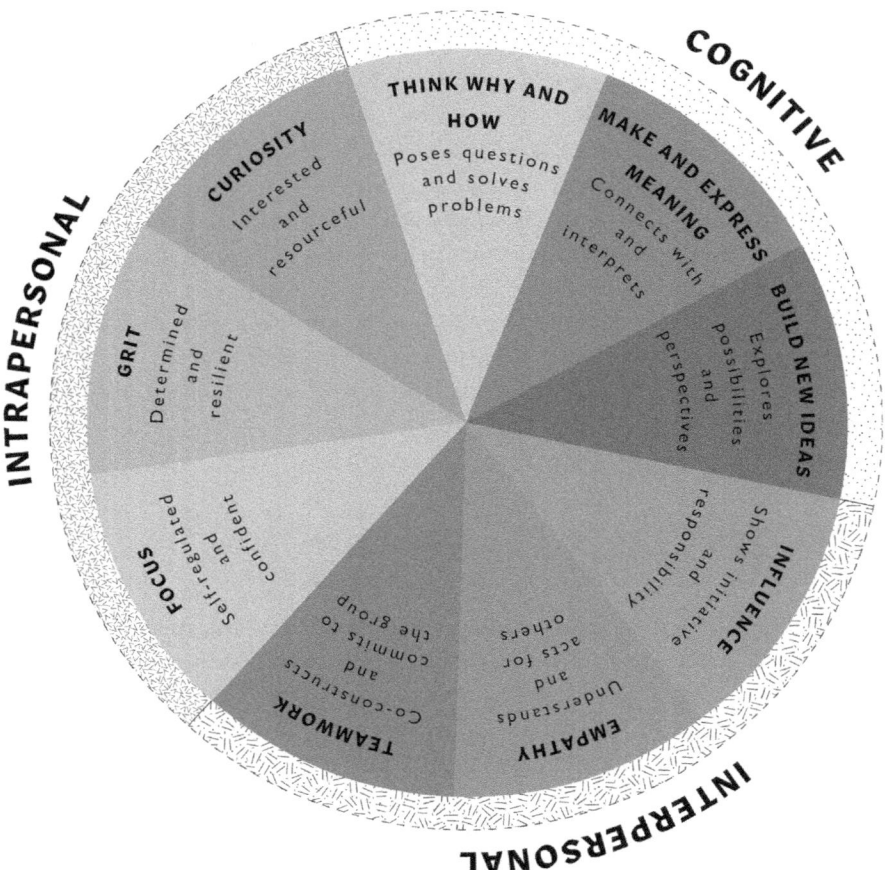

Figure I.2 The Learning Disposition Wheel synthesizes the capacities that develop a disposition or inherent qualities for learning and agency.

What is the Learning Disposition Wheel and how is it used in education?

We introduced the Learning Disposition Wheel in *Transforming Schools: Creativity, Critical Reflection, Communication, Collaboration* and the wheel continues to be used in education (at all levels) to transform learning, pedagogy and learners. The research in the US-based National Research Council's *Education for Life and Work: Developing Transferable Knowledge and Skills in the 21st Century* underpinned the wheel's development. This report draws on a substantial research base in cognitive science, educational and social psychology, economics, child and adolescent development, literacy, mathematics and science education, psychometrics,

Table I.1 The 4Cs: Creativity, critical reflection, communication and collaboration. The following figures are the property of 4C Transformative Learning and are used with their kind permission: 1.1, 1.2, 2.1, 4.2, 6.2, 6.4, 6.5, 6.6, 6.7 8.2, and 8.4.

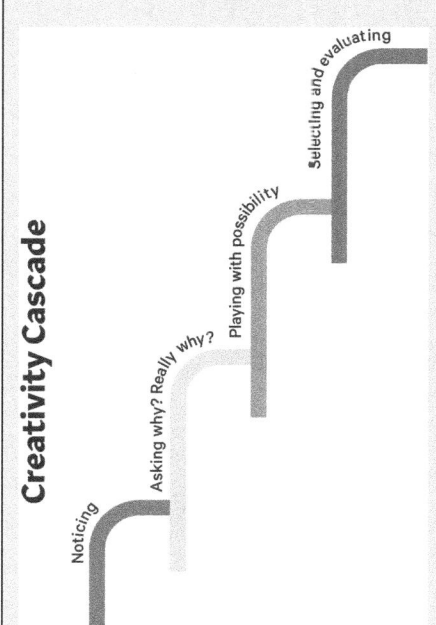

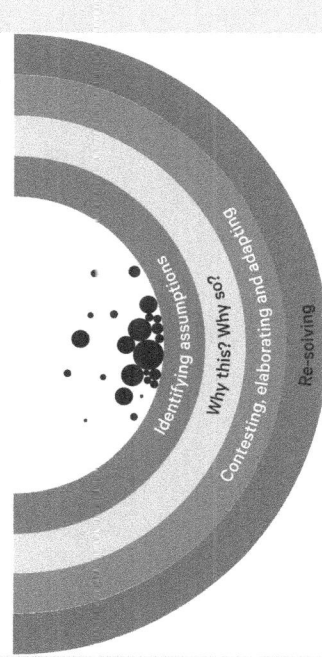

CREATIVITY
to craft and to inspire

Creativity is to imagine and problem-solve with possibilities by exploring the unusual and unexpected. It is not to fear failure, to learn from mistakes and to know there is a creative response to everything. Creativity engages our imagination to imagine, iteratively design and enact new approaches and processes in response to complex challenges. To develop creativity, educators can become meta-aware of the opportunities creativity enables to reform and reshape the process, strategies and cultures of schools. The Creativity Cascade coherence maker provides a schema for this approach (pictured here).

CRITICAL REFLECTION
to question and navigate

Critical reflection is to question, elaborate, analyse and explain. It is to develop thinking processes beyond asking 'what?' to asking 'why, how and what if?' To reflect critically is to first notice and then reflect on and resolve problems through wise action. Critical reflection asks educators to question their assumptions, reform and reframe ideas and then collaboratively reconfigure and resolve them leading to transformative action. The Critical Reflection Crucible coherence maker provides a schema for this capacity (pictured here).

(Continued)

Table I.1 (Continued)

COMMUNICATION
to voice and to message

Communication is to empower and respect all voices as authentic. Communication is about conveying messages and receiving them. Communication is critical in transformation as it allows educators to develop values, strategies and plans collaboratively and then convey that to the school community and into other networks. The Communication Crystal Coherence Maker provides a schema for this capacity (pictured here).

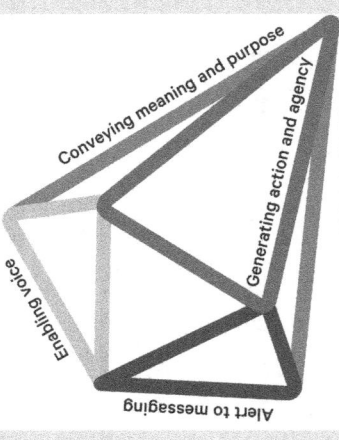

COLLABORATION
to co-construct and challenge

Collaboration is engaging, negotiating and celebrating all participants to develop understandings and skills. Collaboration requires trust and openness to challenging and being challenged by others. Educators require collaboration to build and sustain relationships that drive reimagined processes in learning, pedagogy and curriculum. The Collaboration Circles Coherence Maker provides a schema for this capacity (pictured here).

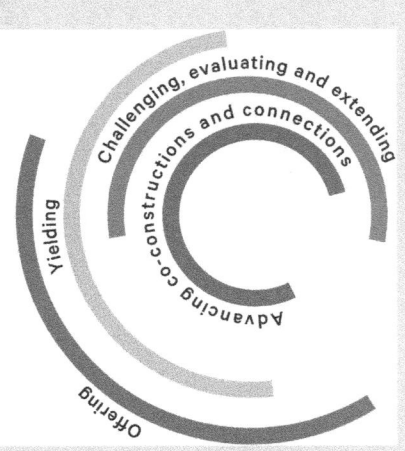

educational technology and human resource development. The report identifies three broad domains for capacities in learning:

- The cognitive – the capacity to think and reason.
- The intrapersonal – the capacity to self-regulate emotions and behaviours.
- The interpersonal – the capacity to relate to others.

The NRC report developed a classification scheme to describe human competencies by aligning a content analysis of twenty-first-century skills with taxonomies of cognitive, intrapersonal and interpersonal skills and abilities from differential psychology (systems that classify human behaviour and their underlying processes). The report recognized that twenty-first-century skills are not new, unique skills that are suddenly of value today. They argue they are competencies or skills that have been essential to realizing human potential for centuries.

From the report's research and classification scheme, we developed a metalanguage for the wheel based on consultation with teachers, students and parents in our praxis. In the Learning Disposition Wheel, the capacities in the three domains are:

- Cognitive
  - Think why and how (poses questions and solves problems)
  - Make and express meaning (connects with and interprets)
  - Build new ideas (explores possibilities and perspectives)
- Intrapersonal
  - Focus (self-regulated and confident)
  - Grit (determined and resilient)
  - Curiosity (interested and resourceful)
- Interpersonal
  - Influence (shows initiative and responsibility)
  - Empathy (understands and acts for others)
  - Teamwork (co-constructs and commits to the group)

The National Research Council report argues that the three domains (the cognitive, intrapersonal, interpersonal) are integrally interrelated and developed together. How we think and reason, how we manage our emotions and how we relate to others are mutually self-reinforcing. How we develop curiosity, for instance, depends upon all the other dispositions. Self-Determination Theory that is evident in the wheel also illustrates how competence (the cognitive), autonomy (the intrapersonal) and relatedness (the interpersonal) are inextricably interdependent. The Learning Disposition Wheel is represented as a circle to illustrate the interconnectedness and reliance each disposition has on the other. The 4C capabilities are also evident in the Learning Disposition Wheel: creativity is *build new ideas*, critical reflection is *think why and how*, communication is *make and express meaning* and collaboration is *teamwork*. The dispositions in the wheel only make sense when they are physically experienced, practised and embedded as a continually evolving way of being in learning and pedagogy.

How is the Learning Disposition Wheel used in schools?

The Learning Disposition Wheel is used to focus on developing appropriate and effective pedagogy, curriculum and assessment. The wheel can be a diagnostic, feedback reporting and evaluation tool where teachers can deeply notice and analyse the strengths and yet-to-be strengths of learners as a classroom cohort or as individuals. This informs and shapes pedagogy and curriculum learning design. Identified strengths in the wheel are used to build yet-to-be strengths and focusing on the yet-to-be strengths begins to develop other dispositions in the wheel.

For instance, if pedagogy is used to develop *focus* (self-regulation and confidence), other skills such as *empathy* (understanding and acting for others) or *make and express meaning* (connecting with and interpreting) may be developed. If *teamwork* is identified as a yet-to-be strength but learning in the class reveals that a lack of *empathy* is affecting their capacity to collaborate, the pedagogical focus turns to empathy to strengthen teamwork. The dispositions are taught and learnt explicitly through curriculum and pedagogy that facilitate self-direction, self-regulation and agency. Critically, the Learning Disposition Wheel provides a common language in schools and organizations to talk about learners, learning and agency building. As we overview the chapters in this book, we would like to outline some ways to understand the scope of this book.

Some caveats and limitations

In the chapter 'Pedagogies and Politics: Drawing on the 4Cs – Normal Pig', authors Justine Bruyère and Noelle Yoo comment 'we did not earn a medal, a trophy, or win any awards, our efforts did result in a critical hope for classrooms – a sign of what could be'. We cannot think of a better way to sum up our intention for this book. These contributions are not intended to be exemplars necessarily. Rather, they are designed to show the real struggles and joys of transformation through the eyes of those trying to make hopeful change. The work detailed in these chapters is not necessarily transferrable to other contexts, but they are offered in the hope that you will find the insights useful as you pursue your own tangled path to transformation. Some of the case study schools have gone backwards, some have leapt forward and some have plateaued. Such is the nature of transformation. All they offer is a way to understand how a group of educators worked to make transformation possible.

These contributions also demonstrate that transformation comes in all shapes and sizes. As we suggested earlier, it is the .4 per cent that makes all the difference. In these pages, you will see that in reality. The contexts of the case study schools and programmes demonstrate through their glorious inherent variation and diversity that transformation cannot be rolled out because our cultures and approaches differ and so must our approach to transformation. That is worth keeping in mind as you dive into the rich variety of these chapters that we will preview now.

Overview of chapters

We open our book with a discussion of how leadership can drive beneficial educational change. In the opening chapter. 'Transforming Leading Through Coherence' former school Principal Susan Orlovich and Educational Leadership Researcher Christine Grice explore leadership learning through building coherent and shared understandings at Miranda North Public School in NSW, Australia. They draw on 4C coherence makers as a way to build and develop leadership capability across all staff. In the next chapter, 'Pedagogies and Politics: Drawing on the 4Cs', we change national contexts to consider how embodiment might be used in learning as a tool for critical reflection. In this chapter, Educators Justine Bruyère and Noelle Yoo explore difficult subjects through the Learning Prism.[3] Their chapter highlights the paradox of struggle and hope that is a hallmark of this kind of work.

'Connection, Creative Chaos and Vulnerability: Reflections on Transformative Praxis' takes us to Aotearoa to explore Mitey, a whole-school professional learning approach to mental health. Researchers and arts practitioners Moema Gregorzewski, Jean M Uasike Allen and Peter O'Connor discuss the programme and its role in bringing Freire's definition of transformation; an interplay between action and reflection, to life. Their chapter reminds us that all transformation is only possible through affective human connection.

Returning to Australia, Denise Lofts, Principal and Miranda Jefferson, Co-Founder of 4C Transformative Learning and co-editor of this book, explore how teachers can engage in professional learning that supports them examine pedagogy. 'Transforming Pedagogy: How Do We Take The Jump?' considers how pedagogy can be understood more deeply. It further explores how schools can be transformed by connecting the practice and theory of pedagogy with the person of the teacher and the person of the student. The chapter explores the experience of Ulladulla High School on the NSW South Coast and how teachers and leaders engaged in deep, collaborative and critically reflective learning designed to support their ongoing growth and identity as professionals and a transformative change in teaching and learning. Another approach that engages with collaborative practice is explored in the next chapter, 'Transforming Learning as Walking on Water'.

Principal of Hurstville Public School (HPS), Mark Steed, and Michael Anderson, co-editor of this collection and co-founder of 4C Transformative Learning, explain how collaborative practice made beneficial change possible. HPS used the Communities of Practice[4] approach to transform attitudes, behaviour and practices. The chapter concludes with a discussion of the five key drivers that made transformation possible.

In the next chapter, Mitch Ulacco, P-12 Head at St Eugene College, and Michael Anderson discuss an approach to shifting school culture towards transformation in 'How Schools Transform Through Creative Disruption'. At St Eugene a process of Creative Disruption was employed through learning festivals to expose teachers and leaders to the possibilities of change. They conclude their chapter by observing that Creative Disruption provides a pause and a space for critical reflection on teaching and learning, curriculum, values and other aspects of school culture. Moving to the UK, Paul Sutton, founder of C&T, Max Dean, assistant director of C&T, and Margaret Jones, former administrator at Fort Royal Community Primary School in Worcester, UK, explore the theme of hope. 'Time to Be Seen: Transforming Learning Through Community Engagement for Children with Special Educational Needs Using Drama and Technology' exemplifies how hope can become action. Engaging with the Prospero digital learning platform, they provide transformative and innovative experiences for students with special needs at Fort Royal School. This blending of technology, drama and learning provides a powerful way to engage learners in transformative experiences.

Our next chapter explores one of the unproductive trends in schooling over the last few decades: the division of learning and assessment. In our view, assessment should be integrated fully with learning in schools to ensure the 'cart' doesn't 'lead the horse'. In 'Transforming Assessment: Assessing the "Unassessable"' Debbie Hunter, principal of Oatley Public School, and Miranda Jefferson explore how dispositions for learning such as grit and curiosity can be assessed, and how the way learning is assessed can foster self-regulatory motivation to learn. The chapter challenges a few myths in education, such as learning and assessment are separate, and that the dispositions for learning cannot be assessed. They conclude that transforming assessment practices can build agency in students and teachers. In the next chapter, Principal Alison Rourke and Teacher Educator Kelly Freebody discuss how inquiry can form the basis of ongoing teacher education. 'Transforming Teacher Education: The Power of Praxis and Inquiry' explores the 4Cs approach through a case study of Fairy Meadow Demonstration School in NSW, Australia. They examine the role of unlearning and building new understandings through a Spirals of Inquiry[5] approach. In the final chapter, Miranda Jefferson and Michael Anderson offer some reflections on the themes that have emerged from this collection of discussions on the 'how' of transformation.

Conclusion

These stories confirm that transformation is joyous, complex and at times difficult, but it is achievable. Schools can change, organizations can achieve growth. This matters because our schools are the place where possibility is discovered, imaginations are invigorated and character is formed. If we are to have productive communities (in all senses of that word), we require our schools to not sleepwalk but to be awake to the possibilities of creative interruptions to ensure they are fit for purpose for today and tomorrow.

Notes

1. S. Ryan, 'Mindful Supervision', in *Passionate Supervision*, ed. P. Simon (London: Jessica Kingsley, 2008), 71.
2. M. Jefferson and M. Anderson, *Transforming Education: Reimagining Learning, Pedagogy and Curriculum* (London: Bloomsbury Publishing, 2021).
3. M. Jefferson and M. Anderson, *Transforming Schools: Creativity, Critical Reflection, Communication, Collaboration* (London: Bloomsbury Publishing, 2017).
4. J. Lave and E. Wenger, 'Learning and Pedagogy in Communities of Practice', in *Learners and Pedagogy*, eds. J. Leach and B. Moon (London: The Open University, 1999), 21–33.
5. H. Timperley, L. Kaser, and J. Halbert, *A Framework for Transforming Learning in Schools: Innovation and the Spiral of Inquiry*, Vol. 234 (Melbourne: Centre for Strategic Education, 2014).

References

Chesner, A., S. Ryan, J. Read, D. Owen, J. Hewson, J. Wilmot, J. Wilmot, L. Zografou, J. Encke, and P. Hawkins 2007. *Passionate Supervision*. London: Jessica Kingsley Publishers.

Jefferson, M. and M. Anderson 2017. *Transforming Schools: Creativity, Critical Reflection, Communication, Collaboration*. London: Bloomsbury Publishing.

Jefferson, M. and M. Anderson 2021. *Transforming Education: Reimagining Learning, Pedagogy and Curriculum*. London: Bloomsbury Publishing.

Lave, J. and E. Wenger, 1999. 'Learning and Pedagogy in Communities of Practice'. In J. Leach and B. Moon (eds.), *Learners and Pedagogy*, 21–33. London: Sage Publications

Pellegrino, J. W. 2017. 'Teaching, Learning and Assessing 21st Century Skills'. In *Pedagogical Knowledge and the Changing Nature of the Teaching Profession*, 223–51. OECD Publishing. https://doi.org/10.1787/9789264270695-12-en.

Sardar, Z. 2010. 'Welcome to Postnormal Times'. *Futures* 42(5): 435–44.

Timperley, H., L. Kaser, and J. Halbert 2014. *A Framework for Transforming Learning in Schools: Innovation and the Spiral of Inquiry* (Vol. 234). Melbourne: Centre for Strategic Education.

Transforming Leading through Coherence

Christine Grice and Susan Orlovich

1

Coherence in critical reflection to identify shared vision and values (p. 18)

Making coherence of collaboration (p. 20)

Coherence in reflective practice using the Leadership Wheel (p. 21)

Structuring pedagogical change in practice through the coherence makers (p. 24)

Ways forward: Leading and sustaining transformation as a process (p. 27)

Leading learning in a school takes creativity, collaboration, communication and critical reflection. Leading is not the solo act of a principal but grows and develops within and between teams. This chapter explores how reflective practice is a foundational team process for imagining and enacting transformative practices. Drawing on the work of our case study school, Miranda North Public School, in Sydney, Australia, we provide insights into the practices outlined in the 4C trilogy of books[1] and how the Leadership Wheel coherence maker[2] was used to support the development of leadership for transformation. The chapter also examines how leadership teams may use coherence makers to support critical reflection and collaboration in pedagogical transformation. Our case study begins with a metaphor for transformation that emerged from the school's community garden.

In mid-2017, an encounter between the principal, a parent and her child in the school playground germinated the idea of building a community garden that could transform part of the school into a green space that nurtured food, one which the community could collectively harvest and enjoy. Before long, a small group of interested gardeners had become focused on what a reimagined playground could look like and began asking, who could it feed and nurture? What tools and learning about plants and gardening practices are needed? How do we keep the garden healthy and thriving? These questions stimulated the team's desire to consider what was already in existence and imagine what could be created.

So, the school sourced gardening tools and the student and community gardeners began work in imagining and creating their community garden. The garden team were curious to explore how they might transform their playground and, at the same time, were building their capabilities for establishing and nurturing a sustainable vegetable garden. However, the establishment of the garden had its challenges. The team soon realized that they each brought different strengths or yet-to-be strengths to the garden project, they had differing ideas about what the garden could look like and they didn't yet share a common view of what they wanted to achieve. To address these challenges, the team set to designing a garden plan that illustrated their shared vision of the garden. They identified what they needed to learn and skills they need to develop for growing vegetables and committed to coming together regularly to reflect on how the garden was developing and make changes to meet emergent needs.

It was over several months of collaboration and through reflection upon the developing needs of the gardeners and garden, that the team grew a thriving community garden, achieving their shared vision for a nurturing, transformed playground. The garden's success was borne of collaborative practices that identified and developed the capabilities needed for transformation of the environment, and practices that embedded ongoing reflection to ensure that the shared vision was being realized. Interestingly, the development of the community garden shared many of the elements and practices of the transformational learning journey the school was embarking upon with the 4Cs. Today, the school's living and growing playground continues to illustrate that transformation is growing, spreading and changing over time. We introduce the metaphor of the community garden to offer coherence to the case study and present the features of shared vision; collaboration; critical reflection, and leadership capability development; each of which was central to the pedagogical transformation at Miranda North Public School.

The heart of the Miranda North case study lies in the journey of transforming leading, driven by the guiding principle of coherence. It tells how school leaders recognized the imperative for a more holistic and interconnected approach to learning and how they navigated the complexities of aligning their vision, strategies and practices to provide coherence in the journey. We explore how practices that bring coherence to the process of transformation allow leadership teams to better understand the practical steps in leading change. The case study begins by examining how the leadership team started the transformation process by critically reflecting on current practices, identifying and challenging the school's underlying educational assumptions, and playing with the possibility of reimagining a learning environment that would identify and develop the capabilities needed to thrive. Next, it explores how they introduced new individual and collective practices that could build an authentic and thriving educational environment at the school. Throughout the case study we highlight how the leadership team utilized coherence makers inherent to the 4Cs approach[3] throughout the transformation process to reflect, challenge, deepen or reimagine the learning environment with individuals and teams of teachers. The chapter concludes with offering ways forward and considerations for leading and sustaining transformation as a process in other school contexts.

Miranda North Public School is a government-funded school in southern Sydney. The school serves a community characterized by high expectations for achievement and sits above the national average for measures of socio-educational advantage. In 2017, student learning and well-being data suggested that learning in the school was academically successful, and assessment measures, such as national assessments, could have pointed to maintaining the status quo in the way learning was curated and offered to students. Instead, the school wanted to move beyond attainment and grow other aspects of learning for its students.

Teachers wondered how they could foster deeper and more authentic learning experiences that would effectively equip students for their future and establish meaningful connections between school learning and the world of their students. They became curious about how they may nurture their students' learning dispositions and capabilities to thrive in their learning and life.[4] School leaders were committed to leading the transition towards a more deeply authentic learning environment; however, they were challenged by the complex task of transforming pedagogy in the school and didn't yet share a common understanding of the 4C capabilities. The leadership team also wondered about what leading capabilities they may need to develop in themselves and others to effect such change, and the individual and collective practices that could be harnessed to support the transformation journey. The leadership team's grappling with these ideas created the impetus and momentum for them to search for coherence in leading pedagogical transformation.

In the 4Cs approach, Jefferson and Anderson[5] offer a coherence maker for each of the capabilities (creativity, critical reflection, communication, collaboration). The 4C coherence makers are a conceptual schema of each of the capabilities and make visible the processes and concepts inherent in the capability that may be difficult to grasp or complex. In the transformative journey of learning at Miranda North, coherence makers played a pivotal role in providing a safe and brave space for the process of educational transformation. These coherence makers offered a scaffold that supported teachers and school leaders in navigating the complexities of aligning their vision with practical strategies and practices.

At Miranda North, the coherence makers were a critical tool for school leaders and teachers to support their reflective practice. They were instrumental in helping to reveal opportunities for deeper analysis and action. The coherence makers assisted teachers and leaders to better understand the complexity of the capability through simplicity and offered an ordering of the steps or stages in enacting the capability in ways that were commonly understood by all. In Miranda North's case, they were the lenses through which the leadership team explored the school site, examined its existing practices and analysed the arrangements that enabled or constrained the transformative practices. To focus and guide the reflection at Miranda North, they drew particularly upon the 4C coherence makers for critical reflection, collaboration and the Leadership Wheel[6] to assist them in the transformation process. Finding coherence in the transformation approach was instrumental in the change process and critical to the school's 4C journey.

Coherence in critical reflection to identify shared vision and values

Developing a shared vision and values for schooling at Miranda North was one of the early processes the leadership team and teachers explored through reflection. Although the school leaders shared some common understandings about effective teaching, learning and pedagogy, these understandings were not clearly articulated, visible or shared with others in the learning community. In starting the school transformation journey in the 4Cs, the school leaders knew that a process for identifying shared vision and values was the necessary place to begin. In leading transformation, Jefferson and Anderson[7] adopt a definition of vision as a 'shared understanding for schooling'. They describe a process to engage all participants in the development of a shared vision through 'collaborative vision making'. At Miranda North, their process for collaborative vision making aimed to establish a common understanding of and aspiration for learning across the community of students, staff and parents/carers. Once developed, the vision could be articulated and enacted through their collective practice. The leadership team valued this process as one of establishing a strong and shared foundation for beginning the transformation journey.

The school's leadership team drew upon the elements of the critical reflection coherence maker[8] as a lens to deeply notice the environment so they could identify assumptions held within the community about learning, teaching and pedagogy. Some of the assumptions included beliefs about the learning needs and interests of the students (What is it that they want students to learn?), the teaching methodologies of the teachers (What types of learning will meaningfully engage all learners?) and the school's pedagogical approach (How is learning curated for deep knowledge and transfer?). These assumptions were rarely questioned and often thought to be implicitly understood. The reflection on assumptions was followed by drawing on the critical reflection coherence maker to ask, 'Why this? Why so?' where they began to uncover and articulate the values that teachers shared for students to thrive in and beyond the school environment. By asking 'why', teachers were able to articulate the reasons they held for particular values about learning and schooling for their students, describe the vision they held for their learners and identify commonalities. Jefferson and Anderson[9] argue 'sustainable change is achieved by a team of people who are either participants in the creation of the vision or are attracted to the vision for change or both'. It was the process of articulating shared values for learning that illuminated to school leaders that a commitment to the transformation process had been achieved. There was a clear appetite for change, and it was commonly shared among the teaching team.

Educational leadership literature frequently suggests that the principal's vision drives change within a school.[10] However, a shared, co-constructed vision enables change to be authentic and owned by all. The reflection process drawn upon to develop shared vision and values was pivotal in identifying common 'big ideas' or assumptions about learning that the learners strongly valued within the community. In addition, it provided the focus and impetus for changing structural practices, teacher and student learning practices and developing partnership practices beyond the school.

For example, a common desire echoed across the community was the development of 'empowered' learners who become increasingly 'agentic' in their learning. By providing an opportunity for students, staff and community to critically reflect on why empowerment and agency were significant to each group, the school began to develop an increasingly shared idea of what learning could be at Miranda North. Similarly, the value of deep learning for all community members emerged as a shared and common feature that was profoundly cherished, as was the notion of authenticity in learning, that learning needs to be 'real' and connected to the lives of their learners. Finally, identifying the school's held assumptions about learning and interrogating why these assumptions were significant and tightly held saw the emergence of a vision statement shared among all members of the community

It became clear to teachers and school leaders that a common value of agency in learning and the curation of authentic learning experiences that enable deep learning were central themes to the school's vision and transformation journey. These themes would ultimately shape the school's inquiry in learning. Jefferson and Anderson[11] explain that inquiry allows educators to consider theory and research in their own context. Furthermore, they argue that 'inquiry empowers teachers to develop and evaluate new practices and drives contextualized responses to achieve deeper learning for students'.[12] To focus Miranda North's inquiry, the school's vision was supported by a whole-school driving question, 'How can we create authentic learning environments that empower learners to be challenged by the 4Cs and enable deep learning?' By presenting the vision as a question, an inquiry approach to the transformation was enabled and a process for problem shaping, investigation and making findings was established. As the shared vision had been collaboratively constructed, all learning community members shared the desire to achieve the common vision by seeking answers through exploring practices, reflecting on practices and action.

Developing shared vision and values was a significant and profound process, highlighting the school's collective endeavour and commitment. It provided the anchor for their transformation journey and reminded the leadership team that transforming is growing, spreading and changing over time. As a result, the leadership team revisited the vision and driving question often.

Making coherence of collaboration

We know that collaboration is necessary for enacting change in schools.[13] However, genuine collaboration is rare as change is often 'done to' rather than 'done with' people.[14] After developing the shared vision and driving question, the leadership team drew upon the collaboration circles coherence maker[15] to create a representation of the vision for change. Teachers and school leaders had shared, through critical reflection upon their practice, that they were comfortable working together cooperatively but felt less confident in enacting authentic collaboration in their stage or staff teams. Therefore, in creating their shared vision, teachers were keenly supported and guided by the stages outlined in the collaboration circles coherence maker to assist them to play, imagine and create together in ways they had not experienced before. Throughout the process, it was common to see teachers revisiting the physical representation of the Collaboration Circles and using it to guide their next steps or to revisit earlier steps when the collaboration became challenging. The coherence maker was an empowering tool that enabled the practice of collaboration to engage all teachers in a growing understanding of what it is to authentically collaborate 'with' each other.

By creating a tangible, tactile representation, teachers made visible their shared vision and amplified and clarified its meaning and key elements for all learners in the community. It allowed teachers to collectively consider what each teacher meant by terms such as 'authentic', 'empower' and 'deep' in ways that grew a shared understanding and provided impetus and enthusiasm for action. In addition, it allowed the leadership team to closely notice the elements of the vision that would benefit from further exploration and deepening of understanding.

Together, the teachers positioned the collaboratively created artefact in a central place in the school to encourage dialogue and discussion about the shared vision for transformation. This was a significant moment in the transformation journey as it signalled clarity and shared commitment to the school's direction in transforming its pedagogy. School leaders shared a sense of pride, joy and excitement and celebrated this moment as an early milestone in their 4C journey.

The 4C collaboration tools, such as the collaboration circles coherence maker,[16] enable a continuous process of working together and problem-solving. Using the coherence maker allowed teachers to consider the processes for successful collaboration as the transformation journey got underway. It did so by offering a supportive scaffold to guide teachers as they engaged in team planning, learning design and learning curation. The collaboration circles coherence maker was also used to introduce new practices that could build collegiality and agency. For example, to enable teacher voice, teachers drew upon techniques that could help structure conversations by highlighting who had spoken and allowing everyone an opportunity to contribute. To amplify the steps of the process, the leadership and stage teams used materials for each participant to 'offer' as they suggested an idea, identifying who had spoken and providing a representation of their 'offering' to the group. This practice was followed by focusing on 'yielding', where again, teachers engaged with joining and elaborating upon an offer made by an individual in the collaboration. Tactile and visible practices to support yielding included drawing on questioning scaffolds that enabled deep consideration of an individual's offering and facilitated the connection of the offer to the thinking of the individual.

The impact of employing such scaffolded practices was the opportunity for the collective group to reflect 'on' the collaborative practice while engaging 'in' the practice. An awareness of how the collaboration was being facilitated was gained, and the way participants engaged in the process was illuminated. For example, by making the practice of offering and yielding visible, by using blocks that identified which individuals had made an offering or had yielded, the leadership team could then guide reflection and 'noticing' of whose voices were heard and whose had not yet been. Such reflection built a collective awareness of the established practices within the school that had previously been invisible, including communication patterns, such as who had an opportunity to have voice enabled and who had remained silent.

According to Jefferson and Anderson:

> collaboration leads to the co-construction of something that evolves from the interdependence and mutuality of everyone's influence. Everyone in a collaborative process has a role to play, and in that role must feel equal and empowered to realise a shared and co-constructed vision. Paradoxically they should be empowered, but also feel vulnerable.[17]

As a deepened understanding of collaboration was emerging among teachers, new collaborative practices began to surface. The emergence of these new practices was apparent when teachers used the collaboration circles coherence maker as a metacognitive tool to support the collaboration of their stage teams. They did this in planning for learning and learning design as well as to guide the stage team's critical reflection upon what had been achieved in a learning project. For instance, as teachers shared a common understanding of the process or order of collaborating, they were aware of hearing all voices in the group, allowing for the offering and yielding of ideas, subsequent problem-solving and co-ownership of shared ideas. Some of these practices had already existed; however, they became more differentiated and adapted to meet new and emergent needs as they became evident in the transformation journey.

Coherence in reflective practice using the Leadership Wheel

As the school's embrace of the 4Cs approach in transformation gathered momentum, the leadership team noticed that the shared vision was well established, articulated and commonly understood within the community. They could also see, through noticing practices, that teachers and school leaders were introducing more scaffolded collaboration opportunities in stage and school teams. At the same time, however, despite some changes in teacher practice, the leadership team had a developing realization that the practices inherent in leading the transformation of pedagogy were increasingly complex, would require a shared leadership approach and could be strengthened by a deepened understanding of themselves as leaders (see Figure 1.1).

To enact a shared approach to leadership at the school, the team met regularly and engaged in ongoing reflective practice to ensure that they were adaptive and responsive to new practices and challenges as they emerged in stage teams and collectively as a school. The leadership team drew upon a coherence maker called the Leadership Wheel[18] to help make coherence of the reflective practice and provide a focus and guide for the leadership reflection. The team was committed to the ongoing reflective practice as a process to help collaboratively navigate the shifts and changes that were emerging during the transformation and embraced the wheel to describe their strengths and focus for development.

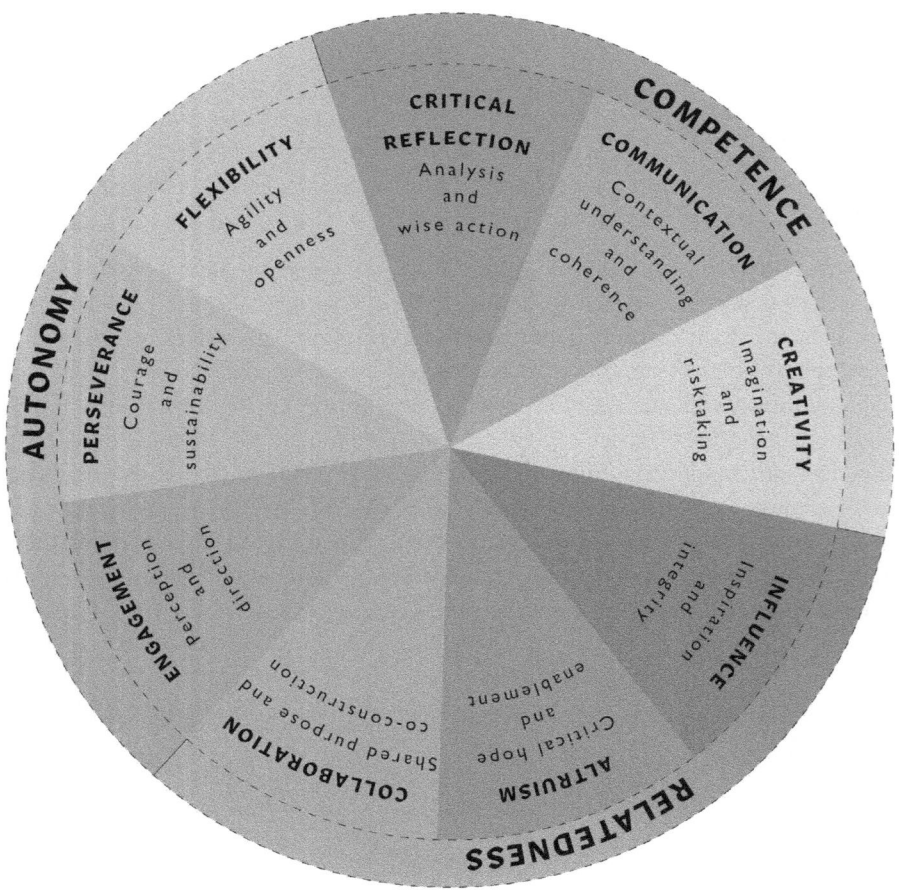

Figure 1.1 The Leadership Wheel.

The Leadership Wheel has three domains, each of which is interrelated and reflects the psychological needs of Self-Determination Theory (SDT).[19] The domains are represented on the Leadership Wheel as autonomy, relatedness and competence. According to Jefferson and Anderson,[20] each domain illuminates three capacities, which are needed to lead transformation. Further, they argue, 'the Leadership Wheel describes capacities that are learnt skills and processes that develop our sense of self-concept and the self-concept of the people we lead'.[21] The leadership team at Miranda North were both intrigued and curious about how they may learn more about their capacities and assist those they lead to develop them.

Through reflective practice using the Leadership Wheel, the leadership team considered how the leading capacities illustrated in the wheel could be developed in both them and others for personal growth and transformation to occur. For instance, they reflected on challenges that were being experienced in their stage teams and the capacities that could be developed to mitigate the challenge. Moreover, they used the capacities in the wheel as a focus for curating learning experiences for their stage and school teams. Using the Leadership Wheel enabled deep self-reflection and provided a common language to describe the attributes of competence, relatedness and autonomy. The visual and tangible nature of the Leadership Wheel allowed the connection between the capacities to be illuminated, realized and explored.

As school leaders began considering the practices that constituted the school culture, they were able to explore the relationship between their leading practices, their team's leadership capacities and the emotional, pedagogical and relational climate of the setting. In addition, regular reflection opportunities allowed each leader to critically reflect upon their leading practices, the development of their own leading dispositions and the practices which were emerging or changing within their stage or school teams. Such analysis allowed for the identification of potentially constraining practices and considering the dispositions that may be drawn upon to respond to the challenge.

For example, one leader identified that to build the collaboration capacity in her staff team; she would also need to strengthen her own capacity of 'engagement' by closely perceiving the team's needs and articulating the team's direction. Jefferson and Anderson[22] describe this approach to leadership as a 'practice of mobilising others to tackle tough challenges and create a vision for a better future' and argue that 'leadership is to diagnose what is needed in a classroom, school and community and establish a clear and structured purpose to achieve that vision'. Using the Leadership Wheel allowed the school leaders to adopt a new practice of diagnosis and action and to curate experiences in response to the diagnosis.

Furthermore, using the Leadership Wheel made visible or explicit the understanding that leading is both a capability that could be developed and a practice that may enable transformation. This realization allowed an agentic and shared approach to leading and 4C learning. The school leaders became aware that constraining leading practices, identified through critical reflection, could be replaced by practices that would foster the 4C transformation. Moreover, the reflective practice was instrumental as it allowed the individual, collective and site practices to be considered as 'ecologies of practices'[23] and the interdependent features of the site to be better understood.

Once the critical reflection had offered substantial evidence of practices that influenced and shaped the culture, the work of rethinking, reimagining and making collaborative decisions for change began. One of the places that leaders started their action was to consider the leadership capacities they needed to develop for themselves and others. For instance, a deep realization that emerged from reflective practice was that the capacity of 'engagement' could be cultivated as a practice to build 'influence', the ability to inspire and challenge others with vision and action. In addition, leaders identified that the capacity of 'influence' had emerged as a 'yet-to-be' strength of teachers through deeply reflecting on the experience of developing the shared vision.

The practice of identifying the strengths and 'yet to be' strengths of themselves and others inspired the leadership team to introduce 4C processes at the small group, stage and whole staff level to build the capacity of 'influence' in others. Collaboratively, the leadership team then planned for processes that would allow staff with a strong disposition for fostering efficacy to learn with others and provided experiences involving teamwork, learning together and collaborative classroom visits. This practice is reflected by Jefferson and Anderson[24] who describe 'an environment of collaboration and experimentation, leading by inspiring, motivating and learning in a shared endeavour with others' as one that is critical to develop action and agency in others, and to enable the transformation.

When teachers knew that it was safe to take risks in the classroom and maintain trust, they could be learners together and begin to influence the transformation process themselves, harnessing the power of agency. This emergent realization encouraged the leadership team to introduce new practices for professional learning by structuring classroom-situated teacher learning.

Structuring pedagogical change in practice through the coherence makers

Leadership reflective practice continued as the pedagogical transformation was occurring and an emergent area of focus became the structuring of professional learning for teachers. The process involved reimagining professional learning to become situated in the student learning environment (i.e. the classroom), engaging with student learners and providing the opportunity to deeply notice, reflect and identify actions. This reimagined learning for teachers involved opening classrooms to small groups of teachers who focused on the needs of student learners and their learning experience. It placed students and their learning needs at the centre of the professional learning focus and allowed teachers and students to be learners together in ways they had not experienced before.

An introduced leadership team process that deepened reflection was the practice of collectively noticing the spaces in which the transformation was occurring. This deep noticing involved reflecting on aspects such as being alert to how students and teachers were utilizing spaces; the nature of communication and language being used in the spaces, such as how voice was being enabled in the classroom and other spaces; and the nature of relating or relationships evident between learners (students and staff learners). For instance, in reflecting on the collaborative classroom visits and the 'noticings' of learning spaces observed, the leadership team drew upon the Leadership Wheel to help identify capacities that could grow the capability of the teachers as leaders of learning in the classroom. For example, the capacity of 'collaboration', which is the ability to facilitate shared purpose and co-construction, emerged as a capacity to be strengthened. This focus emerged from reflecting on the teachers' desire to collaborate for learning design and to be challenged by their contextual understandings of the site and student learning needs.

Reimagining staff meetings to allow all voices to be heard was another structural change resulting from the leadership team's reflective practice. The leadership team noticed that only some voices were heard during administrative staff meetings, while others remained silent. A 'huddle' was introduced to disrupt this phenomenon, where all staff had an opportunity to listen and seek out ideas, share agendas and focus on the elements of deep, effective communication. In addition, 4C strategies were drawn upon to encourage and elicit contributions from all teachers and to help raise awareness of how sharing the communication space and being alert to messaging of others could contribute to authentic collaboration.

The leadership team understood that for new ways of communicating to be effective, new capacities needed to be developed. They used reflective practice to identify the capacities needed for better communication practices. For example, the capacity of 'creativity', the ability to push thinking and actions out of the comfort zone into the unknown, was identified as an area for focus. To develop the creativity capacity in others, the school leaders introduced processes into meeting times to grow staff confidence and ability to think and imagine in ways that could reinvent the traditional school structures. These communication practices provided coherence and understanding of collaborating, learning and listening together.

For the school leaders, structuring pedagogical change was a challenging and exciting time in the transformation journey. It required them to revisit the Leadership Wheel regularly to identify new and emergent needs as the school practices changed and new ones were introduced. In addition, leaders recognized that scheduling regular reflective practice was critical at this stage of the transformation to ensure that the process remained collaborative, that emerging learning needs were met, and that all members of the community were included.

Collaboration with the wider community began to emerge as an area of focus for the leadership team as the transformation in communication practices began to occur. When reflecting on how the changes in practice would be shared and communicated with the broader school community, the leadership team identified the capacity of 'communication' as necessary for development in teachers so they could engage deeply and effectively with the wider community of parents and caregivers. This capacity became a focus for teachers and leaders to ensure that the change was well communicated and that all facets of the community felt part of, enabled by and included in the change process.

Such awareness led to changes in practices, including monthly 'parents as partners in learning' workshops where parents and carers experienced 4C learning through experience and reflection. The workshops were led by students and staff and situated in both classrooms and specialized workshops. The focus of the learning included exploring the 4Cs approach, the dispositions for learning and introducing the strategies that learners across the school employed to build the dispositions and enable the capabilities. In addition, collaborative planning and development forums incorporated processes enabling open communication and reflection. The coherence makers played a significant role in making explicit the processes and features of the dispositions and capabilities to enable the community to experience the 4Cs approach. Moreover, the coherence makers provided order and safety for some newly introduced practices.

Leading reflective practice offered a coherent, commonly understood and democratic process to examine the school's practices through deep noticing and identifying assumptions. It also enabled an opportunity to consider existent practices from various perspectives and challenge the 'status quo'. It helped the leadership team understand how and why they may have maintained and enabled existing practices and, where change or deepening of practice was needed, identify how they could do things differently. Reflective practice also allowed the leadership team to identify and assess the leading capacities for transformation that could be grown throughout the setting to enable agentic learning and the transformation process.

The 4C tools may provide coherence for the process of reflection and returning to values, but they are only effective if people are willing and ready to inquire with others. Working together with reflective tools, with teachers and with students is not straightforward. Practices are not static, and dichotomies and conflicts occur where culture, curriculum and leadership interact. Rather than being mutually supportive, practices can be at odds with one another, almost contradicting each other, until a consensus is reached. Coleman[25] describes this process between people as contiguity, the intertwined interaction of the inquiring self with and between others and their thoughts that create artefacts that are constantly changing people and their work together.

In Miranda North's case, the collaboration circles coherence maker tool was harnessed most effectively when it was used in conjunction with regular and ongoing reflective practice. Ongoing reflective practice was critical in discerning whether the elements of trust and an openness to a range of perspectives existed in the environment. Furthermore, in conjunction with the Leadership Wheel coherence maker, it was essential to illuminate the strengths and 'yet-to-be' strengths that could be harnessed and developed so that collaboration may flourish. Miranda North Public School's transformation approach to curriculum and pedagogy now reflects the assumption that an agile and contextually refined curriculum should challenge its learners to enable agency and relevance. This assumption guides their emergent approach to learning design, where creativity, critical reflection, communication and collaboration are integrated. The school's adopted processes and practices reflect the belief that a collaborative approach to learning design best serves the needs of the student and teacher-learners. It also recognizes that democratic processes that allow both leaders and teachers to create learning experiences (for students and teachers) that are diverse and specific to the needs identified in their context, enable transformation. The coherence makers supported the democratic nature of the reflection process by establishing a shared understanding, encouraging inclusive engagement, promoting critical examination and supporting collaborative exploration. Through this democratic approach to reflection, the transformative journey at Miranda North became a collective effort, driven by the diverse perspectives and contributions of leaders and teachers.

Like the tools used in Miranda North's community garden, the 4C tools offer coherence in the complexity of a transformation process, where everyone is invited and expected to lead learning, and the tools support the task at hand, made easier by them. Several years after the school garden was first established, it is now nurtured by students and community alike, who share the values, vision and practices of growing and harvesting the plants for a more sustainable future. The garden has enjoyed several seasons of rich harvest, and the student and community gardeners work with confidence and care, knowing they are capable of sustaining an environment that continues to change, evolve and nurture the community.

Ways forward: Leading and sustaining transformation as a process

In sustaining the 4C transformative practices, schools must continue to return to their purpose, vision and values. Some suggestions for sustaining the transformation process include:

- critically reflecting on the transformative capabilities of values and learning to identify whether the practices and practice traditions in the setting continue to reflect the purpose and vision or if they require deep examination.
- drawing on the Leadership Wheel to identify the capacities that may be harnessed, yet to be developed, or are critical to enabling the next steps in the transformation process.
- building opportunity for all learners (staff and student learners) to critically reflect on pedagogy and curriculum to consider whether the practices are democratic, collaborative, self-directed and contextually relevant.
- reflecting on the teacher education practices to analyse whether the practices continue to enable renewed perspectives and roles for all teachers through

reflection and inquiry and to identify the learning required to further the transformation.
- utilizing the coherence makers as frameworks to support the complex tasks of transformation in the setting by offering clarity or coherence to complex ideas or concepts.

School culture and leadership are both influential during reform,[26] meaning that a transformative school learning culture is dependent upon transformational leadership and learning practices. The ways that 4C practices are utilized can alter cultures of learning and who is leading the learning itself, thereby altering both. This leads us to make a case for leading agentic learning in transformative ways, with ideas about leading learning that are not necessarily aligned with the transformational leadership literature.

Can we possibly say that transformation is sustainable and that transformation itself is a point of permanent arrival or a dynamic process of permanent changing at the same time? Transforming is the very nature of schooling through both sustaining and changing. The leadership and learning practices that invite change described in this chapter are about taking brave action. This may lead readers to wonder how these practices can create sustainability over time. These transforming practices create sustainable agentic learning. We are not suggesting that we simply create schools that adopt a series of 4C tools to adjust their learning trajectory. Rather, we suggest that by using these tools or processes, we create a coherence to the learning practices or capacities for all learners, and educators, who are themselves learners, that can be repeated in people's lives into the future. The processes or tools offer a coherence in this process of transformation. Agentic learning is the whole purpose of education. The processes that are collectively adopted over time become the very capabilities that enable learning and enable the leading of learning in schools.

Notes

1. M. Jefferson and M. Anderson, *Transforming Schools: Creativity, Critical Reflection, Communication, Collaboration* (London: Bloomsbury Publishing, 2017).
2. M. Jefferson and M. Anderson, *Transforming Education: Reimagining Learning, Pedagogy and Curriculum* (London: Bloomsbury Publishing, 2021), 203.
3. Jefferson and Anderson, *Transforming Schools*.
4. Jefferson and Anderson, *Transforming Schools*, 8.
5. Jefferson and Anderson, *Transforming Schools*.
6. Jefferson and Anderson, *Transforming Schools*.
7. Jefferson and Anderson, *Transforming Schools*, 155.
8. Jefferson and Anderson, *Transforming Schools*.
9. Jefferson and Anderson, *Transforming Schools*, 155.
10. M. Fullan, 'The Elusive Nature of Whole System Improvement in Education', *Journal of Educational Change* 17, no. 4 (2016): 539–44.
11. Jefferson and Anderson, *Transforming Education*, 187.

12 Jefferson and Anderson, *Transforming Education*, 188.
13 P. Hallinger and R. H. Heck, 'Leadership for Learning: Does Collaborative Leadership Make a Difference in School Improvement?', *Educational Management Administration & Leadership* 38, no. 6 (2010): 654–78.
14 N. Mockler, 'Teacher Professional Learning in a Neoliberal Age: Audit, Professionalism and Identity', *Australian Journal of Teacher Education (Online)* 38, no. 10 (2013): 35–47.
15 Jefferson and Anderson, *Transforming Schools*.
16 Jefferson and Anderson, *Transforming Schools*.
17 Jefferson and Anderson, *Transforming Schools*, 132.
18 Jefferson and Anderson, *Transforming Education*.
19 E. L. Deci and R. M. Ryan, *Self-determination Theory* (Rochester, NY: University of Rochester Press, 2012).
20 Jefferson and Anderson, *Transforming Education*, 203.
21 Jefferson and Anderson, *Transforming Education*, 206–7.
22 Jefferson and Anderson, *Transforming Schools*, 206.
23 S. Kemmis, C. Edwards-Groves, J. Wilkinson, and I. Hardy, 'Ecologies of Practices', in Practice, *Learning and Change*, ed. P. Hager, A. Lee, and A. Reich (London: Springer, 2012), 33–49.
24 Jefferson and Anderson, *Transforming Schools*, 206.
25 K. S. Coleman, 'An a/r/tist in Wonderland: Exploring Identity, Creativity and Digital Portfolios as a/r/tographer', *Unpublished doctoral dissertation, Melbourne, Australia: Melbourne Graduate School of Education*, 2017.
26 H. May, J. Huff, and E. Goldring, 'A Longitudinal Study of Principal's Activities and Student Performance', *School Effectiveness and School Improvement: An International Journal of Research, Policy and Practice* 23, no. 4 (2012): 1–23.

References

Anderson, M. and M. Jefferson 2018. *Transforming Organizations: Engaging the 4Cs for Powerful Organizational Learning and Change*. London: Bloomsbury Publishing.
Browning, P. 2013. 'Creating the Conditions for Transformational Change'. *Australian Educational Leaders* 35(3): 14–17.
Coleman, K. S. 2017. *An a/r/tist in Wonderland: Exploring Identity, Creativity and Digital Portfolios as a/r/tographer*. Unpublished doctoral dissertation, Melbourne, Australia: Melbourne Graduate School of Education.
Deci, E. L. and R. M. Ryan 2012. *Self-determination Theory*. Rochester, NY: University of Rochester Press.
Freire, P. 2000. *Pedagogy of the Oppressed, 30th Anniversary Edition* London: Continuum. (Original work published 1970).
Grootenboer, P., K. Ronnerman, and C. Edwards-Groves 2017b. 'Leading from the Middle: A Praxis- Oriented Practice'. In P. Grootenboer, C. Edwards-Groves, and S. Choy (eds.), *Practice Theory Perspectives on Pedagogy and Education*, 243–63. Singapore: Springer.

Hallinger, P. 2007. 'Research on the Practice of Instructional and Transformational Leadership: Retrospect and Prospect'. *ACEL Monograph Series* 40(7): 2–6.

Hallinger, P. and R. Heck 2010. 'Collaborative Leadership and School Improvement: Understanding the Impact on School Capacity and Student Learning'. *School Leadership and Management* 30(2), 95–110. doi:10.1080/13632431003663214.

Jefferson, M. and M. Anderson 2017. *Transforming Schools: Creativity, Critical Reflection, Communication, Collaboration*. London: Bloomsbury Publishing.

Jefferson, M. and M. Anderson 2021. *Transforming Education: Reimagining Learning, Pedagogy and Curriculum*. London: Bloomsbury.

Kemmis, S., C. Edwards-Groves, J. Wilkinson, and I. Hardy 2012. 'Ecologies of Practices'. In P. Hager, A. Lee, and A. Reich (eds.), *Practice, Learning and Change*, 33–49. London: Springer.

Kemmis, S., J. Wilkinson, C. Edwards-Groves, I. Hardy, P. Grootenboer, and L. Bristol 2014. *Changing Practices, Changing Education*. Wagga: Springer.

May, H., J. Huff, and E. Goldring 2012. 'A Longitudinal Study of Principal's Activities and Student Performance. School Effectiveness and School Improvement: An International Journal of Research'. *Policy and Practice* 23(4): 1–23.

Mockler, N. 2013. 'Teacher Professional Learning in a Neoliberal Age: Audit, Professionalism and Identity'. *Australian Journal of Teacher Education* 38(10): 35–47.

Mockler, N. and J. Sachs 2012. 'Rethinking Educational Practice Through Reflexive Inquiry: An Introduction'. In N. Mockler and J. Sachs (eds.), *Rethinking Educational Practice Through Reflexive Inquiry: Essays in Honour of Susan Groundwater-Smith*, 1–8. Dordrecht: Springer.

Robinson, V. M. J., C. A. Lloyd, and K. J. Rowe 2008. 'The Impact of Leadership on Student Outcomes: An Analysis of the Differential Effects of Leadership Types'. *Educational Administration Quarterly* 44(5): 635–74.

Ross, J. 2012. 'Performing the Reflective Self: Audience Awareness in High-Stakes Reflection'. *Studies in Higher Education* 39(2): 219–32, doi:10.1080/03075079.2011.651450.

Silins, H. and R. Murray-Harvey 2000. 'Students as the Central Concern'. *Journal of Educational Administration* 28: 230–46.

Trimmer, K., R. Dixon, and J. Guenther 2019. 'School Leadership and Aboriginal Student Outcomes: Systematic Review'. *Asia-Pacific Journal of Teacher Education* 49(1): 20–36. http://dx.doi.org/10.1080/1359866X.2019.1685646.

Pedagogies and Politics

Drawing on the 4Cs and *Normal Pig*

Justine Bruyère and Noelle Yoo

2

Student voice (p. 34)

Our classroom (p. 34)

Environment: Creativity (p. 36)

Environment: Critical reflection (p. 37)

Environment: Communication (p. 38)

Environment: Collaboration (p. 38)

Day 1: A normal lesson (p. 39)

Day 2: Normal collaboration and communication (p. 40)

After day 2: Normal pivot (p. 41)

Day 3: Normal creativity (p. 42)

> **Day 4: Normal critical reflection** (p. 43)
>
> **Normal worries** (p. 44)
>
> **Emerging themes** (p. 45)
>
> **Learning reflections** (p. 45)
>
> **Ways forward** (p. 46)
> Teaching is tough (p. 46)
> The curriculum needs the 4Cs (p. 46)
> Draw the outside world inward (p. 47)

In every chess game the pieces, the board and the rules are the same – no variation. As the game begins, one has only a few possible moves – the pawns, maybe a knight or a bishop. Some players boast a two-turn checkmate. If you can avoid checkmate for six moves there are over nine million possibilities at play. And, following the eighth move, there are more than two hundred and eighty million positions and outcomes. As you play, the possibilities keep growing. As common saying rings, there are more ways to play a game of chess than there are atoms in the universe. In many ways, teaching is akin to the game of chess. The curriculum, the number of students and even the time allotted in the school day have little variation. And, at least at the beginning of the year many of us are accomplishing the first six moves – learning names, getting to know students, completing initial assessments, building community and so on. After that, though, we reach the beginning of what becomes limitless possibilities in classroom lesson delivery. Deciding just how to move the players on the board can be daunting, or, if you look at teaching the way Noelle Yoo and Jenn Meader did, you might find that it's more like a game with infinite possibilities. During the 2020–1 school year, rather than delivering the curriculum in a locked-set of prescribed moves, Noelle and Jenn decided to move in new ways using a few of the millions of possibilities they had not yet attempted in the classroom. That school year, they worked with their mentor, Justine Bruyère, to use embodiment as a tool for critical reflection, to help build collaboration and communication, and as a way for students to experience creativity through the curriculum.

In the spring of 2020, the whole world changed. More specifically, in America, the global pandemic, west coast wildfires, the murder of George Floyd at the hands of the police, the BLM movement, a rise in Asian American and LGBTQI hate crimes and widespread political unrest made for worrisome and even frightening days. Some students knew very little about the sociopolitical issues of the time, parents were intentionally shielding them from the news. Others only gathered fragmented pieces of what was happening around the world, so they struggled to make sense of what they knew. And still more, there were students who were totally awake to the hostility and hatred that surrounded them, even in the third grade. Knowing how to navigate and express oneself in this world is not a naturally acquired art, quite the opposite. In this highly politicized world, children need help imagining possibilities, questioning narratives, navigating stories of the oppressed, and acting on solutions for the future. At times like this, (perhaps more than ever before) a 'revolutionary transition of schooling that moves [students] from places of knowledge transmission and/or acquisition to places in which co-creativity, ingenuity, and imagination are central to learning'[1] is needed.

In our analysis, we drew heavily on Jefferson and Anderson's[2] Learning Prism as our conceptual lens. Looking through this lens allows us to share how we made sense of our lesson delivery process and learning outcomes. The Learning Prism (see Figure 2.1) provided a language for describing how knowledge, new understanding and wisdom might influence 4C lesson delivery and in turn transform learning.[3] This framing provided a powerful analytic tool helping us not only to understand what 'schools need to move beyond a tendency towards conformity'[4] but also to critically consider the ways that the Learning Prism might bring about change in us, as educators. Within, we follow Noelle and Jenn as they use embodiment and 4Cs practices to help students problem find, play with possibility, respond to complex situations and critically reflect in a year filled with debate and great divide. The authors analyse interviews, video recordings and student artefacts to explore transformation for both students and teachers.

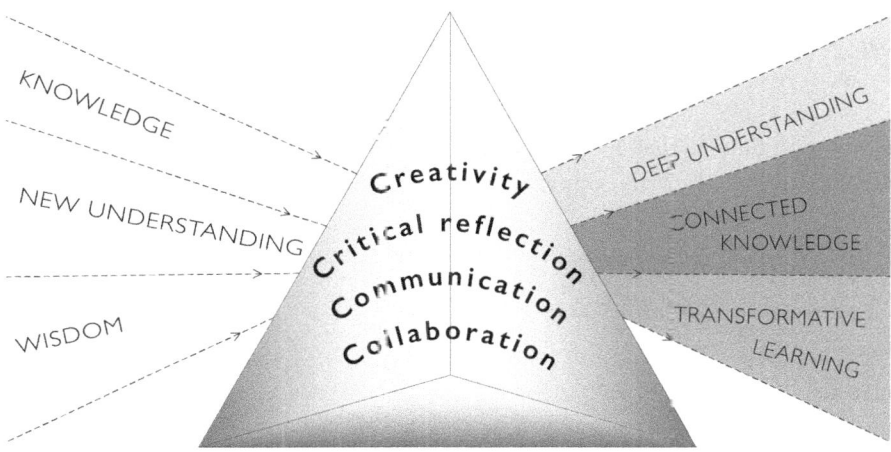

Figure 2.1 'The Learning Prism'.

Student voice

'What does normal mean?' Noelle asked the class of third graders on a crisp February day.
'The same as everyone.'
'Same beliefs.'
'Calm and listening.'
'In America, normal is blonde hair and blue eyes.'
'Saying to someone who does not speak the same language, "That's not normal!"'

Normalcy, it turns out, is something the students in this third-grade classroom accepted and even desired. The desire to be normal is understandable considering how often students are ranked against norms – norms according to their height, weight and even their intelligence. 'There is probably no area of contemporary life in which some idea of a norm, mean, or average has not been calculated.'[5] Students even feel oppressed or othered if they don't have 'blonde hair and blue eyes', if they don't own the new cool gadget or speak perfect English.

Sameness has become a social and political device informing hierarchies. Jefferson and Anderson[6] note that change is only possible when we transform habits and mindsets. In our work together, we wondered how planning, executing and reflecting on our lessons using the Learning Prism[7] could lead to immeasurable understanding while moving away from the status quo and towards transformative learning. Together we discussed the ways that we could use children's texts to craft and inspire, to question and navigate, to voice and to message, and to co-construct and challenge.[8] Knowing this group of keen, active and enthusiastic third-grade learners, we planned a series of units with the Learning Prism as our lens.

A few of our chosen texts were *Before You Were Mine* by Maribeth Boelts[9], *Stormy* by Guojing[10], *A Normal Pig* by K-Fai Steele[11] and *The Other Side* by Jacqueline Woodson.[12] Drama conventions such as slow motion, adding narration, hot seating and corridor of voices were used to accompany the texts.[13] And finally, the Learning Prism, in communion with these texts and drama devices, helped us to consider how to connect knowledge to real-world issues, how to strive for deeper understanding and how to look at schooling not as it is and always has been but as a space for learning as we have rarely seen it.[14]

Our classroom

The classroom where Noelle and Jenn taught is situated in a north-eastern university town in the United States. The third graders represented a range of ethnic, racial and economic groups. Noelle and Jenn were sharing their first year in a teaching relationship. Justine and Noelle had met in August 2018 when Noelle was enrolled in her teacher education course at Vanderbilt University's Peabody College. Since that time, Noelle and Justine had a collaborative teaching relationship where idea sharing, data collecting, reflecting, presenting and publishing were the norm. Noelle and Jenn were eager to work collaboratively on this project, a wonderful illustration of their ambition and desire to 'free learning for transformation'.[15]

Using embodiment techniques, we journeyed together to create shared imaginative experiences where students could confront the world outside of the classroom with the safety of knowing Noelle and Jenn were at their side. Through the participatory, creative-based modelling of the lessons our hope was that students could 'grow in a different way, moving them forward to new, collective understandings' that could help each of them to find new personal meaning.[16] Throughout the school year, Noelle, Jenn and Justine worked to use drama in the classroom to 'provoke wide-awakeness and an awareness of the quest for meaning, which has so much to do with feeling alive in the world'.[17] Together, we met via Zoom twice per month to consider not just what to teach but also the ways we might teach it. Knowing that students would be asked to critically reflect, we also imagined how students could examine and respond to texts using the Learning Prism as a lens.

The work described here will zoom in on what it means to be normal and specifically on our combined efforts with the children's text, *A Normal Pig* by K-Fai Steele.[18] Briefly, in this text a pig named Pip (the only pig with spots in her class) is embarrassed when other pigs at school make fun of her lunch, greens and dried seaweed. Back at home Pip begs for a 'normal lunch'. Rather than changing her lunch, Pip's parents take her to the city centre where many different kinds of pigs happily interact. Pigs with grey skin, pigs with pink skin, pigs with light spots and dark spots and even pigs with stripes get along just fine. Through this experience, Pip reconsiders her desire to be 'normal'. Diversity, difference and considering perspectives surface when reading this text.

Before delivering the lesson Jenn and Noelle addressed the 'elephant in the room', they were worried the third-grade students might not take the message of *Normal Pig* seriously. For Noelle, the message of this text hit home. It was March 2021, shortly after the devastating murder of eight Asian American women in Atlanta, Georgia. As an Asian American woman herself, she was troubled by the reality of hate and racism in America. Noelle remembered being verbally harassed on the train for being Asian. From that point forward she didn't feel safe walking outside by herself. Noelle worried for the safety of her family and friends because of the skin they were born into. With her group of third graders, she desired an opening to discuss Asian and Asian American hate in a way that would be honest, meaningful and inspire activism.

In meetings early on, Jenn and Noelle also shared their worries that creativity and criticality would be overshadowed by a desire to answer correctly. They asked, how can we respond to work that lacks depth? How can we really set the stage for this learning to bring out the best outcome? Together we pondered the idea of teacher responsivity and criticality with important texts, several ideas surfaced including our desire, as educators, to create

(1) environments ripe with opportunities for creativity
(2) environments ripe for critical reflection

(3) environments ripe with communication
(4) environments ripe for collaboration (for teachers and students alike).

Next, we will share a bit about what these ideas have collectively come to mean to us.

Environment: Creativity

As a team, we discussed the curriculum and what it lacked for Noelle, Jenn and the third-grade students. The curriculum checked off the correct objective and outcome boxes, but what it lacked was creativity. More specifically, exercises where students could express themselves using their bodies. The Learning Prism, we came to understand, works hand in hand with embodiment practices, laying the groundwork for creative learning.[19] Embodied practices have the potential to engage students in deeper and more profound ways, helping them to create from a place of sense-making rather than a place of memorization. According to Sternberg[20], creativity and innovation are closely tied, creative environments offer space for counter thoughts, moving beyond assumptions and stereotypes. In our case, we desired to better understand how creativity could complement the learning, playing a central role in the lessons. We chose to use embodiment as a mode for creative expression to imagine, play, fail, retry, and construct new understandings of misconceptions.[21] Embodiment, to us, means learning in action, with our bodies and minds in motion. We see drama, dance, reflection, imagination and more as evidence of the embodiment. And in our set up for these lessons we imagined the body as a tool for portraying children's interpretations of text, for portraying children's creative understandings.[22] To put it another way, learning through the use of embodiment is students '"putting thinking into the body", and "the body into their thinking"'.[23] The embodiment lessons did not come with a plan housing carefully developed steps and teacher prompts. Instead, this work required Noelle and Jenn to take on additional responsibilities tying our Learning Prism lessons to the outcomes and objectives set by their school. Jefferson and Anderson[24] suggest how teachers might actively structure creative learning, noting

> There is nothing magical or mystical about this process. It is structured, effective pedagogy applied to the needs of students.
>
> Creativity learning starts with:
>
> - Noticing – deep perception that flows into asking why, then digging deeper;
> - Asking why? Really why? – asking penetrating complex and connected questions;
> - Playing with possibility – imagining and engaging with the palate of possibility; and then
> - Selecting and evaluating, which is a process of choice and discernment married with deep and perceptive evaluation (from the students themselves and from others).[25]

To do this, Noelle and Jenn knew they wouldn't be on the outside of the action looking in at what the students created; instead as we worked together, they knew their role would be to imagine with the students, predicting where the learning might go and carefully listening to their positions, needs, feelings and reactions to text.[26]

Environment: Critical reflection

To inform lesson planning and environment, we looked once again at the Learning Prism. That particular day of our preparation, student behaviour was Noelle and Jenn's main concern. The more we unpacked, though, the more it became clear that we weren't really talking about student behaviour; we were talking about setting the tone for critical reflection. 'To teach for wisdom is to use critical reflection as a 4C capability to inform decisions and actions in all learning. It is to recognize explicitly that how we use knowledge infuses the way we teach.'[27] Collectively we asked, how do we want to use the Learning Prism and 4C knowledge we have so that we could teach about Asian American hate, about racism, and about inclusivity and difference? 'This kind of reflection allows students to see the world as "joined up" rather than seeing human experience as granular and disconnected. In other words, they see a connection between their own assumptions and preconceptions and the role of institutions and power structures in shaping those preconceptions.'[28] Our goals, after that day, were vested in more than just delivering knowledge, we hoped to create spaces where the product from learning was a wisdom to appreciate differences in the world and the power to make change happen.[29] As we grappled with the enormity of our hopes, we knew we had to share more than just this one text and we knew we would be teaching these lessons for the rest of the year. Our role would also be to draw real understanding (while creating critical learning opportunities) of pandemic related hate, violence against Asian Americans and other realities that have been facing people of colour and Asian communities in America for centuries into the learning.

The truth is, schooling often pulls students away from this kind of criticality, saying students are too young, this content is too mature for students or that school is supposed to be fun not depressing.[30] James Baldwin, in his now famous 'Talk to Teachers', noted that one of the 'paradoxes of education was that precisely at the point when you begin to develop a conscience, you must find yourself at war with your society'.[31] Rather than only asking students about the setting, plot and characters in texts, we hoped to foster thinking about texts in divergent ways. Our questions explore questions such as,

- Why do you hold these views?
- What's informing and influencing (media, news, parents, friends) your thinking?
- Why might people disagree on this subject?
- Can you understand both sides?[32]

These types of questions do not have answers that can be found in a text. Therefore, we are able to uncover what students believe, how their beliefs were formed, if the beliefs are based on evidence and whether students can weigh (evaluate, assess?) others' beliefs.[33]

Environment: Communication

As we further considered the Learning Prism and this particular classroom, our conversation grew around cultivating openness and dialogue. In classrooms very few things matter more than student voice and safety.[34] If students do not feel emotionally safe, studies show communication is negatively influenced.[35] Next to a child's home, school is the most likely place they will regularly visit to gain an understanding of the world. Noelle and Jenn described students who experienced difficulty expressing themselves on paper and specifically through fill-in-the-blank tasks. These exercises, they explained, resulted in student silence and defeat – two outcomes Noelle and Jenn weren't comfortable with. If our goals as educators are vested in the creation of classrooms that are safe for critical communication, places where students are able to engage in 'democratic habits of thought and action',[36] then we must be alert to how messaging strengthens communication as we construct knowledge.[37]

Our approach leveraged communication to engage students while exploring and expressing knowledge.[38] More specifically, using *Transforming Schools* as our guide, 'we began our 4C approach to learning and transformation with a focus on communicating through the body, and the voice. This is known as embodied cognition or enactment'.[39] The embodiment we carried out used text to create a pathway into the story, a pathway that led to the reconstruction of the text. The embodiment was evidence of student ideas. We hoped students might play with the possibility that exists when someone speaks out – perhaps a word of support or a line of defence – to make a difference, altering the text in its original form and asking 'What if?'.[40] This form of dramatic play or embodiment generates 'safe and learning rich environment(s) where children create a zone of proximal development to try out their growing capabilities'.[41] The product of playful learning is not predetermined; instead it evolves and is highly dependent upon group communication. To engage in this work groups need to trust one another. Research shows environments where students are communicating, using their bodies, and expressing themselves foster student sense of safety and openness.[42]

Environment: Collaboration

Recognizing heightened forms of participation as a priority, we brainstormed what that might look like in the third-grade classroom. It was more than communication, but what was it? Noelle and Jenn described students talking over one another and instances where more outgoing students made all of the decisions in their small groups.

Again, we looked to the Learning Prism. The prism supersedes antiquated models of education where group work is thought of as every student in a group completing individual tasks and then compiling them into one final product.[43] Instead, we shared a vision of students working in small groups as if they had one mind and many hands. The prism helped us to identify how collaborative efforts could open students to new understandings. This sophisticated collaboration involving 'complex cognitive and social processes such as adaptability, perspective-taking, improvisation, self-regulation, and problem-solving skills as children learn to work with group cohesion, improvising with others and addressing conflicting views' was our end goal.[44]

We believed a focus on collaboration would lay the groundwork for students to make decisions together, mutually building on each other's ideas.[45] Our trio hoped for heightened collaboration not just for the students but also for our small group. The nature of our project required collaboration on everything from considering what 'counts' as learning to reflecting on the lesson planning process. From our 4C research, we knew that sharing, reflecting, changing, debating and understanding were required steps in collaboration.[46] These facets of collaboration, therefore, were embedded in both our work together and in the third-grade lesson delivery. Together, we strived to create

- Open-ended and complex tasks;
- Solo and group goals;
- Strategies for seeking help; and
- Supportive feedback loops.

Even as educators who considered themselves more open and flexible, the 4Cs approach encourages the release of some control, making room for students to grapple with ideas, work alongside peers, seek help and come to new understandings.

Day 1: A normal lesson

We share this lesson with the hope that educators will add, subtract and revise these ideas for their unique classroom settings. We are not attempting to create a one-size-fits-all approach to learning. Instead, we hope to shine a light on one way to use the Learning Prism and the 4Cs as the basis of your teaching. Consider this one of millions of ways to 'play the game of chess'.

On the first day of this lesson and before opening the pages to *Normal Pig*[47] Noelle shared a story from her own experiences in elementary school with her students,

> When I was in 5th or 6th grade, a new classmate joined my school. He was Korean American, just like me. At my school, we ate lunch in a cafeteria – it was a big room with tables and benches where all the kids in our grade could sit with their friends and enjoy lunch together. On his first day, the new classmate's caregiver packed him a Korean lunch of kimchi, rice and a few side dishes – probably to comfort him on what was probably a nerve wracking first day. For

> those of you who are not sure what kimchi is, it's cabbage – seasoned with different sauces and spices and then fermented for a few months. Kimchi is a staple in Korean cuisine and is known in other parts of the world for its many health benefits. Because it ferments for a long time, kimchi has a strong scent that can overwhelm your senses if you've never smelled it before. Have you ever been overwhelmed by the smell of something new? It might be a candle, a new food?

The students then shared smells that surprised them and Noelle continued,

> Well, when this student opened his lunch, many of the kids sitting around him had never smelled kimchi before. They responded by covering their noses, yelling, 'Ew! What is that smell? Make it go away!' The new student was so embarrassed and probably sad that he ran out of the cafeteria. I want you to remember my story as we read Normal Pig. This story is not unusual or even fiction. This is reality, people are often made to feel bad for regular parts of their lives.

The room was quiet and attentive and students were positioned to hear the story. So, Noelle read Pip's story aloud to her class. While reading she and Jenn projected the illustrations on the classroom whiteboard. Students listened intently and there was an understanding that even though the characters in the story were pigs, this book was conveying a serious topic. Noelle's choice to draw her life into the classroom prepared her students for high-quality interactions filled with authentic communication and emotion. From the onset of the story, the students were able to understand that incidents like the one that happens to Pip are happening every day.

As the lesson continued, Noelle and Jenn supported critical reflection by probing students, 'Who holds the power in this story?' and 'What if we changed who held the power? How could that change the story? Could any other answer also be true?' Rather than looking for a particular response, they encouraged questioning of the status quo. Later, sitting in a circle facing one another they asked, 'What's informing your thinking? Have you heard stories like this one on the news or with friends?' 'How can we use this story to see our world differently?' and 'How can we use what we have learned to make real change happen?' The questions were not asked in any sequential order or with the intention of receiving any correct answer. Instead, Noelle and Jenn ebbed and flowed with students in what felt more like a conversation than a scripted question-and-answer session. Student thinking and conversation were guiding what they asked and how they responded to questions posed.

Day 2: Normal collaboration and communication

During a review of the story the next day, a discussion about the lunch room scene in *Normal Pig*[48] ensued. Jenn and Noelle took this moment to zoom in on the image where Pip was being made fun of because of her lunch, they asked, 'Why, really why, is this image and page so important in the story?' Third-grade students who frequently brought ethnic lunches shared their worry and sadness for Pip – and themselves. They were drawing from their personal experiences to inform their reactions. One student remarked, 'That's so mean to make a comment about what someone is eating.' Another student who often brought Indian dishes made by her grandmother added, 'My grandmother makes my lunches with special spices and ingredients and I can't imagine someone treating me that way'. Noelle observed that some students were very quiet, so she leaned in. 'Have you ever encountered food that smells bad or different? I have'. Several students immediately recalled situations where they had smelled something new for the first time and they couldn't help but cover their nose or say, 'ew'. The image of Pip in the lunchroom was a launch point for both communication and tension.

Using the Learning Prism and 4Cs as our Northstar and in response to this productive friction, Noelle and Jenn asked students to imagine a different lunch scene, one where things turned out better or perhaps just differently for Pip. They prompted, 'In your groups, we want you to collaborate using what you wish had happened in the lunchroom to create a different storyline.' Students quickly began working on their scenes. Excitement filled the room as they re-storied *Normal Pig*.[49] Noelle and Jenn hoped to see how open-ended and complex tasks in combination with engaging a palate of possibility could open up this classroom to deep and wide learning.[50]

With Noelle and Jenn's assistance, sometimes acting alongside students, groups of students were rolling up their sleeves imagining what could have been in this story. In a couple of the scenes, Noelle played the role of the bully. Initially, students found her acting humorous. Soon though, they realized she was a bully who was not going to back down. Noelle's commitment to the role of bully brought an authenticity to the scenes that stopped some students in their tracks. Although we have no way of knowing, we agreed that this authenticity would probably not have been there if Noelle had observed the scenes as an audience member. The dramatic retellings, as it turned out, lacked the sincerity Noelle hoped for. Students presented these modified scenes with some signs of critique and hope, overall though, the drama lacked the depth we all wished for. Students were putting a pretty bow on the terrible lunch scene saying, 'Wow, your lunch smells good' or 'Hey, can I try?' The scenes were fairytale-esque and we all wanted more.

After day 2: Normal pivot

We were seeing surface-level responses, students trying desperately to guess what the correct answer was. Yet we knew students were thinking and feeling more than they were showing. Our shared understanding of the Learning Prism taught us that greater opportunities for communication would offer greater opportunities for 'expression of identity and culture'.[51] Noelle and Jenn wanted to create lessons that would amplify student voices and increase 'students' capacity to concentrate, to self-regulate . . . and to learn.[52] This pivot involved two centring steps that also happened to be reminders from our previous sessions together.

(1) A main question informing our work was, 'How do we want to use the Learning Prism and 4C knowledge we have to teach about Asian American hate, about racism, and about inclusivity and difference?' and this should motivate the unit above all else.
(2) A review of Jefferson and Anderson's[53] thoughts on wisdom in learning. 'To teach for wisdom is to use critical reflection as a 4C capability to inform decisions and actions in all learning. It is to recognize explicitly that how we use knowledge infuses the way we teach.'[54]

The first step, we concluded, was to promote more conversation about race and racism through linked text sets. Linked text sets are videos, books, posters, images and more that create a more expansive understanding of topics.[55] But sharing texts in class (due to the volume of curriculum mandates) would not be enough. So, during lunch hour, Noelle decided to host a diverse book club for students. While students ate their lunch, Noelle shared diverse books, talked and made connections between the texts and real life. One of the linked texts Noelle selected was the story *Eyes that Kiss in the Corner* by Joanna Ho[56]. This text celebrates the almond-shaped eyes that many Asian and Asian Americans have. Noelle decided on this text for its celebratory lens on difference. After reading *Eyes that Kiss in the Corner*, Noelle presented students with everyday racism scenarios and asked what they would do in each scene. Whether it was mispronunciation of Asian names, belittling based on Asian features, or poking fun at Asian food, students in the book club were collaborating in more and more authentic ways. This work offered a foundation for students to consider racism through two lenses, (1) How hateful interactions affect Asian or Asian American children, and (2) What actions students could take to support and protect Asian or Asian American children.

Day 3: Normal creativity

Following the book club meetings, Noelle and Jenn set up the embodied cognition by querying, 'Who in this text do you most want to know better? Is there anyone you have questions for? A character who you don't understand and you wish you could find out more? Maybe you wonder why they behaved in a certain way?' Students called out character names and the name Pip was called out the most. Next, Noelle notified the class that Pip was among the group. The students nervously looked around the room – Noelle repeated, 'Pip is here somewhere . . . hmm, where did Pip go?' Jenn added, 'Oh, I'm sure Pip is here, I just saw her with the group (looking at students), where are you Pip?'. At this moment, a student reluctantly raised her hand and asked, 'I'm right here?' Noelle and Jenn had a quick celebration and invited Pip to the hot seat. Hot seating is a drama tool for learning where characters, played by students, are interviewed in-role by their classmates.[57] This tool invited students to uncover more about the character, explore motivation and consider new perspectives.

Once Pip took her seat, students considered their questions. They thought alone and then shared a question they had with a partner. This process of selecting questions for Pip required them to think not only of the text as it was but also to evaluate and discern what it could be.[58] The third graders were excited and curious to learn more about Pip. They asked, 'How did you feel when the kids were making fun of your lunch?', 'Why didn't you tell your mom why you wanted a normal lunch?' and 'Do you wish your friends had done something different?' Pip responded as the lonely, misunderstood pig. Most of the classroom fell in love with Pip, whimpering for Pip and wishing for her to know how much they all cared.

Seeing that students were opening up, Noelle and Jenn asked if the class would like to interview other characters from the text; they replied with a resounding yes. This time students already knew how the character for the hot seat was selected and a mean pig was quickly chosen. Students asked, 'Did you think about how Pip would feel before you said those things?', 'Why did you say those things to Pip?', 'Did you regret it?' and 'What did your friends say after you said those things to Pip?' These third graders were yearning for the mean pig to see his error and to feel remorse. In our drama hot seat, he shrugged off the incident as a joke. He apologized but insisted that the incident was being blown out of proportion and none of his friends had said anything to him after the incident. The classroom was, once again, tense. The mean pig was not realizing how hurtful he had been and many students were visibly upset. This, Noelle and Jenn decided, was the perfect moment to consider action-oriented steps.

Day 4: Normal critical reflection

There were students on both sides – those who empathized with the rejection of an unfamiliar smell and wanted to understand how they could still be honest without hurting Pip's feelings and those who championed Pip – desiring for Pip to be true to herself in her response to the bullies. As the conversation deepened students communicated experiences where they (a) tried something new and didn't like it, (b) tried something new and did like it, (c) didn't try something new because they were worried they would be made fun of, (d) tried something new and were made fun of or (e) tried something new and felt accepted. Students approached the scenario through a risk-taking lens – connecting their lives and experiences to those in the story. They drew hard lines in defence of Pip.

> 'It doesn't matter if you don't like the smell. You should think about Pip. How would you feel if someone said those things about your lunch?'
> 'If a smell bothers you, maybe you can move and eat somewhere else. But you can't tell people not to eat something they like.'
> 'When people are rude about Pip's food, you're making her feel bad. It's not okay to make someone feel bad just because they like something that you don't like.'

It was clear that students acknowledged their role in protecting and supporting 'the different' in their world. On this final day devoted to *Normal Pig*, students had free choice to complete written reflections about *Normal Pig* (alternate stories, comics, flash forward, posters about bullying and racism) or return to small group work and reimagine the cafeteria scene. Roughly one-third of the students chose to create posters and advertisements about racism and bullying in schools – they included tips and ideas about how children could be more inclusive at lunch and after school. The other two-thirds of the class re-storied *Normal Pig* one last time.

Group presentations showed students collaborating, communicating, critically reflecting and creating together. One group of students chose not to change what the new pig said to Pip, but instead, classmates intervened and confronted the new pig. Another group played out a scenario where the new pig didn't say mean things but responded authentically and with curiosity saying, 'I've never smelled something like that before. What are you eating? Is it good?' A final group of students planned for Pip to walk to another table in the cafeteria, when the mean pig began to bully. At the new table, she and her lunch were accepted. These third graders understood the many possibilities when dealing with racism. For some students, watching these interpretations of how they could confront bullying was a lightbulb moment. They expressed knowing that there were many ways to help when witnessing oppression. One student confessed, 'I didn't know that there were lots of things I could do when I saw someone being mean'. Another student further explained, 'I only really thought about telling a teacher which doesn't really work'.

Normal worries

Due to the pandemic, the school week was reduced to four instead of the usual five days. The pressure of being at an independent school where lots of voices spoke into the types of learning and work Noelle and Jenn did in the classroom created some anxiety. During our Zoom meetings they expressed having some freedom but realized how much time was required to do this work justice. Jenn and Noelle felt a push and a pull. On one hand they were trying to meet the needs of the school curriculum, appease parents and exceed any expectations set by administration – all with one less day each week. On the other hand, they saw the existing gaps in the curriculum and desperately wanted to make change in their classroom. To combat this, Noelle and Jenn constantly reflected on the purpose of this work and the transformations they were seeing in students. Noelle elaborated,

> We had to trust that what we were doing was ultimately going to help all of our learning goals as educators, especially as it related to our school's social justice mission and our own priorities of social emotional learning. While we had to make minor adaptations to the scope and sequence we had initially mapped out for the year, the skills and learning we were hoping to see reflected in the kids' authoring were still met through the critical embodiment. In fact, we felt this

inspired true action from the students in a way that we hadn't seen with other projects we had planned before. The kids felt a real purpose for their authoring and researching, and they enjoyed owning that responsibility and autonomy. (Yoo, personal communication, 4 December 2021)

At this time in the world, perhaps more than any other time in our lives, we see the Learning Prism and the 4Cs as necessary, not extra. Our world is growing in complication and frustration; imagining how students will be prepared to respond to the world beyond our classrooms without creativity, critical reflection, communication and collaboration is strenuous. The 4Cs give students (of all ages) the ability to search for and confront meaning.[59]

Emerging themes

As a trio, we set out to bring the Learning Prism into this third-grade classroom. Almost by surprise, the 4Cs also engulfed our meetings and our work efforts together. Delivering these lessons required us to be collaborative, to think creatively, to critically reflect and to communicate openly with one another. Our hope in the third-grade class was to un-silo the learning while helping students to see the connections from social studies to literacy and to the world beyond the walls of the classroom. To do this, we knew we could not arrive with a script or end-product blueprints; instead we would need to support questioning and drive connections while creating space for reflection. The 4Cs were a perfect foundation for both classroom learning and structuring our planning time.

Learning reflections

Reflecting means looking back and giving serious thought to moves we make and why we make them. This year of work together, according to Noelle, was an investment in self and in students.

Before the Learning Prism and 4C work, we unfortunately thought more about the constraints of our learning environment than we did the possibilities. COVID brought in even more constraints and worries. There was always this hope for something more, but we didn't know the path. This approach and the 'why' for the approach make it worthwhile. It required a lot of time, learning, unlearning, and making mistakes but good things came and we began to see more possibilities in every lesson. Learning moments we never would have had. (Yoo, personal communication, 4 December 2021)

As educators, the 4C approach provided the grounds for use of new tools, questioning the status quo, taking risks, and working together in community. 'The work was empowering,' Jenn commented, 'It has changed the way I will teach forever'.[60]

Community is more than people working in the same building or even in the same classroom, it is 'discovered through people feeling empowered in coming together in the pursuit of shared meaning'.[61] Time spent in our community brought us to problem-posing, dialoguing, creating and most of all transformation.

The Learning Prism does not represent just one thought nor is it a tool that teachers use for a single subject area at one particular time in the week or school year. We like to think of the Prism and the 4Cs as the backpack that we put all of the learning into. So, if your schedule includes math, science, language arts, social studies and social emotional learning, then all of these subjects will be encased in 4C learning.

Ways forward

This research nudged and stretched learning differently for each of us. Mainly we learnt about how tough teaching is right now, we recognized that the curriculum as it exists needs the 4Cs and we recognized the need to draw the political world into the classroom. In the coming pages we will tell more about each of these learnings.

Teaching is tough

Many opinions on how teaching should play out for students exist, one of the prevailing and current methods involves highly standardized curriculums, intense early phonics programmes and rigorous testing. Teachers are working day and night to keep up and keep funding dollars flowing into their underfunded schools. And they know, we all know, that the only way to keep community schools operating is to 'turn test scores around' and 'close the gap' – deficit minded language we're not comfortable with.[62] Noelle and Jenn had participated in assessments, participation and even arts-related professional development. But neither had any learning where they simultaneously learnt the theory and the practice with a guide.

The curriculum needs the 4Cs

Traditional roles and even practices were brought into question, and we continuously cycled questions like 'How do traditional practices gate keep students?', 'How can we centre the student, not the teacher, in the learning?' and 'How are these practices (either with the 4Cs or without) empowering students? If they are not, where can we immediately make changes?' Our questioning took courage, especially for educators whose livelihood depended on employment at a school that wasn't always centring or empowering the student. The three of us knew that teachers who question the way it has always been will rarely be welcomed with open arms, 'they are not valued or legitimized by the mainstream. It takes courage and critical reflection to interrogate the status quo of our school institutions, and in that reflective discourse the tool of praxis illuminates our understandings and sustains transformation.'[63]

Draw the outside world inward

The nudging and stretching extended well beyond pedagogy. We realized how the political world was impacting students and that, despite the overwhelm of our curriculum, we had to contribute to students' sociopolitical understandings of the world, not as saviours but as companions in problematizing the complexity of the world. As adults, we found navigating how to approach racism, sexism and oppressions based on body size, neurodiversity, citizenship and wealth (to name a few) to be important for our own understandings. We do not pretend to be experts in these areas, instead we work to consult experts and here, we direct you to some of our mentors in diverse thought: @Ebonyteach, @debreese, @BLoveSoulPower, @MattRKay, @DrIbram, @MisterMinor @davidekirkland @ValerieKinloch @TchKimPossible and @GholdyM; and the voices of @tweetsomemoore, @LatinoSexuality, @Jess5th and @Jimanekia.

The outside world, as it turns out, was impacting the three of us in ways we were both acknowledging and ignoring. Increasingly burdened throughout the pandemic with a 'leave the outside world outside' anthem, the exasperation was setting in. The truth is, around every corner, educators in the United States are undervalued. News headlines illustrate the consequences of bringing who you are as a human to your classroom. The *Washington Post*[64] ran an article detailing the firing of a Tennessee educator for teaching white supremacy in history. That same month, *USA Today*[65] told of a Michigan teacher forced out of the profession based on his sexuality and desire to hang a gay pride flag in his classroom. And finally, in 2022, the *Daily Mail*[66] wrote of a teacher who blamed Asian Americans for Covid screaming 'Go back to China!' Alarmingly, many teachers today can relate to the story of Pip, the idea of being 'normal' might even seem appealing. Normal, after all, doesn't make headlines. Shortly after this research was complete, Noelle and Justine both left education for the world outside of a traditional classroom.

To return to our chess game analogy, over the ten months in which this project took place, we have grasped a surprising realization – players can win, lose or draw in education. Within the game of chess, a player can declare a draw when the pieces on the board are in the exact same position more than three times or if fifty consecutive moves have not resulted in a captured piece. In the case of our Learning Prism exploration, we see our efforts as a draw. While we played a good game where students came to new understandings and uncovered ways to better understand the world and each other, no permanent changes were made. The curriculum remains fixed, measuring memorization and single right responses, as it was before this project and despite Noelle's offers to continue this work on a larger scale, no attempts have been made to continually pursue this work.

For many deeply committed educators, fuelled by connections between social justice issues and learning, the political work of curriculum, community connections and lesson delivery is simultaneously energizing and exhausting. For the three of us, during a wildly political year, the 4C project connected what was happening throughout the world to this third-grade classroom in life-giving ways. The project connected all of us to the process of becoming conscientious, people first, worldly citizens. However, it was also exhausting and in situations like this it's easy to become hopeless, even distressed – thinking, there is too much work to do and not enough people to do the work. These depressed notions of where education is and the obstacles standing in the way of where it should be, though, only help oppressors. Here, we suggest educators link their work to the work of larger organizations and movements. We also project self-care, taking breaks and sustainable efforts.

Though we did not earn a medal, a trophy or win any awards, our efforts did result in a critical hope for classrooms – a sign of what could be. And, these efforts also illuminated a 'journey of learning access to knowledge and responsibility for the access'.[67] The work is not yet done and as each of us moves forward in education, all in different ways, we take with us the importance of critical reflection, creativity, communication and collaboration embedded in a hope for tomorrow.

Notes

1. M. Jefferson and M. Anderson, *Transforming Schools: Creativity, Critical Reflection, Communication, Collaboration* (Bloomsbury Publishing, 2017), 3.
2. Jefferson and Anderson, *Transforming Schools*.
3. Jefferson and Anderson, *Transforming Schools*.
4. Jefferson and Anderson, *Transforming Schools*, 179.
5. Lenard J. Davis, *Enforcing Normalcy: Disability, Deafness, and the Body* (New York: Verso, 1995), 23.
6. Jefferson and Anderson, *Transforming Schools*.
7. Jefferson and Anderson, *Transforming Schools*.
8. Jefferson and Anderson, *Transforming Schools*.
9. M. Boelts, *Before You Were Mine* (New York: Candlewick Press, 2007).
10. Guojing, *Stormy: A Story About Finding a Forever Home* (Vancouver, Canada: Schwartz & Wade Books, 2019).
11. K. Steele, *A Normal Pig* (New York: Balzer + Bray, 2019).
12. J. Woodson, *The Other Side* (Brooklyn, NY: G. P. Putnam's Sons, 2001).
13. J. Neelands, *Structuring Drama Work: A Handbook of Available Forms in Theatre and Drama* (Cambridge: Cambridge University Press, 1990); C. O'Neill and A. Lambert, *Drama Structures: A Practical Handbook for Teachers* (Nelson Thornes, 1982).
14. Jefferson and Anderson, *Transforming Schools*.
15. Jefferson and Anderson, *Transforming Schools*, 19.

16 D. Booth, '"Imaginary Gardens with Real Toads": Reading and Drama in Education', *Theory into Practice* 24, no. 3 (1985): 193–8.
17 M. Greene, 'Curriculum and Consciousness', *Teachers College Record* 73, no. 2 (1971): 253–70, 123.
18 Steele, *A Normal Pig*.
19 Jefferson and Anderson, *Transforming Schools*.
20 R. J. Sternberg, 'Creative Thinking in the Classroom', *Scandinavian Journal of Educational Research* 47, no. 3 (2003): 325–38.
21 R. A. Beghetto, *Killing Ideas Softly?: The Promise and Perils of Creativity in the Classroom* (Arizona: IAP, 2013); Jefferson and Anderson, *Transforming Schools*.
22 M. Perry and C. Medina, 'Embodiment and Performance in Pedagogy Research: Investigating the Possibility of the Body in Curriculum Experience', *Journal of Curriculum Theorizing* 27, no. 3 (2011): 84–99.
23 Jefferson and Anderson, *Transforming Schools*, 111.
24 Jefferson and Anderson, *Transforming Schools*.
25 Jefferson and Anderson, *Transforming Schools*, 83.
26 R. K. Sawyer, 'Creative Teaching: Collaborative Discussion as Disciplined improvisation', *Educational Researcher* 33 (2004): 12–20; Jefferson and Anderson, *Transforming Schools*.
27 Jefferson and Anderson, *Transforming Schools*, 36.
28 Jefferson and Anderson, *Transforming Schools*, 94.
29 Jefferson and Anderson, *Transforming Schools*.
30 G. Muhammad and B.L. Love, *Cultivating Genius: An Equity Framework for Culturally and Historically Responsive Literacy* (New York, NY: Scholastic Incorporated, 2020).
31 J. Baldwin, 'A Talk to Teachers', *Teachers College Record* 110, no. 14 (2008): 17–20.
32 Jefferson and Anderson, *Transforming Schools*; V. M. Vasquez, *Negotiating Critical Literacies with Young Children* (Washington, DC: Routledge, 2014).
33 Jefferson and Anderson, *Transforming Schools*.
34 Jefferson and Anderson, *Transforming Schools*.
35 C. A. Pohan, 'Creating Caring and Democratic Communities in Our Classrooms and Schools', *Childhood Education* 79, no. 6 (2003): 369–73.
36 J. Dewey, *Education Today* (New York: G. P. Putnam's Sons, 1940).
37 Jefferson and Anderson, *Transforming Schools*.
38 Jefferson and Anderson, *Transforming Schools*.
39 Jefferson and Anderson, *Transforming Schools*, 109.
40 Neelands, *Structuring Drama Work*; O'Neill and A. Lambert, *Drama Structures*.
41 Jefferson and Anderson, *Transforming Schools*, 133.
42 E. Fairweather and B. Cramond, 'Infusing Creative and Critical Thinking into the Curriculum Together', in *Nurturing Creativity in the Classroom*, eds. R.A. Beghetto and J.C. Kaufman (New York: Cambridge University Press, 2010), 113–41; Jefferson and Anderson, *Transforming Schools*; T. Toivanen, R. L. Salomaa, and L. Halkilahti,

'Does Classroom Drama Support Creative Learning?: Viewpoints on the Relationship Between Drama Teaching and Group Creativity', *The Journal for Drama in Education* 32, no. 1 (2016): 39–56.

43 Jefferson and Anderson, *Transforming Schools*; B. Rogoff, 'Developmental Transitions in Children's Participation in Sociocultural Activities', *Human Development* 39, no. 1 (1996): 4–27.

44 L. Alcalá, B. Rogoff, and A. López Fraire, 'Sophisticated Collaboration Is Common Among Mexican-Heritage US Children', *Proceedings of the National Academy of Sciences* 115, no. 45 (2018): 11377.

45 Jefferson and Anderson, *Transforming Schools*.

46 Jefferson and Anderson, *Transforming Schools*.

47 Steele, *A Normal Pig*.

48 Steele, *A Normal Pig*.

49 Steele, *A Normal Pig*.

50 Jefferson and Anderson, *Transforming Schools*.

51 Jefferson and Anderson, *Transforming Schools*, 105.

52 Jefferson and Anderson, *Transforming Schools*, 104.

53 Jefferson and Anderson, *Transforming Schools*.

54 Jefferson and Anderson, *Transforming Schools*, 36.

55 K. E. Pytash, K. E. Batchelor, W. Kist, and K. Srsen, 'Linked Text Sets in the English Classroom', *The ALAN Review* 42, no. 1 (2014): 52–62.

56 J. Ho and N. Naudus, *Eyes that Kiss in the Corners* (Solon, OH: Findaway World, LLC, 2021).

57 P. Aubusson, R. Ewing, and G. F. Hoban, *Action Learning in Schools: Reframing Teachers' Professional Learning and Development* (Sydney, Australia: Routledge, 2009).

58 Jefferson and Anderson, *Transforming Schools*.

59 J. R. Temple, '"People Who Are Different from You": Heterosexism in Quebec High School Textbooks', *Canadian Journal of Education/Revue canadienne de l'éducation* 28, no. 3 (2005): 271–94.

60 J. Chock-Goldman and H. Meader, 'Crisis Intervention', in *The Art of Becoming Indispensable: What School Social Workers Need to Know in Their First Three Years of Practice*, eds. T. Cox, T. Fitzgerald and M.E. Alvarez (Oxford: Oxford University Press, 2021), 133.

61 Jefferson and Anderson, *Transforming Schools*, 24.

62 H. R. Milner IV, 'Race, Talk, Opportunity Gaps, and Curriculum Shifts in (Teacher) Education', *Literacy Research: Theory, Method, and Practice* 66, no. 1 (2017): 73–94.

63 Milner IV, 'Race, Talk, Opportunity Gaps, and Curriculum Shifts in (Teacher) Education', 27.

64 V. Strauss, 'Tennessee Teacher Fired for Teaching About Critical Race Theory', *The Washington Post*, 6 December 2021, https://www.washingtonpost.com/education/2021/12/06/tennessee-teacher-fired-critical-race-theory/.

65 USA Today, 'Michigan Teacher Leaves Job Over Mandate to Remove LGBTQ Pride Flag', 30 November 2021, https://www.usatoday.com/story/news/nation/2021/11/30/michigan-teacher-leaves-job-over-mandate-remove-lgbtq-pride-flag/8804975002/?gnt-cfr=1.
66 https://www.dailymail.co.uk/news/article-10474247/Teacher-fired-city-official-husband-suspended-racist-rant-Asian-American-couple.html.
67 D. Heathcote, 'Learning, Knowing, and Languaging in Drama: An Interview with Dorothy Heathcote', *Language Arts* 60, no. 6 (1983): 695–701.

References

Alcalá, L., B. Rogoff, and A. L. Fraire 2018. 'Sophisticated Collaboration Is Common Among Mexican-heritage US Children'. *Proceedings of the National Academy of Sciences* 115(45): 11377–84.

Baldwin, J. 1967. 'Negroes Are Anti-Semitic Because They're Anti-White'. *New York Times Magazine*, 26.

Beghetto, R. A. 2013. *Killing Ideas Softly?: The Promise and Perils of Creativity in the Classroom*. Oregon: IAP.

Daily Mail 2022. *California Christian School Teacher is Fired and her City Official Husband is Suspended for Racist Rant at Asian-American Couple Blaming Them for COVID and Screaming: 'America is a Free Country! Go Back to China!'*. 3 February.

Davis, Lenard J. 1995. *Enforcing Normalcy: Disability, Deafness, and the Body*. New York: Verso.

Ewing, R. A. and J. N. Saunders 2019. 'The School Drama Partnership: Beyond an Artist-in-residence Program'. In Robyn Ewing and John Saunders (eds.), *Education and Theatres*, 149–63. Cham: Springer.

Fairweather, E. and B. Cramond 2010. 'Infusing Creative and Critical Thinking into the Curriculum Together'. In R.A.Beghetto and J.C. Kaufman (eds.), *Nurturing Creativity in the Classroom*, 113–41. New York: Cambridge University Press.

Greene, M. 1971. 'Curriculum and Consciousness'. *Teachers College Record* 73(2): 253–70.

Heathcote, D. 1983. 'Learning, Knowing, and Languaging in Drama: An Interview With Dorothy Heathcote'. *Language Arts* 60(6): 695–701.

Heathcote, D. 2012. 'The Fight for Drama, The Fight for Education'. *The National Association for the Teaching of Drama* 28(1): 1–9.

Jefferson, M. and M. Anderson 2017. *Transforming Schools: Creativity, Critical Reflection, Communication, Collaboration*. Bloomsbury Publishing.

Muhammad, G. 2020. *Cultivating Genius: An Equity Framework for Culturally and Historically Responsive Literacy*. Scholastic Incorporated.

Neelands, J. 1984. *Making Sense of Drama: A Guide to Classroom Practice*. Heinemann.

Neelands, J. 1990. *Structuring Drama Work: A Handbook of Available Forms in Theatre and Drama*. Cambridge University Press.

O'Neill, C. 1995. *Drama Worlds: A Framework for Process Drama*. Portsmouth, NH: Heinemann, 67.

O'Neill, C. and A. Lambert 1982. *Drama Structures: A Practical Handbook for Teachers*. Nelson Thornes.

Perry, M. and C. Medina 2011. 'Embodiment and Performance in Pedagogy Research: Investigating the Possibility of the Body in Curriculum Experience'. *Journal of Curriculum Theorizing* 27(3): 84–99.

Pohan, C. A. 2003. 'Creating Caring and Democratic Communities in our Classrooms and Schools'. *Childhood Education* 79(6): 369–73.

Pytash, K., K. Batchelor William Kist, and K. Srsen 2014. 'Linked Text Sets in the English Classroom'. *ALAN* 42(1): 6–12.

Rogoff, B. 1996. 'Developmental Transitions in Children's Participation in Sociocultural Activities'. *Human Development* 39(1): 4–27.

Sawyer, R. K. 2004. Creative teaching: Collaborative discussion as disciplined improvisation. *Educational Researcher* 33(3): 12–20.

Connection, Creative Chaos and Vulnerability

Reflections on Transformative Praxis

Moema Gregorzewski, Jean M Uasike Allen and Peter O'Connor

3

- **The wider context of Aotearoa** (p. 54)
- **Mitey: A whole school arts-based approach to mental health education** (p. 55)
- **The nature of transformative praxis** (p. 58)
- **Connection, creative chaos and vulnerability: Reflections on transformative praxis in Mitey** (p. 59)
- **Immediacy in a mediated world: Creating genuine human connections** (p. 59)
- **Carefully scaffolded chaos: Teaching as a creative process** (p. 60)
- **Reciprocal vulnerability** (p. 62)
- **Conclusion** (p. 64)

In 2021, we evaluated the use of arts-based pedagogies and practices in four primary schools in Aotearoa. All four schools were taking part in Mitey, a whole-school professional development approach to mental health education. We were interested in exploring how the transformation of teachers' pedagogical practice could create impact on a wider agenda to support the mental health and well-being of staff and students. We begin this chapter by situating our evaluation in the wider cultural, political and historical context of Aotearoa. We then discuss our conceptualization of mental health. Next, we discuss the theoretical underpinning of Mitey, its uniquely Indigenous ways of understanding mental health and its reliance on arts-based pedagogies. We subsequently frame the critical pedagogical approach we take to understanding notions of and possibilities for genuine transformation in schools. We explore how one teacher, Paul, reflects on his experience of Mitey and his perception of how his praxis has transformed. We suggest that the possibility of genuine transformative praxis in schools results from creating whole-school systems that enable authentic human connections, creative chaos and reciprocal vulnerability in classrooms.

The wider context of Aotearoa

Aotearoa, like many other nation states, continues to grapple with the ongoing impacts of its colonial history. In the last forty years, radical neoliberal policies have exacerbated the ongoing trauma this colonial history has caused for Māori, the Indigenous people of Aotearoa and settler populations. One in four children in Aotearoa live in material hardship and one in five children live with 'food insecurity'. Māori and Pacific children are disproportionately overrepresented in these statistics. Aotearoa's family violence ranked an appalling fifth out of the thirty-four OECD member countries in 2015.[1] Research shows that some victims suffer more than fifty incidents of domestic violence before getting help, with 'children [. . .] present at two-thirds of all family violence incidents attended by Police'.[2] Children make up 20 per cent of all violent deaths. Aotearoa has one of the highest youth suicide rates in the world and 23 per cent of young people report symptoms of depression. Covid-19 has further layered a further trauma on all children. Pacific and Māori communities have experienced disproportionate numbers of infections, hospitalizations, deaths and severe economic pressures.

The World Health Organization (WHO)[3] defines mental health as 'a state of well-being in which the individual realises his or her own abilities, can cope with the normal stresses of life, can work productively and fruitfully, and is able to make a contribution to his or her community'.[4] While this definition positions mental health as more than just the absence of mental disorders, it has been challenged by Galderisi[5] and Tiatia-Seath, Tupou and Fookes[6] as being embedded in socioeconomic terms. According to the authors, WHO's conceptualization of mental health posits that 'to be mentally well, is to be productive'.[7] This concept of production aligns clearly with dehumanizing neoliberal ideology focused on the individual as a form of capitalist production.[8] We also question the use of 'normal stresses of life'. After all, what is deemed normal? In the Aotearoa context, due to its colonial history, white middle-class colonial ideals often dictate norms. We argue, however, that the oppressive situation in which many citizens of Aotearoa find themselves is a temporary situation. As Freire[9] proposes, we may change an oppressive status quo collectively by engaging in dialogue and naming our realities. As an arts-based approach, Mitey responds to Freire's proposition. It is based on an Indigenous model of mental health that, rather than limiting itself to individualistic notions of health, acknowledges the need for and the possibilities of genuine social change.

Mitey: A whole school arts-based approach to mental health education

The Sir John Kirwan Foundation (hereafter referred to as 'the Foundation') desired to respond to these deep-seated social issues discussed above. In 2019, the foundation approached the Te Rito Toi Centre for Arts and Social Transformation at Waipapa Taumata Rau, the University of Auckland, to design a whole-school approach to mental health education specifically for Aotearoa primary schools. As a result, a cross-disciplinary team at the university worked alongside trial schools, a web design company and foundation staff to co-design Mitey. It is the first whole-school mental health education approach in Aotearoa schools to have been shaped by peer-reviewed research.

In January 2021, the university team and the foundation launched Mitey's Wellbeing Review Tool and the Mitey website www.mitey.org.nz. The Wellbeing Review Tool is a survey gathering the status quo of mental health education in each participating school. It ascertains needs across all aspects of school life, including policy and governance, community relationships, staff well-being and classroom pedagogical and curricular approaches. The Mitey website features a public-facing presence and an intranet for those schools who contract into the freely provided, philanthropically supported essential resources for schools.

In February 2021, Mitey 'coaches' and senior teachers with curriculum expertise began to implement the approach. Employed by the foundation, Mitey coaches train teachers in schools by unpacking Mitey's underpinning pedagogical principles and understanding of mental health and modelling learning experiences in class. When the coaches work in collaboration with schools, they codesign a unique approach in each school by establishing a plan of action based on the well-being review tool results. The coaches model, co-teach and observe teachers in classrooms as they work through the lesson plans provided via the Mitey website. The coaches provide advice and support senior leadership, governance groups and the wider school community.

Contemporary international literature emphasizes that mental health is a community responsibility, not just a personal matter, and that the promotion of mental health is a collaborative social action.[10] In Mitey, everyone belonging to the wider school community – *all* school staff (including non-teaching staff), students and their whānau – become central players in children's socioemotional development and mental health[11]. Focusing on both the individual and the environment, Mitey adopts a holistic, proactive perspective that considers the social-ecological situatedness of each participating school.[12]

Acknowledging its unique historio-cultural situatedness in Aotearoa, Mitey is underpinned by the Mana Model.[13] The model identifies five dimensions of mana, or power,[14] that children need to thrive. These dimensions relate not only to the child as an individual but also to their family, school and community. Mana whānau emphasizes that children need to believe that they are central and valued within their whānau (wider family) and school. In this way, they can develop a sense of self and contentment. Mana ūkaipō describes the feeling of belonging and connection to the environment and to others. Mana ūkaipō celebrating difference as enriching and unique and porposes that children need to know their cultural knowledges and histories. Mana motuhake acknowledges the importance of nurturing a positive sense of identity and providing role modelling in children's lives. Mana tū focuses on children's need to develop understanding and skills to deal with adversity. Mana tangatarua calls on educators to foster the development of the skills, knowledges and confidence that enable children to navigate mental well-being within multiple worlds and cultural contexts.

To explore how Mitey can catalyse transformative praxis, it is important to consider that the approach is *not* a targeted programme that focuses on preventing or treating mental illness. Other contemporary mental health promotion programmes in schools constitute such 'targeted initiatives' delivered to selected children who show signs or symptoms of negative mental health. Such programmes focus on attempts to 'fix' children at risk. Many didactically disseminate messages about unhealthy or disruptive habits, such as behaving defiantly, taking drugs or bullying. Others engage children in isolated activities that temporarily improve their well-being in the short term. Examples of such practices are positive affirmation games or resilience skills training. However, if an initiative only targets a distinct percentage of children, it may fail to provide for children who have mental health struggles but do not show symptoms. It may also fail to provide for those who might have poor mental health in the future.[15]

Mitey's design aims to enable teachers to integrate the social and emotional learning of *all* children into their everyday life and activities at school. In this way, Mitey is a universal, embedded whole-school approach to mental health education. As a universal approach, Mitey responds to Le Galès-Camus'[16] warning that the ubiquitous, exclusive preoccupation with those labelled 'ill' undermines the provision of educational initiatives that promote and sustain positive mental health for all. Contemporary research emphasizes that universal approaches promoting positive mental health for all are effective.[17] As Holt[18] argues, children on all points of the mental health spectrum benefit from mental health-promoting initiatives. Children with risk factors or mental health issues benefit more from universal approaches in which they work together with others rather than from approaches that target only them.[19] It is as important, then, that schools develop proactive strategies that promote mental well-being for all. In this way, schools can ensure that school staff can recognize the needs of children with mental health issues and refer them to targeted support or treatment.[20] Universal approaches minimize stigma and discrimination, the biggest barricades hindering people from seeking help when struggling with negative mental health.[21]

Arts-based and experiential approaches to teaching and learning are central to the learning experience sequences developed. Mitey is based on a stepped progression of learning. It consists of a framework outlining clear achievement objectives embedded in four scaffolded units, or levels. These are, in turn, composed of a number of carefully sequenced drama pedagogy-based learning experiences. The Mitey framework outlines the skills, knowledge and understanding about mental health expected to be taught and learnt at each curriculum level.

Mitey's Level 1 unit, entitled *My Kākahu*, illustrates how Mitey is conceptualized and implemented as a whole-school approach explicitly anchored in the Mana Model. *My Kākahu* provides teachers with a series of clearly scaffolded learning experiences that provoke students to explore their own identities, feelings and the identities and feelings of others. A kākahu is a Māori cloak traditionally woven from feathers and flax. Throughout the ten learning experiences constituting *My Kākahu*, students create a variety of paper feathers. For example, learners create feathers representing what they like doing. Learners also reflect on what makes a good friend and how they can be a good friend to others. They create feathers with one of the qualities of a friend and how the friend makes them feel. The scaffolded learning experiences challenge learners to explore ideas about their feelings and aspects that make them the same and different from others. For example, learners create self-portraits, which are used throughout the unit to elicit reflections and discussions. Using drama education strategies to explore a picture book about friendship, courage and the value of differences, teachers encourage students to explore how thoughts can lead to feelings and actions. Learners also unpack the idea of what it means to be brave and create feathers representing moments in their lives when they were brave.

In the seventh learning experience, learners encounter Mitey's mascot, a balloon dog from outer space. Teachers engage in the drama education strategy Teacher in Role. Here, the teacher takes on the role of the balloon dog Mitey, who has just arrived on earth from outer space and wants to know more about who the learners are, where they are from and what these peculiar things called feelings are. Using song and visual art, learners identify and represent different feelings and create a vocabulary of emotions together. They talk to Mitey, the balloon dog, and explain what different feelings mean to them, where they feel them in their body and how others might see them feel that way. Again, learners create visual representations of their explorations onto feathers. Progressively, the learners and their teacher collaboratively weave each feather into a kākahu. This communal cloak becomes a representation of what makes the class who they are, and of what helps to support them as a community of learners. The unit encourages learners to regard their and each other's similarities and differences as valuable, productive and protective. It was during discussion of this seventh learning experience that one teacher, Paul, articulated his experience of the Mitey approach.

That's why I've chosen
    to spend that time
        where we should have been
            doing guided reading
                I should have been
                    sitting down with a group
                      and asking them
                        to show their work
I should have been
    doing a
        writing warm up
            and doing some
            grammar and
                punctuation practice
                and some
                      structured literacy---
But what we did today
                was
                              magic.

When Paul spoke of the 'magic' that happened with his 7- and 8-year-old students, he recalled sitting cross-legged on his classroom floor with his students. They sat in a circle, watching each other engage in countless attempts at bringing the Mitey mascot to life. Dozens of miniature balloon dogs were about to be born into this world. Paul recalled whole-hearted laughter reverberating from all directions of the classroom as myriad half-formed balloon creatures vanished into thin air with unapologetically vociferous pops and bangs. Paul recalled students experiencing him fail in both laughter and despair and try again with outrageous resilience and courageous belief. He remembered students supporting him accomplish those awfully intricate twists and fiddly twirls that turn formless, limp rubber and invisible air into perky little paws in an ever-growing playground of liberating chaos and reciprocal commitment. Paul recalled looking up from his playfully distorted, dancing fingers to reframe the scene, to see his students afresh. They were no longer inchoate beings in need of adult interventions. Rather, they emerged as fellow cocreators, who, immersed in the heightened state of embodied awareness of this human co-presence and laid bare vulnerability, seemed to have felt this magic too (Research memo).

This 'magic' Paul speaks of, we argue, is an example of transformative praxis.

The nature of transformative praxis

Paolo Freire[22] understood praxis as an iterative cyclical interplay between action and reflection, informed by and informing both theory and practice. Freire[23] argues education will be transformative when teachers 'live the plenitude of their praxis, that is, if their action encompasses a critical reflection which increasingly organizes their thinking and thus leads them to move from a purely naïve knowledge of reality to a higher level, one which enables them to perceive the causes of reality'.[24] We conceptualize educational transformation as a humanizing process resulting from social and political change.

The transformation sought by Mitey is essentially about making school structures and ethos more human. Based on critical conceptusalizations of educational transformation and pedagogy, Mitey recognizes that the relationship between teachers and students sits at the heart of all learning in schools. Mitey engages school communities to collaboratively embark upon a journey towards health and well-being. This mutual journey encourages teachers to learn and learners and communities to teach.[25] Whole-school communities engage in rich and meaningful learning about the world, their places within it and the places they would like to occupy. We argue that Mitey catalyses transformative praxis because it embraces and promotes pedagogical practices that privilege (1) the immediacy of genuine human connection, (2) carefully scaffolded creative 'chaos' and (3) a sense of 'reciprocal vulnerability'.

Connection, creative chaos and vulnerability: Reflections on transformative praxis in Mitey

'My class have a lot of behavioural problems', Paul told me straight away as I interviewed him at his school in May 2021. 'A lot are high needs'. he put it both exhaustedly and lovingly as we sat cramped in the small office space off a narrow, seemingly endless corridor next to the staff room. 'They have the potential to be one of the toughest, but also one of the sweetest classes I've ever had' (Research memo).

Immediacy in a mediated world: Creating genuine human connections

During our interview, Paul highlighted that Mitey fostered what he called 'the human connection' not only between his students, but also between his students and himself. Paul emphasised that nurturing genuine human relations was crucial 'in an age where those kids are headed, sorry, but they're headed more for disconnection. You know, everything virtual walking around like this---' As he spoke, Paul eerily morphed into a hunchback creature that stared obsessively at the stiff end of its own arm, hidden underneath the table. Paul lamented that students' sense of presence was perpetually distorted by social media. When the crooked critter finally redirected its gaze back towards me, it whispered, 'They crave it'. Paul nodded as he slowly turned back into himself. 'They want more of it.' (Research memo).

The exploration of human experience and expression via social relations and connection sits at the heart of critical pedagogy. Critical pedagogue bell hooks[26] identifies the kind of human connection Paul discusses above as a form of pedagogical love. hooks articulates that teaching with love entails engaging in commitment, responsibility and trust. When such an engagement occurs, educators can provide students with powerful learning experiences. It was this human connection, or pedagogical love, for which Paul seemed to ache:

> The urgency in his voice grew as he continued, 'We need it rather than be given a big book that we have to walk around with and say, hang on, let me just check if I'm allowed to do that first---' As Paul continued, he transformed once again. This time, his spine straightened in the blink of an eye, like an arrow hurtling to its destination. His voice grew loud, stern, and alarmed: 'Oh no, no, no, no, no! There's no learning intention associated with that!' A moment of silence followed. We let it pass. Paul let himself sink back into his chair. His gaze examined the bare table. He contemplated. What was it about Mitey that allowed him to make these genuine connections with his students, which humanised his classroom, which freed him from the chains of rigid learning intentions that at all times seemed to keep a watchful, warning eye over him and his pedagogical practice? Eventually, Paul raised his gaze. 'That's the thing, that is it!' I looked back at him in suspense. It was not long before I caught an almost perfectly camouflaged sparkle return to his eyes. 'It's--- creative!' (Research Memo).

We explore creativity as an enabling factor of educational transformation next.

Carefully scaffolded chaos: Teaching as a creative process

As Paul's reflections on his experiences of Mitey progressed, he repeatedly concluded that he could only be an effective and inspiring role model and mentor if students experienced his teaching practice as a creative process. Paul explained that this entailed being spontaneous and resilient, openly taking risks, reacting to setbacks and flexibly adapting his practice to unforeseen circumstances. Crucially, he came to realize that collaboration with students was vital to understanding and implementing teaching as a creative process. This realization can be understood within a critical pedagogical framing as a move towards reconciliation.[27] Here, teachers and students are no longer positioned within an educational hierarchy. Rather, they understand that they are simultaneously teachers and learners within a process of inquiry. Paul's reflections propose that his experiences of Mitey resonate with Freire's vision of schools not as places purposed on liberating whole-school communities via set programmes but rather as spaces where such communities of learners, teachers and families can develop solidarity with one another and defiantly reimagine their realities.[28]

Paul stated that the flexibility provided by Mitey's clear but open structure was another key player in enabling him to conceptualize his teaching practice as a creative process and to act accordingly in his classroom. Paul termed the flexibility and adaptability possible within Mitey's solid structure 'chaos'. He enthusiastically emphasized that

> It enables the kids to see you react to any setbacks, any change of plans, they see you adapt, they see you be resilient, and they see you as someone that they trust. Maybe being a little bit out of your depth for a while, but then they get to see a heavy sense of how you work, you know, they get to see this. boom. They get to see this creative 'oh right and this is why I trust this person for six hours a day, you know, this is why this person is my mentor right now.' Because if they can do it, I want to learn how to do that. It's inspiring to them. [. . .] you need it, you definitely need it (Research memo)

Paul proposed that the 'chaos' inherent in Mitey acknowledges the unpredictability of human interaction and the creative, dynamic nature of teaching and learning. To Paul, Mitey was a 'map', not a prescription. Mitey did not dictate rigidly predetermined processes. Paul's reflections assert that the four unit levels' explicit achievement objectives linked to the Aotearoa New Zealand Curriculum, along with the levels' clearly defined learning outcomes, constitute an effective, stable scaffolding. However, this structure did not prescribe the nature and pace of pedagogic engagement. As Paul highlighted, sometimes '[t]here's a problem. Things are not going according to the script'. Mitey's clear scaffolding, a carefully sequenced stepped progression of learning, allowed him to 'chuck the script out' when necessary, while continuing to deliver purposeful mental health education. Mitey allowed him to adapt the pace at which he worked with his students, to slow down the curriculum, and to harness valuable moments for future learning. Paul's reflections suggest that these moments of pedagogical practice constituted what Freire[29] calls an act of freedom, where creative power works for students and teachers to become more conscious of the world around them in all its messiness, creativity and chaos.

During the communal balloon dog creation lesson, Paul and his students did not start their scheduled Mitey learning experience. Instead, they prepared for the next session by creating balloon animals. Paul stressed that because of this extraordinary ('magic') experience, his students were personally and emotionally invested in the character Mitey, the imaginary dog from outer space. Consequently, they engaged passionately in the learning experience the following day, when they explored what feelings were and how they were at play in their own lives. Paul had been certain that students would not take the drama strategy involved (Teacher-in-Role) seriously and, consequently, disengage. When Paul encountered this perceived 'problem', he 'chucked out the script' and engaged his students in the collaborative creation of balloon dogs.

This instance of reciprocal vulnerability and compassionate support constituted a pivotal learning experience for both Paul and his students, and for all of them as a class community. The creative 'chaos' catalysed and sustained by Mitey's stable structure gave Paul opportunities to engage in acts of spontaneity and the deconstruction of traditional power hierarchies ingrained in mainstream schools. Paul could share power and decision-making with his students. As he avidly reported, 'the kids loved it. Being able to share some of that power, share some of that decision making, make suggestions and find that those suggestions were really, really good.' From a critical pedagogical framing, Paul's sharing of power with his students is key to his movement in pedagogical practice from a banking model to a problem-posing educational stance.[30] Here, teachers and learners encounter each other holistically, not as knowledge depositors and empty pitchers, but as multidimensional human beings endeavouring to grapple with the world within and around them collectively. According to Paul, the pedagogical shift needed to conceptualize school communities as more human also involved a movement in levels of vulnerability of all in the classroom. We explore Paul's reflections on reciprocal vulnerability next.

Reciprocal vulnerability

Paul reflected that Mitey's successful implementation required him to be vulnerable. He defined vulnerability as speaking honestly about emotions with his students, including 'talk[ing] about how you're suffering'. Paul explained that bringing his own vulnerability into the classroom and expressing feelings was new to him. Being vulnerable, he shared, was particularly difficult for him as a man. He lamented that 'it's not expected'. At the same time, Paul asserted that he had always aspired to inspire his male students to be vulnerable and talk about personal struggles and emotions, encourage reciprocal support and instil a sense of hope for difficult times. Hope is a key concept in critical pedagogy that transforms educational spaces. It is a practice that bell hooks[31] articulates as a pedagogy in itself. She argues that if we do not have hope we cannot imagine, and if we cannot imagine, we cannot bring new possibilities into being. We conceptualize Paul's focus on instilling a sense of hope within his class as a crucial constituent of his emerging transformative practice through the Mitey approach. Before engaging in Mitey, Paul had striven to be 'frank and honest'. He had shared tales and personal experiences with his learners. As Paul put it, he had been wearing his heart on his sleeve. This had always been important to him, particularly because he wanted to reach the boys in his class. He wanted them to have the mentor he himself had never had. Mitey, however, catalysed a move beyond superficially sharing personal anecdotes towards openly acknowledging, exhibiting and sharing his own vulnerability. Paul also shared that his students had never 'had to be' vulnerable prior to Mitey, to apologize, to admit mistakes and to be empathetic and self-reflective. As he explained, 'they've never had to be vulnerable and turn around and do things like, I made a mistake, I'm really sorry. I hurt your feelings

I didn't mean to make you cry. Sometimes I feel like that as well. When I have those feelings, please forgive me'. Paul's observations indicate that he perceived an increase in his students' ability to recognize and positively respond to mental health matters in themselves and others. Paul noticed that students increasingly thought before they spoke. He suggested that they were more cognizant of the impact their words could have. He stated that his students were beginning to use kinder words with each other. He had also noticed that students exhibited less hesitation to want to share and participate, a shift he attributed to the fact that, since starting Mitey, teachers 'get involved in sharing things about us as real people'; '[w]e are modeling it [. . .] They're seeing us as vulnerable as well'. In this way, Mitey provided the basis for a pedagogy of reciprocal vulnerability.

Paul's reflections suggest that he started to reframe his own vulnerability, and that of his students, as an asset. He began to model this active process of shifting perspectives to his students. He engaged in a pedagogy of reciprocal vulnerability, a way of not only teaching and learning, but also knowing and being in the world with oneself and others. Critical activist scholars such as Cammarota and Fine[32] argue that all knowledges are relational. In other words, they are embedded in social interactions. This assertion provokes us and educators like Paul to recognize and raise the status and value of social interactions in the classroom. In the case of Paul's class community, knowledges emerged as deeply relational and social interactions as highly valuable, since their acknowledgement allowed a sense of reciprocal vulnerability between Paul and his students to form, surface and proclaim its own validity and pedagogical worth.

The Mitey coaches were an integral part in paving the way for reciprocal vulnerability to unfold. Along with other teaching staff interviewed at his school, Paul characterized the coaches as open, approachable, understanding, non-judgemental and inspiring. As Paul reflected,

> So, I really appreciate that. Sometimes you do get professionals that come through to PD [Professional Development]. And you know that they're just running the script through. You know, but [the coaches] have both been amazing with it and from the point of view that they remember our names. And they've only seen us a handful of times this year, you know, three or four times, but they remember. And that means a lot. They'll talk to you about different things, they will model approaches that they'll do, they're willing to put themselves on the line. And I rate that so high, I really do, I rate that huge.

Paul's reflections propose that the coaches were willing to be vulnerable themselves. They modelled a pedagogy of reciprocal vulnerability by engaging in spontaneity, flexibility and risk-taking. We suggest that engaging in a process-focused and open-ended arts- and drama-based approach to teaching and learning encouraged the coaches to embrace improvisation, adaptability and unknown possibilities. Paul emphasized that he needed time to observe the coaches in action to grow confident and comfortable with the idea of facilitating Mitey himself. He appreciated that the coaches gave him the opportunity to sit back and observe their pedagogical practice in the classroom. Mitey's scaffolded modelling approach to professional development, along with the coaches' sincere interest in establishing and sustaining a genuine reciprocal relationship with Paul, provided him with the space, pace and human connection he felt he needed to grow his confidence and trust – and to eventually facilitate and adapt Mitey's learning experiences himself.

Conclusion

We have often wondered if Paul would have framed and named his world the way he did if we had never interviewed him. Perhaps our conversation constituted a crucial first step for Paul in recognizing, naming and framing the profound shift towards a transformative praxis that was unfurling so slowly, quietly, almost invisibly within and around Paul, strategically camouflaged within the rigidity of everyday curriculum demands.

Paul's reflections on the shifts in his pedagogical practice catalysed by the creation of affective human connections and courageous reciprocal vulnerability resonate with the interviews we conducted with other Mitey teachers. They all became neither fixers nor counsellors, but facilitators of collaborative learning and catalysts for communal reflection. In carefully scaffolded creative 'chaos' within their classrooms, learning communities like Paul and his students could try out embodied, affective explorations of their experiences kanohi ki te kanohi, face-to-face. As Paul modelled his vulnerability to his students, he witnessed them grow emotionally receptive and lay bare their own humanity. Reciprocal vulnerability on the basis of genuine relationship-building made seeing, naming and reframing possible. We surmise that Paul and his students began to act as co-creators of knowledges whose earnest engagement and unveiled vulnerability demand a radical reconceptualization of what schooling should first and foremost be: spaces that are compassionate, creatively chaotic and humanizing.

Notes

1 R. Gammon, *Family Violence: New Zealand's Dirty Little Secret* (Massey University News, 2016), http://www.massey.ac.nz/massey/about-massey/news/article.cfm?mnarticle_uuid=C61AEFE4-B1D7-0794-48A1-CFA90FEDDEFF; A. Grant, 'Vulnerable Children Act 2014', *Auckland University Law Review* 22 (2016): 401–8; Z. Henley, 'Cross-agency Plan to Deliver World Leading Interventions for People Who Use Violence Within Their Family', *Practice: The New Zealand Corrections Journal* 4, no. 2 (2016), https://www.corrections.govt.nz/resources/research_and_statistics/journal/volume_4_issue_2_december_2016.html.

2 Ministry of Justice, *Reform of Family Violence Law Paper One: Context and Supporting Integrated Responses* (2016), 1, https://www.justice.govt.nz/assets/Documents/Publications/fv-reform-paper-1-context.pdf.

3 World Health Organization (WHO), *Mental Health: Strengthening Our Response (2018)*, https://www.who.int/news-room/fact-sheets/detail/mental-health-strengthening-our-response.
4 World Health Organization (WHO), *Mental Health*, para. 2.
5 S. Galderisi, A. Heinz, M. Kastrup, J. Beezhold, and N. Sartorius, 'Towards a New Definition of Mental Health', *World Psychiatry* 14, no. 2 (2015): 231–3.
6 J. Tiatia-Seath, T. Tupou, and I. Fookes, 'Climate Change, Mental Health, and Wellbeing for Pacific Peoples: A Literature Review', *The Contemporary Pacific* 32, no. 2 (2020): 400–30.
7 World Health Organization (WHO), *Mental Health*, 404–5.
8 P. Freire, *Pedagogy of the Oppressed* (London: Penguin Books, 1996).
9 Freire, *Pedagogy of the Oppressed*. New York, Bloomsbury
10 H. Herrman, S. Saxena, and R. Moodie, *Promoting Mental Health: Concepts, Emerging Evidence, Practice: A Report of the World Health Organization, Department of Mental Health and Substance Abuse in Collaboration with the Victorian Health Promotion Foundation and the University of Melbourne* (Geneva: WHO Press, 2004).
11 D. Holt, *Promoting Positive Mental Health in the Primary School: Theory into Practice* (Milton Park, Abingdon: Routledge, 2020), https://doi.org/10.4324/9780429504051
12 J. A. Durlak, R. P. Weissberg, A. B. Dymnicki, R. D. Taylor, and K. B. Schellinger, 'The Impact of Enhancing Students' Social and Emotional Learning: A Meta-Analysis of School-Based Universal Interventions', *Child Development* 82, no. 1 (2011): 405–32, https://doi.org/10.1111/j.1467-8624.2010.01564.x.
13 A. Macfarlane, M. Webber, H. McRae, and C. Cookson-Cox, *Ka Awatea: An Iwi Case Study of Māori Students' Success* (Te Rū Rangahau: University of Canterbury, 2014).
14 J. C. Moorfield, *Mana* (Te Aka Māori Dictionary, 2022), https://maoridictionary.co.nz/word/3424.
15 J. Glazzard, 'A Whole-School Approach to Supporting Children and Young People's Mental Health', *Journal of Public Mental Health* 18, no. 4 (2019): 256–65, https://doi.org/10.1108/JPMH-10-2018-0074.
16 C. Le Galès-Camus, 'Foreword', in *Promoting Mental Health: Concepts, Emerging Evidence, Practice. A Report from the World Health Organisation, Department of Mental Health and Substance Abuse, in Collaboration with the Victorian Health Promotion Foundation (VicHealth) and The University of Melbourne (2004)*. World Health Organization (WHO), *Mental Health*.
17 A. Graham, R. Phelps, C. Maddison, and R. Fitzgerald, 'Supporting Children's Mental Health in Schools: Teacher Views', *Teachers and Teaching: Theory and Practice* 17, no. 4 (2011): 479–96, https://doi.org/10.1080/13540602.2011.580525.
18 Holt, *Promoting Positive Mental Health in the Primary School*.
19 K. Weare and W. Markham, 'What Do We Know About Promoting Mental Health Through Schools?', *IUHPE – Promotion Education* 7, no. 3–4 (2005): 118–22.
20 G. Danby and P. Hamilton, 'Addressing the "Elephant in the Room". The Role of the Primary School Practitioner in Supporting Children's Mental Well-Being', *Pastoral*

Care in Education 34, no. 2 (2016): 90–103, https://doi.org/10.1080/02643944.2016.1167110.
21 Weare and Markham, 'What Do We Know About Promoting Mental Health Through Schools?'.
22 P. Freire, *Cultural Action for Freedom* (New York: Harvard Educational Review, 1970), 476–521.
23 Freire, *Cultural Action for Freedom*.
24 Freire, *Cultural Action for Freedom*.
25 P. Freire, (1998). *Pedagogy of Freedom* (New York: Rowman and Littlefield Publishers, 1998).
26 b. hooks, *Teaching Community: A Pedagogy of Hope* (New York: Routledge, 2003).
27 Freire, *Pedagogy of the Oppressed*.
28 G. E. Fischman, 'Un/Taming Freire's Pedagogy of the Oppressed', in *The Routledge International Handbook of Critical Education*, ed. M. W. Apple, W. Au, and L. A. Gandin (New York: Routledge, 2009), 232–9.
29 Freire, *Pedagogy of the Oppressed*.
30 Freire, *Pedagogy of the Oppressed*.
31 hooks, *Teaching Community*.
32 J. Cammarota and M. Fine, *Revolutionizing Education: Youth Participatory Action Research in Motion* (New York: Routledge, 2008).

References

Cammarota, J. and M. Fine 2008. *Revolutionizing Education: Youth Participatory Action Research in Motion*. New York: Routledge.
Danby, G. and P. Hamilton 2016. 'Addressing the "Elephant in the Room". The Role of the Primary School Practitioner in Supporting Children's Mental Well-being'. *Pastoral Care in Education* 34(2): 90–103. https://doi.org/10.1080/02643944.2016.1167110.
Durlak, J. A., R. P. Weissberg, A. B. Dymnicki, R. D. Taylor, and K. B. Schellinger 2011. 'The Impact of Enhancing Students' Social and Emotional Learning: A Meta-analysis of School-based Universal Interventions'. *Child Development* 82(1): 405–32. https://doi.org/10.1111/j.1467-8624.2010.01564.x.
Fischman, G. E. 2009. 'Un/Taming Freire's Pedagogy of the Oppressed'. In M. W. Apple., W. Au, and L. A. Gandin (eds.), *The Routledge International Handbook of Critical Education*, 232–9. New York: Routledge.
Freire, P. 1996. *Pedagogy of the Oppressed*. London: Penguin Books.
Freire, P. 1998. *Pedagogy of Freedom*. New York: Rowman and Littlefield Publishers.
Galderisi, S., A. Heinz, M. Kastrupt, J. Beezhold, and N. Sartorius 2015. 'Towards a New Definition of Mental Health'. *World Psychiatry* 14(2): 231–3.
Gammon, R. 2016. 'Family Violence: New Zealand's Dirty Little Secret'. *Massey University News*. http://www.massey.ac.nz/massey/about-massey/news/article.cfm?mnarticle_uuid=C61AEFE4-B1D7-0794-48A1-CFA90FEDDEFF.
Glazzard, J. 2019. 'A Whole-school Approach to Supporting Children and Young People's Mental Health'. *Journal of Public Mental Health* 18(4): 256–65. https://doi.org/10.1108/JPMH-10-2018-0074.

Graham, A., R. Phelps, C. Maddison, and R. Fitzgerald 2011. 'Supporting Children's Mental Health in Schools: Teacher Views'. *Teachers and Teaching: Theory and Practice* 17(4): 479–96. https://doi.org/10.1080/13540602.2011.580525.

Grant, A. 2016. 'Vulnerable Children Act 2014'. *Auckland University Law Review* 22: 401–8.

Henley, Z. 2016. 'Cross-agency Plan to Deliver World Leading Interventions for People who use Violence Within Their Family'. *Practice: The New Zealand Corrections Journal* 4(2). https://www.corrections.govt.nz/resources/research_and_statistics/journal/volume_4_issue_2_december_2016.html.

Herrman, H., S. Saxena, and R. Moodie 2004. *Promoting Mental Health: Concepts, Emerging Evidence, Practice: A Report of the World Health Organization, Department of Mental Health and Substance Abuse in Collaboration With the Victorian Health Promotion Foundation and the University of Melbourne*. WHO Press.

Holt, D. 2020. *Promoting Positive Mental Health in the Primary School: Theory Into Practice*. Routledge. https://doi.org/10.4324/9780429504051.

hooks, b. 2003. *Teaching Community: A Pedagogy of Hope*. New York: Routledge.

Le Galès-Camus, C. 2004. 'Foreword'. In *Promoting Mental Health: Concepts, Emerging Evidence, Practice. A Report From the World Health Organisation, Department of Mental Health and Substance Abuse, in Collaboration With the Victorian Health Promotion Foundation (VicHealth) and The University of Melbourne*. World Health Organization.

Ministry of Justice 2016. *Reform of Family Violence Law Paper One: Context and Supporting Integrated Responses*. https://www.justice.govt.nz/assets/Documents/Publications/fv-reform-paper-1-context.pdf.

Moorfield, J. C. 2022. *Mana. Te Aka Māori Dictionary*. https://maoridictionary.co.nz/word/3424.

Tiatia-Seath, J., T. Tupou, and I. Fookes 2020. 'Climate Change, Mental Health, and Well-being for Pacific Peoples: A Literature Review'. *The Contemporary Pacific* 32(2): 400–30.

Weare, K. and W. Markham 2005. 'What do we Know About Promoting Mental Health Through Schools?'. *IUHPE – Promotion & Education* 7(3–4): 118–22.

World Health Organization (WHO) 2013. *Mental Health: Strengthening our Response*. https://www.who.int/news-room/fact-sheets/detail/mental-health-strengthening-our-response.

Transforming Pedagogy
How Do We Take the Jump?

Denise Lofts and Miranda Jefferson

A case study: Ulladulla High School (p. 71)

A Bildung and Didadtik approach to pedagogy (p. 76)

Teacher professional learning (p. 80)

Concluding reflections: Taking the jump with pedagogy (p. 83)

We aren't attracted to extreme sports and adrenaline rushes like skydiving (although Denise is a surfer and Miranda is a body boarder) but we do love the challenge of taking a jump with pedagogy. We both loved being teachers in creativity rich classrooms (Denise with Visual Arts and Miranda with Drama and Filmmaking) and now we want schools to be rich and creative with pedagogy. It's not often that skydiving and pedagogy are mentioned in the same sentence, but perhaps there is more in common between the two than we realize. For teachers to transform or even explore and develop their pedagogy seems to take courage, determination and the ability to take risks. In our experience we have found that there is often a struggle for teachers to understand and discuss pedagogy, and a reluctance to question the way pedagogy is understood and enacted in schools. This chapter is about how teachers can be supported and challenged in professional learning to take the leap into exploring their pedagogy. To discuss, explore and

Figure 4.1 Teaching can be compared to an extreme sport like skydiving. It is highly skilled and involves risk-taking in exploring new pedagogies to create the right conditions for students to learn.

discover pedagogy may not appear transformational; however small shifts in teaching practice and understanding are the ongoing steps that transform student and teacher learning.

We begin by introducing a tool that supports teachers to describe and reflect on their teaching practice and to design learning experiences. It is a coherence maker called the Pedagogy Parachute (see Figure 4.2, from Jefferson and Anderson's *Transforming Education*[1]), and it enables teachers to discuss and explore their pedagogy. The Pedagogy Parachute illustrates how effective teaching is an extreme sport that is highly skilled and involves creative risk-taking to curate optimal learning experiences.

We use Ulladulla High School as a case study to examine how their approach to teacher professional learning is critical to the sustainable exploration and ongoing transformation of pedagogy in their classrooms. One of Ulladulla High School's intentions is to transform the students' experiences of learning through the way they do teacher professional learning. The European approaches of 'Bildung' and 'Didadtik' are used to explain how pedagogy in self-direction can engage and build capacity in students as learners and teachers as professionals. And we describe how processes in critical reflection and collaboration can engage the teacher as a 'whole person' when exploring their pedagogy. We argue that building teacher identity and agency through professional learning is critical to developing the identity and agency of students in learning.

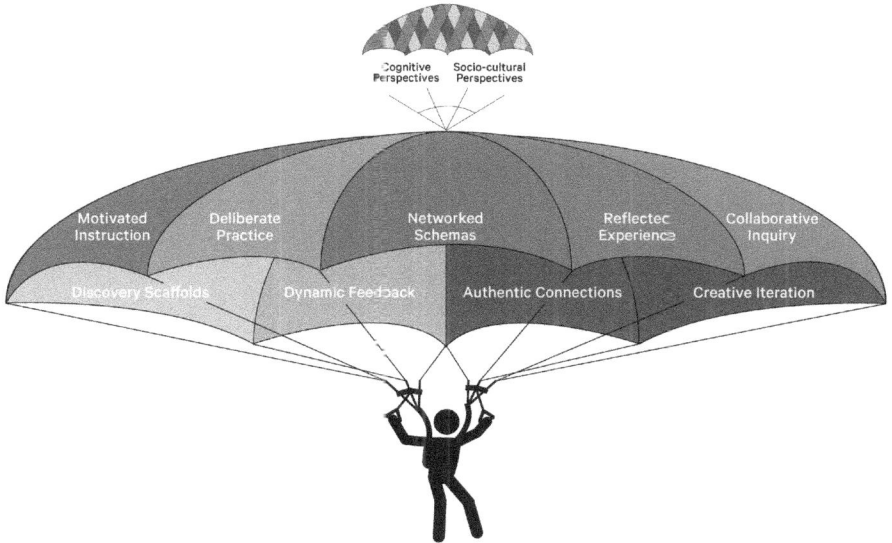

Figure 4.2 The Pedagogy Parachute (from Jefferson and Anderson's *Transforming Education*) is used by Ulladulla High School as a tool to explore and deepen their pedagogy.

A case study: Ulladulla High School

Denise is the principal at Ulladulla High School, a regional, co-educational school (1,262 students) on the south coast of New South Wales on Murramarang Land[2] in Australia. The school draws students from a large rural and coastal area and has a committed school community of leaders, teachers and administrative staff who live and work in the community. The school has been on an upward enrolment trend. The parent carer community is mostly from skilled trade, office and service industries and predominantly English-speaking and born in Australia. It is an inclusive school community with twelve support classes[3] and has a significant enrolment of Aboriginal Students at 8.5 per cent or 104 students. The school is committed to promoting First Nations cultural heritage. Throughout the chapter, Ulladulla High School's experience with pedagogy is explored through Denise's observations. Her reflections are italicized responses to questions that illuminate how the research and concepts discussed in the chapter are applied in the school setting. Denise begins by describing how the metalanguage of the Pedagogy Parachute is used to explore pedagogy in the professional learning at Ulladulla High.

Denise, how does the Pedagogy Parachute support teachers to explore pedagogy?

Experiencing the Pedagogy Parachute for the first time challenges the most experienced educator to take a step back and engage a reflective lens on their own practice. It is a complex scaffold, although an accessible tool for a mentor to

> support a new teacher or an experienced teacher to re-engage their classroom, whether it be for planning, reflecting and evaluating learning experiences.
>
> Teachers can often articulate the target (outcome) of their teaching and describe what they are trying to achieve, however, the complexity of what happens in the teaching and learning experience is often hard to authentically describe and understand. The Pedagogy Parachute is a coherence maker that enables understanding of what pedagogy teachers choose to use, making deliberate and contextual decisions. I have noticed teachers, seeing and describing, often for the first time, a deeper view of the learner and a conscious understanding of the learning experience and the student's growing agency in that process.
>
> Even the notion of a parachute conjures up ideas of 'this is going to be a wild ride, with a bit of freefall'. The Pedagogy Parachute provides a platform of language that builds curiosity and conversation about the very cornerstone of a teacher's work. It deliberately identifies and differentiates the practices contained in pedagogy. As they say, if you can name the emotion, you are more likely to understand it and more likely to apply it contextually. This applies equally to the complex craft of teaching. The Pedagogy Parachute articulates the very art of teaching. It is a deeply considered schema that brings precision to our craft.
>
> These questions were posed to my executive team – 'What is your definition of pedagogy?', 'What is transformative pedagogy?' 'What was the difference and why does it matter?' These were hard questions but discussing them was important. We believe transformative pedagogy is authentic learning experiences that are socially and personally transformative. Through curated learning experiences the 4CTL team[4] led us to unpack the metalanguage embedded in the Pedagogy Parachute and it all made sense. It supports teachers to bring meaning to what they do and a language that provides ways to address the questions we ask when designing learning. It is a way for teachers to describe, collaborate, talk about and understand the learning experiences they curate.

The Pedagogy Parachute used by Ulladulla High is based on Jefferson and Anderson's research in *Transforming Schools* (2021), informed by sociocultural and cognitive perspectives in education. It describes pedagogical elements that support the development of self-determination and self-regulation in students learning experiences. The elements in the Pedagogy Parachute are:

- Networked schemas (learning frameworks)
- Motivated instruction (generative communication)
- Discovery scaffolds (emergent learning)
- Deliberate practice (systematic proficiency)
- Dynamic feedback (interactive assessment)

- Authentic connections (meaningful, real-word relevance)
- Collaborative inquiry (co-constructed problem shaping and solving)
- Creative iteration (sequential generation)
- Reflective experience (interpretive perception)

'Flying the Parachute' is a metaphor for explaining how teachers can use and manipulate the elements of pedagogy appropriate to the *why* and *what* of the learning. The Parachute provides teachers with a metalanguage for analysing teaching methodology and may reveal the habitual defaults of established practice. Teachers may ask: Are we using too much instruction? Do students need more practice, feedback, scaffolds or authentic connection in their learning? Should this particular learning be an inquiry, an experience, or framed through a schema? What do the students need to deepen or transfer their learning? How can they develop skills to self-regulate and self-determine their learning?

Within the Parachute framework there are progressions for teachers to develop their pedagogic practice, and this is illustrated in Figure 4.3. The element *discovery scaffolds* for example, begins with teachers *using scaffolds* and progresses to teachers *facilitating discovery scaffolds*. Understanding and applying *scaffolds*[5] is an integral step to the higher-order practice of teachers implementing *discovery scaffolds*[6] as a methodology for deeper and autonomous learning. With experience, reflection and inquiry, teachers develop expertise in the depth and breadth of pedagogical practice and can integrate and imagine the possibilities of all the pedagogical elements in the Parachute.

The development of teacher skills and understandings is intertwined with the development of learner agency and self-direction. The continuum in pedagogical knowledge mirrors a continuum of learners' skills in self-regulation and self-direction. For example, an expert teacher may be able to facilitate *discovery scaffolds* but if the learners do not yet have the skills to self-regulate, the teacher begins with *scaffolds* to guide and prompt their learning.

All the elements of the Parachute are general pedagogical knowledge[7] relevant to all areas of learning across a curriculum. The elements are of equal significance and work together to create deep learning experiences for students. Some learning may emphasize certain elements in the Parachute more than others, depending on the needs of the students and 'why' 'what' is being learnt. For example, science learning may involve more *collaborative inquiry* and arts learning may involve more *creative iteration*. The intention of the Pedagogy Parachute is to support teachers with an explicit language and understanding of often what they do intuitively and to encourage teachers to 'take a jump' to explore and challenge their pedagogy. Taking a jump with pedagogy can be a struggle for teachers as Denise has discovered at her school. Here, she tells a story about introducing new pedagogical processes in their professional learning, illustrating how hard it is for teachers to change from established patterns of practice.

Figure 4.3 Developing pedagogic practice.

What made you realize that it is hard for teachers to change their practice?

We all understand that schools are very busy places. Creating the space for teachers to be 'uncomfortable' and challenge their practice has been ongoing and evolving in our school's professional learning, not without moments of despair. There was a point during the term, I arrived a little late to our fortnightly 'Collaboration Circles' – the name given to our teacher professional learning teams. With much curiosity and some concern, I noticed something. Instead of honouring and engaging in the planned new pedagogy for their learning, there was something

> else going on. The pedagogical experience was truncated to merely a scribe taking notes from ad-hoc talk. This was far removed from the deliberately considered pedagogical practice that had been curated carefully by the leadership team for the teachers to undertake and learn from.
>
> I was disappointed. Not by the presence of the scribe (who was meticulously writing and prompting the teachers), rather by the absence of agency by the other teacher learners to hold the space as intended and lean into the possible uncomfortableness of a new learning process. I had been optimistic; I had thought as a school we were more evolved in our pedagogical thinking. If this was my group, clearly, we had more work to do. The default way of teaching and learning I witnessed, appeared to be focused on the product (a systemically required artefact of learning), rather than a curated experience of learning intended to build the agency of teachers as learners. Speed and efficiency were the default, and this disappointed me immensely.
>
> However, I realized how hard it is to transform pedagogy with teachers and change habits. There are the decades of educational traditions and 'habitus'[8] (for example, 'this is the way we were taught') deeply embedded. It is hard for teachers to change pedagogy when we have a system focused on learning as product with narrow predetermined outcomes, rather than the evolving process of teaching and learning. The challenge is to imbed both teacher and student agency in the process of learning, beyond narrow, systemic big data targets.
>
> I reflected on how front and foremost a transformative pedagogical experience for our teacher learners needs to be. Our teachers need to experience, see and apply new pedagogy to provide pathways away from a 'default mode' of teaching. If we don't engage with new pedagogy, we steal deep learning experiences from our students and developing them as autonomous and engaged learners. It was a confronting experience. If we truly were to influence and transform pedagogy, we had to rethink the way we engaged and challenged teacher learners beyond their default practices.

Denise's observations that it is difficult for teachers to change their habits reveal the power of patterned rituals in pedagogical practice and the emotional reticence to take risks and try new processes. Teachers developing their pedagogical practice matters to Denise at Ulladulla High School because she has a vision for students (and teachers) that goes beyond test scores and rankings. She reflects on a change in her thinking when she encountered the educational thought leader Yong Zhao and how this helped her to reimagine what teaching and learning in schools could be.

What influenced your vision for learning at your school?

In 2011 early in my principalship, in front of a packed room of Australian school leaders, Yong Zhao spoke with passion about a vision of education and school that excited me. It was focused on a highly relevant, authentic view on the purpose

> of school and education – it was that young people should not be judged by test scores and a mark on a page, rather by their ability and dispositions across many things. The message was simple, yet incredibly complex to action.
>
> He spoke about the skills and attributes needed in a contemporary society. His words reverberated with me. He talked of classrooms that are being transformed through deep learning experiences and where student agency is built through coherent future-focused pedagogy. The students create useful things and develop personal attributes necessary for the world beyond school.
>
> According to Yong Zhao, test scores place students in a mindset of imagining a future that is set. What if their scores are not good – is this the only measure in which we would value a student? It was this thinking that strongly influenced my need to question what my school was truly providing and to create a school vision aligned to the 2008 Melbourne Declaration on Educational Goals for Young Australians.
>
> I want our students to be able to imagine a 'view of a future self' – where teachers introduce them to a world that is beyond their present realm, so that they can imagine themselves in the future. To do that, we must develop self-confidence in everyone's ability, whatever that is, as everyone has something they are good at. We need to foster student's abilities to connect with groups, to make small social connections and then with an adult who cares. We need to give opportunities to students to show what they can do and what they are good at. We need to unlock their capacities to contribute and find the entrepreneurial key that is inherent in all of us.
>
> Leveraging and empowering the agency of students (and teachers as well) is essential to establishing life-long dispositions. For students this is their exit ticket credential to step into the world beyond school. It is important for us to create a school where teachers allow content to emerge and where students are provided opportunities and possibilities to make meaning and pathways of learning through the pedagogical process. According to the notion of a Didadtik approach it involves opening up the curriculum through pedagogy.

A Bildung and Didadtik approach to pedagogy

This vision for Ulladulla High School is about building self-determination in learners and opening up the curriculum through pedagogical practice that creates learning experiences that are relevant to students and their future. The *Didadtik* approach that Denise refers to can support teachers to reconceptualize the role of pedagogy, the learner and 'content' in classrooms. The concept of Didaktik (and Bildung) is from the central and northern European education tradition and it resonates with valuing deeper, student-centred learning with creative, open and responsive pedagogy. The Didaktik approach to pedagogy has a long lineage in the European tradition, going back to Ancient Greece and the Socratic method of learning through questions.

Didaktik as a teaching approach is inextricably linked to the concept of *Bildung* and a particular view of learning.

Bildung's meaning is difficult to translate directly, but the word 'formation' probably comes closest to capturing its essence in English.[9] The verb *bilden* in German means to form or to shape, and hence Bildung is about how knowing and doing something forms an individual's unique identity and capabilities. It describes the activation of potential in learners, rather than the process of learning. It is about character formation and student's finding value, truth and meaning from learning.[10] According to education researcher Stefan Hopmann,

> In Bildung, whatever is done or learned is done or learned to develop one's own individuality, to unfold the capabilities of the I.[11] The purpose of teaching and schooling is in this perspective neither to transport knowledge from society to a learner (curriculum), nor a transpositioning of knowledge from science or other domains to the classroom, but rather the use of knowledge as a transformative tool of unfolding the learners individuality and sociability, in short: the Bildung of the learners by teaching.[12]

Aspects of Bildung are being described by Denise when she explains her vision of building students' sense of a future self, confident in what they are good at, creating things of use and developing a sense of connection with community. Education theorist Wolfgang Klafki highlights Bildung's three main characteristics as:

- self-determination of the individual to make independent, responsible and ethical decisions;
- co-determination and contributing with others to the community;
- and solidarity as action to help others.[13]

Bildung is both individual formation and reflective and responsible social action.

From the theory of Bildung we understand that the prime intention of pedagogy is for learners to build capacity in awareness, wisdom and action, rather than 'learning stuff'. The forming and building of students' potential can unfold in classrooms where the 4C capabilities: creativity, critical reflection, communication and collaboration develop agency and co-agency in learners.[14]

Critical to Bildung is the concept of 'restrained teaching' or Didaktik. According to Stefan Hopmann, Didadtik is restrained teaching because it allows for and is open to the individual growth of the learner's Bildung.[15] Didaktik is also difficult to translate and is not to be confused with didactic in English which is associated with 'telling' (like a lecture) and moralizing. Didaktik teaching focuses on:

- the Bildung unique to every individual learner,
- the meaning of learning experiences and
- responding to the learners and the learning.[16]

To develop the Bildung in learners, the outcome of the learning is not in the content of the teaching but how learners make sense of the world through the learning. The meaning of learning experiences for learners is not knowing things but knowing *why* they are learning *what* they are learning. For example, when learning history, it is ask what can we learn about people by understanding the Ancient Greek world, or what can we learn about ourselves when we create an artwork, or what can we learn about the world we observe around us through science. The 'content' of the learning means something different for every learner if the teaching approach allows for learners to engage with their own unique perspective. In the spirit of Bildung, the vision statement for Ulladulla High School includes that '*all students build the best version of themselves through their own agency as learners and personalised educational pathways to become creative, mindful, entrepreneurial, and innovative young people. . .* '[17] This means teachers asking the 'what and why' of the learning before they curate the 'how' of the teaching process.

In the Didadtik tradition, teachers select and justify the content of learning and then consider the teaching methods. Stefan Hopmann explains that in the Didadtik approach,

> Meaning is what emerges when the content is enacted in a classroom based on the methodological decisions of a teacher, ie. his or her pedagogical freedom. Accordingly, the Didaktik parameter of good teaching is not the degree to which the students master the content as delineated in the curriculum, but rather the question if and how the educative substance could be opened up for the students as intended; more exactly, if and how it became open in their individual meeting with the content in the given teaching process.[18]

The teacher's pedagogical skill is to design learning that allows students to have access to engaging and fruitful encounters with learning that is meaningful to them. For instance, in the Ancient Greece example, the 'why' of learning about people may be explored through the methodologies (the 'how') of *collaborative inquiry* and *authentic connections* in the Pedagogy Parachute. Or in the other example, making an artwork may use *creative iteration* and *reflective experience* to explore the understanding of the inner self. And students explaining their observation of the world through science may involve *networked schemas*, *discovery scaffolds* and *dynamic feedback*. The skill of expert teachers is to 'curate' learning that builds agency and co-agency through experiences that are purposeful, interactive and offer choice for learners. The concept of curation as described by researcher and publisher Michael Bhasker, can help in understanding how teachers curate pedagogy.

> Curation can be a clumsy, sometimes maligned word, but with its Latin root *curare* (to take care of), it captures this irreplaceable human touch. We want to be surprised. We want expertise, distinctive aesthetic judgements, clear expenditure of time and effort. We relish the messy reality of another's taste and trusted personal connection. We don't just want correlations – we want a why, a narrative, which machines can't provide.

Expert educators curate rich opportunities (like a narrative) for students to discover, imagine, be surprised or perhaps be provoked by learning. To curate pedagogy, teachers develop a deep and ever-evolving knowledge about learners and learning deeply, by asking the *why*, *what* and *how* questions of learning. It is expertise that takes time and effort, it sometimes can be messy and there are aesthetic judgements made by teachers to create those experiences. Teachers are the curatorial 'human touch' of learning, but in the end, through transformative pedagogy for deep and self-directed learning, students should be curators of their own learning. Denise reflects on curating learning experiences and the Didaktik approach in her own teaching before she became a principal. She then considers how it currently informs pedagogical practice in the school plan.

> ### How can you explain the Didaktik approach to pedagogy?
>
> *As a visual arts teacher, I was a 'curator of learning'. It came with the territory of Visual Arts – the audience, the individualized response to the world, the framework of artmaking practice, along with creating something from the imagined. My classes were individualized, ever changing and somewhat unorthodox. I never wanted my year nine students stabbing their eyes out with boredom, irrelevance and misunderstanding. I strived for connection, relevance and purpose, with students fuelled by action and by their own agency.*
>
> *Creating something worthwhile for the world was important to me and engaging my students to do this was paramount in fulfilling their learning aspirations, alongside meeting the mandated syllabi. This mantra has continued throughout my educational journey. I lead learning from a place of engagement, authenticity, action, urgency and purpose. Students only get one chance to be a Year 9 student, let us make it the best opportunity to build their agency as a learner.*
>
> *My understanding of Didaktik is that what students experience here and now must be emerging, relevant and evolving in response to the learner's experience. This may appear obvious to many, however, the fixation on test scores and averages narrows the curriculum and steals the joy from learning, as well as the creativity, autonomy and passion of the teacher.*
>
> *Our school plan actively embeds a focus on pedagogical practice that encourages student voice, choice and project-based learning based on a student's experience. It emphasizes pedagogical practice that supports co-teaching, risk-taking, critical reflection and the dispositions of learning. We do not teach to the test and our focus is to show our students there is a bigger, global world in which they can be an integral part.*

A Didaktik approach responds to what emerges in the learning and the emergent needs of the learners. Although teachers have plans and possible outcomes for learning (structures), these plans can be designed to adapt (improvisation) to the individual perspectives of students, which may achieve outcomes different from those intended. Didaktik as 'restrained teaching' is an open or loose process that allows for emergence and different perspectives in the learning. Didaktik is not a mechanical or procedural approach where teachers are 'invisible agents' delivering a curriculum directed by the system. Instead they are animators and curators of learning experiences and sources of animation for the system.[19] In the Didaktik tradition, 'content' is viewed as emerging from how the teacher opens up learning to students and how the students interpret the learning for themselves. There is greater autonomy for teachers and students in the Didaktik tradition and this has implications for how teacher professional learning is also structured and facilitated.

Teacher professional learning

Transforming pedagogy in schools does not just mean evolving the way student learning happens. It also means evolving teacher professional learning. A teacher's learning can also be viewed through the lens of Bildung and Didadtik. Who a teacher is, their unique perspective, their beliefs in teaching, their emotions and attitudes about change or risk, need to be engaged with and reflected upon for any new pedagogical learning to be explored and acted on.[20] This means knowing teachers as unique, individual learners and focusing on how they make meaning of their professional learning experiences through a Didadtik approach. It is to view teacher professional learning as a formative experience that engages the 'person of the teacher' and builds their capacity for self-determination and co-determination through content and design that asks the *why*, *what* and *how* questions of their learning. Here, Denise describes how Ulladulla High School approached meeting the differing needs and motivations of teachers in the schools for professional learning and how they curated those experiences.

How did you and your team approach professional learning?

We can talk much about the transformation of pedagogy in terms, of leadership, influence, culture and classroom climate. However, it was imperative that as a leadership team, we embraced the complexity of our organization and leveraged the diversity of the adults. This was to ensure the curated professional learning experiences for our teachers captured the imagination, passion and the 'person' of each teacher. In doing so, we hoped to enliven their own agency and self-efficacy. 'If you don't feed the teachers, they eat the students' is something I say often.

It was fundamental in each step of the professional learning curation, that both our approach to collaboration and the sense of belonging for our teachers was leveraged; without this consideration we would have missed the target for our students. Ulladulla High School is its own, unique place and it was clear to our leadership team that we needed to make decisions based on our context. We used the unique eco-system of the Serengeti plains of Tanzania (the best-known African savanna) as a metaphor to reimagine professional learning at our school. Many of the animals of the Serengeti can be found nowhere else in the world and this resonated with us, so animal names were used as metaphors to describe groups involved in different aspects of the professional learning.

The capabilities for transforming learning at our school have been enabled by our guiding coalition of leaders and teachers whom we call the 'Giraffes'. This group of eight (teachers, head teachers, deputy principals and principal) looks and consults across the school to consider the long-term strategy to lead and transform professional and classroom learning. We notice and critically reflect on the emerging needs, fears and capacities of our teachers.

In the professional learning partnership with 4CTL, we began to understand we needed to create networks of collaboration at the school and so we set up professional learning teams (the Collaboration Circles). From these professional learning teams, curious, interested and willing teachers popped their heads up to do more learning in new pedagogy. We called this group the 'Meerkats' as they emerged as keen and inquisitive in being involved in driving new learning at the school.

The guiding coalition (the Giraffes) worked together with the Executive leadership team which included all the head teachers across the school. We refer to the seventeen head teachers as the 'Lions', as they have responsibilities in leadership to influence and support teachers to explore their teaching and learning. The guiding coalition (the Giraffes) recognized the capacity in the head teachers (the Lions) to influence classroom pedagogy, to enable the link of pedagogy to curriculum and embed the school strategic plan. This is supported by the pedagogy professional learning group (the Meerkats).

There is agility in the guiding coalition (the Giraffes) and the head teachers (the Lions) being able to deeply notice the emerging vision at the school through the process of ongoing critical reflection embedded in the fortnightly collaboration circles. The professional learning in pedagogy is complex and must be underpinned by authentic reflection processes that enable courage, curiosity, creativity, tenacity, motivation and enthusiasm in teachers.

This ongoing professional learning opportunities were transformative as they enabled deep noticing of real-time evidence with critical reflection. Without this approach, there is no point, you must notice, reflect on what is happening and then make informed decisions towards the next step when transforming pedagogy. When the reflection process is honoured, you can avoid assumptions, prejudice, or predetermined pathways.

Ulladulla High School's professional learning and *why* they did *what* they did and *how* they did it, can be conceptualized and understood in terms of Bildung and Didadtik. The guiding coalition (the Giraffes) and the executive leadership team (the Lions) aimed to develop learning experiences that built teacher's agency and self-efficacy, in other words, their Bildung. The ongoing development of teachers' critical consciousness in self-determination and co-determination as professionals was critical to the learning content and pedagogy of the professional learning. The aim of the leaders was to focus on the teacher as a learner and through reflection respond to the teacher's meaning-making of the learning. This is a Didadtik approach rooted in interpreting, curating and guiding the teachers professional learning through the development of agency and co-agency.

The *why* of the professional learning was to realize their vision for student learning by engaging the imagination and passion of teachers (firstly with the curious and keen Meerkat group). The *what* of the learning was to develop the agency and co-agency of teachers to explore and develop their pedagogy in an authentic way. The *how* of the professional learning was informed by their *why* and *what*, hence using elements or methods from the Pedagogy Parachute such as *authentic connections, discovery scaffolds, reflected experience* and *collaborative inquiry.* The *what* of the learning (in a meta way) was also about learning in the Pedagogy Parachute and providing teachers with a metalanguage to discuss pedagogy collaboratively. Those leading the professional learning (the Giraffes and Lions) used a Didadtik approach by being continually responsive to the teachers' meaning-making of the learning and how the learning informed the teachers' classroom practice.

The leaders responded to teachers as learners with their own unique needs and wants, identity and capabilities. The Bildung characteristics of self-determination through decision-making, contributing to community through co-determination and being active in the support of others was built through collaborative and critical reflective processes in the professional learning. These processes supported and developed the emotional and social functioning[21] of teachers' learning at the school.

Effective professional learning is a complex and dynamic relationship between the 'person of the teacher' (their Bildung) and the practice and theory of teaching (a Didadtik approach). The interaction between practice in the classroom, experiential learning of education theory and the identity of the teacher as a professional can be mindfully curated through pedagogy that supports self-direction and self-regulation.[22] The learning design (the processes and structures) of professional learning at Ulladulla High endeavours to allow for different perspectives, the emergence of ideas and responses to the contextual, differentiated needs of teachers as pedagogues and learners. One aspect of their pedagogical design is to use collaboration and critical reflection as structures and processes for developing co-agency in the professional learning.

Learning is strengthened when there is sense of belonging through a shared endeavour with a community of learners.[23] Trust and intellectual risk-taking, the sharing of concerns and ideas and the confidence in developing competence are supported through collaboration and critical reflection.[24] Critical reflection and collaboration can support good teaching and new pedagogical practice, and nurture teacher's courage, curiosity, creativity, care and commitment.[25] However communities of practice are only successful if they are intensive and sustained.[26] Critical reflection and collaboration can support the building of teacher's professional identity or 'Bildung'. There is no quick fix or silver bullet that transforms teacher practice.[27] It requires deep learning as an ongoing and ever-extending commitment to developing ideas, action and people, rather than technical or procedural one-size-fits-all, 'bolt-on' 'teacher training'. It is about connecting the professional with the personal, and this is what Ulladulla High School has endeavoured to do in their professional learning as they take the jump to explore and transform their pedagogy.

Concluding reflections: Taking the jump with pedagogy

To explore and transform pedagogy entails taking a jump with teacher professional learning and practice. As the Ulladulla case study has illustrated, the jump can be supported by understandings and processes that connect the practice and theory of pedagogy with the person of the teacher and the person of the student (their Bildung). We have discussed how the Bildung and Didadtik approach of northern Europe describes how we can reimagine what learning can mean for both students and teachers. Bildung and Didadtik emphasize the formation of character, competency, criticality and citizenship through what we learn. For our students this is achieved by teachers who consider the essential why, what and how questions about their teaching for their learners in their classrooms. Those leading professional learning with teachers should consider the same questions. Rather than 'being trained', teachers in professional learning can engage in deep, collaborative and critically reflective learning that supports their ongoing growth and identity as professionals by asking why, what and how questions.

The Pedagogy Parachute is a tool that provides a metalanguage for leaders and teachers to develop their pedagogy. Mindfully curated pedagogy is the art of teaching, and Ulladulla High School has demonstrated that schools can commit time and energy to professional learning that supports teachers to explore, discover, share and challenge their pedagogical practice. Ulladulla High's approach has been one that at its core wants to connect with and develop teacher's self-efficacy. Their aim is to engage teachers to develop and transform pedagogical practice towards a school vision that goes beyond the test results of their students. They want to develop students' competencies, agency and sense of social responsibility for their lives beyond school. To do that, teachers must develop and evolve pedagogy to transform learning.

Engagement with and evolution in pedagogy in schools is not easy, it requires a multidimensional, differentiated and long-term approach to teacher professional learning.[28] But according to Denise, '*If the pedagogy parachute is a language, then the only way to encourage our teachers to take the jump, is to talk our way into understanding the complexity of teaching. With that, I say, we need to get the conversation going teachers because the flying future jump will be exhilarating!*.'

Notes

1. Miranda Jefferson and Michael Anderson, *Transforming Education: Reimagining Learning, Pedagogy and Curriculum* (London: Bloomsbury, 2021).
2. Murramarang is the name for the traditional lands and First Nations people in the area.
3. Support classes are for students with moderate to high learning needs.

4   4CTL (4C Transformative Learning) is a professional learning organization that has long-term partnerships with schools to transform their practices, structures and culture.
5   Learning scaffolds are informed by psychologist Lev Vygotsky's zone of proximal development where an expert or more expert peer supports and continues to challenge the potential threshold of the learner from guided learning to independent learning.
6   Educational psychologist Jerome Bruner argues there is power in learners being allowed and able to work things out for themselves and discover their own learning through what he calls 'the development of an attitude toward learning and inquiry, toward guessing and hunches, toward the possibility of solving problems on one's own'.
7   General pedagogical knowledge is defined by educational psychologist Lee Shulman as the principles and strategies of classroom management and organization that are cross-curricular. Lee S. Shulman, 'Those Who Understand: Knowledge Growth in Teaching', *Educational Researcher* 15, no. 2 (1986): 4–14; and Lee S. Shulman, 'Knowledge of Teaching: Foundations of the New Reform', *Harvard Educational Review* 15, no. 2 (1987): 1–22.
8   The French sociologist Pierre Bourdieu used the term 'habitus' to describe and understand how cultural settings such as schools and education systems reproduce the means of their own production. Habitus allows us to see and interrogate the subconsciously unseen social structures that have become embedded and habitual in our psyches.
9   Ian Westbury Teaching as a reflective practice: what might Didaktik teach curriculum Kurt Riquarts, Ian Westbury, and Stefan Hopmann (eds), *Teaching As A Reflective Practice* (New York: Routledge, 2000), 15–39.
10 Jesper Sjöström and Ingo Eilks, 'The Bildung Theory – From von Humboldt to Klafki and Beyond', in *In Science Education in Theory and Practice: An Introductory Guide to Learning Theory, Springer Texts in Education*, ed. Ben Akpan and Teresa J. Kennedy (Springer Nature Switzerland AG, 2020), 55–67.
11 Quote references Wilhem von Humboldt, 'Theory of Bildung', in Riquarts, Westbury, Hopmann, *Teaching as a Reflective Practice.* [1792] 2000.
12 Stefan Hopmann, 'Restrained Teaching: The Common Core of Didaktik', *European Educational Research Journal* 6, no. 2 (2007): 109–24.
13 Brian Hudson discusses Wolfgang Klafki (1995/1998) in 'Comparing Different Traditions of Teaching and Learning: What Can We Learn About Teaching and Learning?', *European Educational Research Journal* 6, no. 2 (2007): 109–24, 135–46.
14 Jefferson and Anderson, *Transforming Education*.
15 Hopmann, 'Restrained Teaching'.
16 Hopmann, 'Restrained Teaching'.
17 Vision statement for Ulladulla HS: https://ulladulla-h.schools.nsw.gov.au/content/dam/doe/sws/schools/u/ulladulla-h/2021-summit-times-/pdf-docs/Student_Handbook_Brand_New_2021.pdf.
18 Hopmann, 'Restrained Teaching'.

19 Hopmann, 'Restrained Teaching'.
20 Teacher professional learning researcher Fred Korthagen argues that changing teaching behaviours can only be effective if teacher's emotions and motivations are involved in the cognition of new learning and practices. Korthagen argues that professional learning needs to consider the 'core qualities' of a teacher by connecting with the 'person of the teacher'. Fred Korthagen, 'Inconvenient Truths About Teacher Learning: Towards Professional Development 3.0', *Teachers and Teaching: Theory and Practice* 23, no. 4 (2017): 387–405.
21 Neuroscientists Mary Helen Immordino-Yang and Antonio Damasio argue that emotion and social functioning have enormous repercussions for the way humans consolidate and access learning. They argue, 'the more educators come to understand the nature of the relationship between emotion and cognition, the better they may be able to leverage this relationship in the design of learning environments.' Mary Helen Immordino-Yang and Antonio Damasio, 'We Feel, Therefore We Learn: The Relevance of Affective and Social Neuroscience to Education Mind', *Brain and Education* 1, no. 1 (2007): 3–10.
22 Korthagen, 'Inconvenient Truths About Teacher Learning'.
23 L. Darling-Hammond and N. Richardson, 'Teacher Learning: What Matters?', *Educational Leadership* 66, no. 5 (2009): 46–53.
24 Korthagen, 'Inconvenient Truths About Teacher Learning'.
25 M. Jefferson and M. Anderson, *Transforming Schools: Creativity, Critical Reflection, Communication, Collaboration* (London: Bloomsbury, 2017).
26 Hammond and Richardson, 'Teacher Learning'.
27 Jefferson and Anderson, *Transforming Education*.
28 Korthagen, 'Inconvenient Truths About Teacher Learning'.

References

Darling-Hammond, L. and N. Richardson 2009. 'Research Review/teacher Learning: What Matters'. *Educational Leadership* 66(5): 46–53.

Hopmann, S. 2007. 'Restrained Teaching: The Common Core of Didaktik'. *European Educational Research Journal* 6(2): 109–24.

Hudson, B. 2007. 'Comparing Different Traditions of Teaching and Learning: What can we Learn About Teaching and Learning?'. *European Educational Research Journal* 6(2): 135–46.

Humboldt's, W. V. [1792] 2000. '57 Theory of Bildung 1'. In I. Westbury, S. Hopmann, and K. Riquarts (eds.), *Teaching as a Reflective Practice: The German Didaktik Tradition*, 57–61. Mahwah: Lawrence Erlbaum Associates.

Immordino-Yang, M.H. and A. Damasio 2007. 'We Feel, Therefore we Learn: The Relevance of Affective and Social Neuroscience to Education'. *Mind, Brain, and Education* 1(1): 3–10.

Jefferson, M. and M. Anderson 2017. *Transforming Schools: Creativity, Critical Reflection, Communication, Collaboration*. Bloomsbury Publishing.

Jefferson, M. and M. Anderson 2021. *Transforming Education: Reimagining Learning, Pedagogy and Curriculum*. London: Bloomsbury Publishing.

Korthagen, F. 2017. 'Inconvenient Truths About Teacher Learning: Towards Professional Development 3.0'. *Teachers and Teaching* 23(4): 387–405.

Shulman, Lee S. 1986. 'Those who Understand: Knowledge Growth in Teaching'. *Educational Researcher* 15(2): 4–14.

Shulman, Lee S. 1987. 'Knowledge of Teaching: Foundations of the new Reform'. *Harvard Educational Review* 15(2): 1–22.

Sjöström, J. and I. Eilks 2020. 'The Bildung Theory – from von Humboldt to Klafki and Beyond'. *Science Education in Theory and Practice: An Introductory Guide to Learning Theory* 55–67.

Transforming Learning
Walking on Water

Mark Steed and Michael Anderson

5

Community of Practice (p. 89)

First steps in establishing a Community of Practice at Hurstville PS (p. 90)
From cooperation to collaboration (p. 91)

Strategies for learning transformation (p. 91)
Exploring the 4Cs (p. 91)
Breaking ground (p. 92)
Forming an effective Community of Practice (p. 92)
Key driver 1 – Challenging and changing traditional leadership structures (p. 93)
Key driver 2 – Learner agency (p. 95)
Key driver 3 – Understanding and recognizing true collaboration (p. 96)
Key driver 4 – Outward facing connections to craft a shared endeavour (p. 97)
Key driver 5 – Strategic and regular reflection on practice (p. 98)

Concluding reflections (p. 99)

The call of the ocean speaks powerfully to many people around the globe and particularly Australians. To enter the salty maelstrom at one of the beaches along the Australian coastline is to be immersed physically, mentally and spiritually in what surfers call the 'blue room'. From early on, Snowy McAlister wanted to experience the feeling of almost walking on water, to no longer be within the wave form but riding on top of it, above the surface, using the wave energy to propel him towards the shore. While surfing is commonplace today it had a mystical quality in the early 1900s.

An early surf pioneer, 'Snowy' (Figure 5.1) was born in outback Broken Hill, New South Wales, in 1904 and moved to beachside Manly, New South Wales, in 1914. For Snowy, this sea change was an awakening that altered the course of his life. Not long after seeing surfing demonstrated, Snowy commandeered his mother's pine ironing board, skipped school and headed for the Manly waves to emulate the skills of surfing pioneer Duke Kahanamokus. McAlister kept driving innovation in board design and building a community, meeting with around fifteen surfers to ride the waves on their new contraptions. Snowy went on to be National Surfing Champion from 1926 to 1928 and became an Olympic surfer in 1928 and again in 1956 (as a fifty-two-year-old). Perhaps unwittingly, he was creating a Community of Practice (CoP) that would long outlive him and his surfing prowess and lead to an international movement. Snowy's talent was to take a concept that was unknown and provide not only the skills but also the communities and structures to generate an international

Figure 5.1 Snowy McAlister with his iconic surfboard.

sporting movement. In many ways the community that Snowy created is similar to the communities required in a transforming school. Amidst the unpredictability of modern day schooling a community can create frameworks and connections to ensure transformation in learning continues to engage, sustain and innovate.

In this chapter, we discuss through a case study of Hurstville Public School (HPS) how educational settings can begin to transform their professional learning culture and practice. We engage with the research around Communities of Practice[1] to discuss and reflect on the experiences of HPS. We identify five key drivers for transforming learning through a community of praxis approach that focuses on leadership, agency, collaboration, building a learning community and reflection. We begin this chapter with a discussion of a Community of Practice approach.

Community of Practice

Snowy's greatest achievements were not championships nor Olympic medals. Critically, his greatest achievement was to generate a group of engaged individuals who collaborated to make surfing the international sport that it is today. Cognitive anthropologist, Etienne Wenger described this kind of group as a Community of Practice as members who 'share a concern or a passion for something they do and learn how to do it better as they interact regularly'.[2] This collaborative and situated approach contrasts with the commonplace 'bolt on' professional learning often delivered *en masse* to teachers or school leaders that takes little or no account of the context nor the likely sustainability and support required to embed and progress the professional learning.[3] A Community of Practice approach seeks to situate and create a community around the learning so that it might take root and flourish in each school's context. Exploring and applying transformative practices through the 4Cs also requires a deep understanding of the context for the learning. While the school transformation may be partially understood in the abstract (from a book or a seminar) these approaches are only deeply understood through application in context. As educational leadership researchers Christine Grice and Christopher Day report[4] professional learning (for transformation or anything else) is likely to work when it is:

- close to teaching practice;
- focused on the workplace;
- supported by the principal; and
- sustained over time.

These qualities are vital to drive an effective Community of Practice.

In classrooms a Community of Practice (CoP) provides opportunities for educators to develop a 'collaborative learning loop that takes these ideas and strategies back to their colleagues and adapt them to their local contexts and their student cohort'.[5]

As CoPs are best understood in their context, we will now turn to a case study at HPS to explore their approach to a Community of Practice to support an understanding of transformative processes. Before we discuss these drivers of transformation, we will explain and describe HPS's context to put this work into perspective.

First steps in establishing a Community of Practice at Hurstville PS

HPS has approximately 1,170 students and over 120 staff members. Almost 97 per cent of families in the school community identify from a language background other than English. The school has always been considered atypical compared with schools in the local area as it:

- is a large primary school (schools in the area have many fewer students on average);
- has four Opportunity Classes (classes for students identified as 'high performing' or 'gifted'); and
- has four Support Unit classes (classes for students with a recognized disability – an intellectual disability or autism spectrum disorder).

When Mark Steed, the principal, began at HPS in 2017, it became apparent to him that while the students were committed to learning and there was evidence of growth, there were significant anomalies regarding the skills that students were developing to support them throughout their lives. Students were not always offered the opportunity to build, refine and extend their skills in communication or in collaboration. The school has always been identified as 'high performing' on traditional measures of success such as standardized tests, however, there were few explicit strategies that engaged students in these areas. Similarly, there were limited opportunities for teachers or students to refine skills in communication and collaboration. Some students actively avoided opportunities to communicate with their peers. Overall, the consistent high achievement of the students against traditional metrics (such as NAPLAN, Best Start etc.) had bred unintended complacency. People in the school were working hard and advocating for students but there was little sense of shared endeavour focusing on refining and reflecting on explicit teaching practice that united the school and drove deep learning.

The second aspect of school culture to clearly emerge was that the school had highly competent practitioners who worked within team structures. The teams identified were loose associations of staff members who shared resources and discussed issues and challenges specifically related to their students. There was scant evidence that the teams had any interrelationship with each other. No obvious approaches existed for the strategic analysis of trends across the entire school regarding student learning, well-being or other identified school priorities. Staff at the school were often part of different project teams that occasionally provided whole-school professional learning. However, the relevance of this professional learning was sometimes elusive. Additionally, there was only a limited analysis of student and school community data. When analysis occurred, it was only reviewed by the leadership team and was superficial. This observation is not a criticism, as this situation could potentially describe about 90 per cent of primary schools at that time. This openness and evidence of cooperation (if not necessarily collaboration) is fertile ground for establishing CoPs. Some of the drivers identified in this chapter created the impetus for the establishment of CoPs at HPS.

The case study presented in this chapter is not intended to represent exemplar practice. HPS, like any school endeavouring to transform has wins, losses, plateaus and dead ends. This case study simply identifies the beginning stages of the work of transformation. In many senses the beginning of transformative process when the work is novel and exciting is the least difficult. The hard work of maintaining and sustaining transformation is the difficult undertaking. HPS is still on a journey and this case study is the account of how it began. Some of the first steps were identifying the difference between status quo practice (cooperation) and transformative practice (collaboration).

From cooperation to collaboration

The broad cooperation observed at Hurstville is apparent in many schools. People work together productively and professionally; however this represents a cooperation rather than a collaborative approach.[6] As Vera Jon Steiner argues, collaboration is a 'shared affair of the mind'.[7] Collaboration shifts practice from working alongside with essentially individual practice to developing 'shared practice'. Critically, a CoP is oriented to sharing and acting in deep collaboration. The problem that Hurstville faced was while there may have been elements of collaboration, the default experience was cooperative yet isolated. To enable transformative practice in schools through a Community of Practice the focus needed to shift to shared frameworks and strategies (such as the Learning Disposition Wheel or Collaboration Circles) that allow shared planning, action and reflection to enable transformative practice in each school. At Hurstville, the 4Cs were the foundation shared framework that allowed for strategic collaboration across the school.

Strategies for learning transformation

Exploring the 4Cs

The school's direction at the time was ambitious, as they had commenced work in 2016 on investigating the 4Cs – communication, collaboration, creativity and critical reflection. Teaching staff members had spent some time examining each of the 4Cs and participated in professional learning around what the 4Cs were and their relevance for student learning. In 2017 it became apparent that the staff member spearheading the 4C project team across the school was experiencing a significant level of doubt and frustration. They were questioning the engagement from staff members and were concerned about the impact on classroom practice and the lack of explicit opportunities for students to develop the 4Cs.

Breaking ground

During Term 3, 2017, the school began a collaboration with 4C Transformative Learning. This collaboration reconceptualized 'learners' in the school as not only students but also teachers, specialist staff, parents and community members. On reflection, it felt that among the group of school leaders, it had been a while since HPS had thought about and reflected on themselves as learners. HPS embarked on a bold plan from this point. HPS needed to know what the 4Cs and learning dispositions would offer the school and critically, students.

They formed a team they colloquially referred to as the 'Groundbreakers', as they intended to break ground and as learners, analyse what they believed were the potential pros and cons of engaging more deeply with the 4Cs. The level of interest and excitement created by the members of the Groundbreakers group was palpable and instigated an emerging climate of generative tension. Generative tension for Hurstville was a heady mix of excitement, anxiety and possibility. Generative tension is vital when sparking the curiosity of learners and also creating a climate in which learners desire to be involved in a learning because they understand its relevance to their needs. It is not unlike the 'Fear of Missing Out' (FOMO) from a learner's perspective. Deeper curiosity is often peaked by a discussion about the learning and why it matters.

Generative tension in situations can lead individuals and groups to moments of greater clarity or a genuine call to action. The twenty-four-member Groundbreakers group featured ten existing members of the school's leadership team and an invited group of fourteen staff from across the school who were lateral thinkers. They suspected that by inviting certain staff members and not explaining why to the wider staff, the situation would create a positive form of tension around this learning. They hoped it would pique the curiosity of other staff. They also suspected that if this new learning was challenging and satisfying, the fourteen staff members selected would informally discuss the work with other staff creating a 'ripple effect'.

Forming an effective Community of Practice

The Groundbreakers were a Community of Practice. In Lave and Wenger's[8] terms, there was a shared passion and enthusiasm for making beneficial change through planning and action in the school. Critically, the make-up of this group not only reflected positional leadership but also leadership capacity. Again, this reflects a view of leadership that is distributed rather than hierarchical and recognizes that leadership is nurtured through curiosity and inquiry rather than solely seniority or rank. The selection of 'lateral thinkers' to the 'Groundbreakers' supported an inquiry approach to action where transformation is understood as a process of discovery and understanding rather than an exclusively 'top down' roll-out. While there was broad engagement with the shared endeavour these CoPs are not 'tension free'. In many ways the generative tension in these groups provides the energy to collaborate or in the words of Collaboration Circles,[9] the offer and yield are the foundation of productive collaborations and communities of practice. In a successful Community of Practice, a sense of generative tension and excitement even occasional anxiety for the task at hand can serve to motivate and cohere the group to the common endeavour. Critically this group considered the work to be done as a reflective inquiry where their own individual and collaborative learning were key.

With some distance this approach has helped them understand and reflect on the *key drivers* for transformative change through CoP at HPS. They crystallized these into five key drivers that included:

1. Challenging and changing traditional leadership structures;
2. Learner agency coupled with positive tension;
3. Understanding and recognizing true collaboration;
4. Outward facing connection to challenge assumptions and to craft a shared endeavour (Learning community); and
5. Strategic and regular reflection on practice.

We will discuss each of these drivers and how they each relate to the development and sustenance of effective communities of practice.

Key driver 1 – Challenging and changing traditional leadership structures

One of the first tasks was to challenge assumptions regarding existing status quo and the structures teachers thought might constrain or limit school transformation. They created a number of school-funded team leader positions that were filled via expression of interest process, based on criteria that fitted our aspirations for transformation. These positions embedded leaders across the school, matching every team, including our specialist teams: English as an Additional Language, Learning and Support and Community Language Team with an Assistant Principal or Team Leader to generate powerful and connected collaborations. This shift grew the school leadership team to seventeen members and challenged them to redefine how they would effectively collaborate as a team of this size. This change to their leadership approach also enabled a different dynamic enabling voice and advocacy from those whose voices had not been heard much in the past.

The changing representation of the Community Language Team was the starkest example. Historically, the Community Language Team had limited representation or advocacy across the school and was considered by some as not being full and/or equal members of staff. This shifted rapidly and the Community Language Team embraced the opportunity to share their voice and contribute more substantially to whole-school planning and discussion. School strategic planning and reflection became something the Community Language Team explored *with* the leadership team, rather than something that simply happened *to* them. This approach challenged historical power structures and connections across the school that had previously hindered or diverted their shared vision for deep, diverse and engaged learning for everyone in the school.

In organizations that are considering transformation, positional leadership structures are often a reflection of the status quo rather than the dynamism required for a shifting and transforming school. As Alvesson and Spicer argue, 'formal structures, rules and routines could be a source of significant stupidity in organisations . . . Structures are often mistaken for guarantees of quality, productivity and reliability . . . Most people have a limited overview and do not make much effort to carefully look behind the surface structures'.[10] Through questioning the titles and roles that existed in the school, an opportunity emerged to think deeply about what leadership really means in transforming learning. HPS created an opportunity for everyone to redefine and rethink leadership structures, not just take them for granted.

For example, the school-funded transformational learning positions allowed HPS the flexibility to drive collaboration at all levels and embed the concept of transformative leadership not as a position but as a capacity. This in turn enabled each leader with space to advocate for their team members and students to provide clear representation and provide a chance for all voices across the school to be heard. Focusing these changes on ongoing collaboration challenged the establishment of any 'fiefdoms' within the school and created new dynamics through the creation of new structures and connections. This was a different way of thinking and ensured that leaders were continually reflecting on what the impact of their decision-making was on the whole school, not just the impact on their respective team or grade.

Etienne Wenger argues that effective collaborative leadership is critical in forming, shaping and enabling a Community of Practice. He argues that in CoPs 'decisions need to be taken, conditions need to be put in place, strategic conversations need to be had. Not all members see value in being involved in these processes. Whether you call them leaders, coordinators, or stewards, someone needs to do it – and it is as well to recognize them for the role they play.'[11] The impetus, the conditions and the frameworks for beneficial change only emerged when the endemic positional leadership structures at HPS were reimagined.

Rather than leadership being absent from CoPs they are critical to ensure transformative practice can take root and grow. Perhaps more critically it is the role of this leadership to sustain collaborative and transformative practices in the face of intransigence, apathy and resistance. To create sustainable CoPs the leaders role is crucial to enable and direct the opportunities for transformative change through collaboration. Agency is at the centre of renewed leadership structures to enable voice for all involved in the transformation process. The next key driver, learner agency, must permeate all practices including leadership to ensure there is a shared investment and vision for change.

Key driver 2 – Learner agency

A key feature of the professional learning was providing agency in the way teaching staff engaged with transformative learning. Staff were offered two pathways named after and explained by a water analogy: they could join the Rapid or River stream. The Rapid (as the name implies) was fast paced non-linear new learning, involving directional shifts, changes, challenges, unlearning and the occasional spill. River was learning at a slower pace with more points of reflection, a longer time frame and opportunities for deeper collaborative discussion. River allowed for time to take in this learning and situate it in the context of the students and the school.

HPS expected most would select the River approach and ten or so people would take on the Rapid option. In the end, forty-four staff members signed up for the Rapid learning approach. It became clear that exploring the dispositions on the Learning Disposition Wheel[12] was challenging staff to reflect on who they were as people and teaching practitioners. This was powerful, as the cascade into classrooms was swift. Teachers were discussing the dispositions on the Learning Disposition Wheel with students and engaging them in a variety of embodied learning experiences to help them gain a deeper understanding of what the dispositions were about and how students may recognize them in others and themselves.

Typically, professional learning can be in many schools or systems a 'take it or leave it' experience.[13] Teachers are not often positioned as agentic learners who can make their own contribution and choices in learning but rather empty vessels who need to be 'filled' with the latest policy or approach. Historically, professional learning at HPS had become something that staff endured. It was not an experience that inspired or challenged them to question their own teaching practice or to analyse any new learning against the current needs of their students. This CoP-based professional learning experience was designed to provide choice in the process, approach and classroom application of the learning. This strategy valued and celebrated the work and collaboration of teachers rather than an external 'expert'. In their research on CoPs in schools and higher education teacher educators Bernadette Mary Mercieca and Jacquelin McDonald[14] argue:

> Teacher agency for all teachers is an important aspect of schools that foster a culture of growth where learning is the norm and a shared enterprise. A culture of growth is evident in schools where there is high human capital (how good we are alone), social capital (how we get better together) and decisional capital (how we get better over time) within the staff and their leaders who work collaboratively.

There is nothing particularly novel about claiming teachers, students and everyone in schools require agency in their learning. Yet the modest agency designed into the Hurstville CoP and advised in research[15] tends to be the exception rather than the rule in professional learning. Engaging in true collaborative practice requires respect for other's perspectives and not a 'one size fits all' approach to developing professional learning. As we see in the next driver this also requires a deep and practical understanding of collaborative practice before action focused transformation can take hold.

Key driver 3 – Understanding and recognizing true collaboration

While exploring the 4Cs and the dispositions, HPS realized that to fully comprehend collaboration as an authentic experience, they required a clear framework that regularly drew all staff members into authentic professional learning. Initially teachers and leaders did not fully understand how to collaborate individually or as a larger group. So, to understand and achieve collaboration they had to explicitly learn the skill and reflect on how they could continue to grow this skill across all teams. They decided on a collaborative planning structure. This model provided each team, including the specialist staff (working across teams), with whole days together with a focus on planning and programming. The emphasis was on developing a collaborative programme designed together from scratch. The collaborative programme began by focusing on the syllabus outcomes the teams were intending for their students to achieve. They also considered deeply the specific needs and context of the learners within their cohorts. In the past it was common for different members of teams to offer up a previously developed programme area with some small-scale adaptions. In these cases, it was cooperative programme development rather than an authentic collaboration with learners needs driving the shared endeavour.

Drawing on Andy Hargreaves work, South African education researcher Adeola Folasade Akinyemi and colleagues[16] argue,

> professional learning communities demand that teachers develop grown-up norms in a grown-up profession – where difference, debate and disagreement are viewed as the foundation stones of improvement. Accordingly, collective learning is also apparent, through collective knowledge creation. Thus, collaboration among teachers foster good working relationship and can be seen as a means of enhancing their professional development.

Adeola Folasade Akinyemi's exhortation[17] that 'difference, debate and disagreement' are foundational to effective professional learning is easier said than done. Hurstville's experience identifies a missing link in collaborative practice – the explicit learning of collaboration. Collaboration Circles[18] was used as the framework to support collaborative practice and learning at HPS. Collaboration Circles explicitly used approaches that allowed and enabled difference and disagreement that celebrated diverse opinions.

The initial staging of 'offer' and 'yield' (the first two elements of Collaboration Circles) provided HPS with a starting point to explore and collaborate around transformative practice through a structured process. The tacit assumption among professionals and students is that collaboration is widely understood and easily achieved.[19] Unfortunately, this assumption is problematic at best and corrosive at worst. While most professionals understand how to cooperate, authentic and productive collaboration takes time and effort to build[20] and requires a deep and sustained commitment.

Vera John-Steiner's definition of collaboration as 'a shared affair of the mind' can only be achieved when processes, frameworks and scaffolds support understanding and action-making. This realization was a powerful driver of change at HPS, as voices that had remained unheard were now being shared, considered and valued. These processes led to a school culture that valued and embedded collaboration as a defining process in the staffroom and the classroom. This learning was valuable and HPS's teachers' responsibility as educators was to provide the benefit of their experience to their neighbouring schools by inviting them to a 'community of practice'. Additionally, this created further productive tension as they now had to consider how best to provide professional learning to their peers. This was a step-up that necessitated an approach that shared and disseminated our learning inside and outside HPS.

Key driver 4 – Outward facing connections to craft a shared endeavour

A Community of Practice was formed organically from five geographically local primary schools, all of whom were beginning to explore the 4Cs. Forming a Community of Practice entailed a move beyond the cooperation to a deeper and inherently more difficult collaborative engagement. This collaborative approach saw leaders from each school come together to explore needs and the possibilities for learners within and across their schools.

The collaboration challenged the teachers and leaders to think beyond the needs of their students to consider their neighbouring schools' contexts. It did not take long for HPS to plan out and enact shared professional learning across the five schools that brought our staff members together on the different school sites and examined how each school was embodying the learning around the 4Cs and the learning dispositions from the Learning Disposition Wheel. The five leadership teams also came together to collaborate on new learning around the different coherence makers to help scaffold our understanding of the 4Cs. It was during this time that the staff member who had led the whole-school 4C strategy previously moved on to another role in another area. HPS knew they needed to have a clear strategic focus on the 4Cs within the school and across the broader Community of Practice so in response to this need they created a school-funded *Instructional Leader – Contemporary Learning* position.

To continually challenge the relevance and rigour of what they were exploring with students, HPS needed to be reflecting with others on a similar trajectory but within a different school/learning context. This helped them to identify commonalities and differences in each school's learning journey. One of the outcomes of engaging with this community was that these connections created more opportunities to exchange and grow ideas outside their own siloed setting. They ensured this by continually providing learning agency and regular opportunities to connect and collaborate. Externalizing their learning and engaging with other schools reframed and challenged what was possible; broader and deeper than the initial conceptual framework of the Community of Practice that supported them to regularly and strategically consider their practice and progress.

A persistent flaw in teacher professional learning is the tendency for individual schools to hold learning for themselves. An inter-school Community of Practice approach provides a feasible and workable way for schools to share and engage with challenges and issues that are shared. In a network of schools, they had the opportunity to share the learning beyond HPS. This 'external audience' also forced them to test and clarify their thinking and practice so that they could share insights that were relevant to the other schools in the Community of Practice.

Key driver 5 – Strategic and regular reflection on practice

HPS was fortunate that the staff member who took on the contemporary learning role possessed a dynamic skill set and was able to develop strong connections between staff across the school and between the school teams across the Community of Practice. This was an enabling leadership role that ensured that reflection was a critical component of the CoP and not an afterthought. This led to a clear focus on exploring teaching practice and regularly reflecting on the needs of the school's learners. This cascaded into exploring the opportunities that were being created by the emerging pedagogy established within each learning space.

As a school, HPS began to understand that a large part of crafting their own learning was the need for regular points of shared reflection that led to identifying tangible actions. They established a framework known as Collaborative Classroom Visit/Deep Noticing and Action – CCV/DNA.[21] Small groups of staff (six or seven people) would work with a facilitator who would use questioning to guide a shared reflection based on a snapshot of practice within a learning space. The snapshot of practice would be no more than fifteen to twenty minutes and the people entering the space would observe but not engage with the practice or the students. This strengthened deep noticing of what was occurring for learners in that particular classroom.

Once the snapshot was complete, the small group and facilitator would join the practitioner who delivered the snapshot and they would begin the reflection by talking about the learning from their perspective. Members of the group would share their noticings and build on ideas from one another while the facilitator posed questions to draw all participants completely into the reflective space.

Once the shared reflection was complete, each member of the group identified an action to explore within their own teaching practice. This action was recorded and shared with the other members of the group. After the shared reflection, each group member followed up with the leader of their team and discussed the action that they had identified and planned for a co-teaching experience in which they explored this planned action with the students they were teaching.

One of the critical indicators of successful transformation is the extent to which student learning is deepened and enhanced.[22] The irony is that so little time is spent beyond the initial teacher education phase on teachers learning deeply about students and their learning. To respond to this gap, HPS began by building the systems and dispositions in their teachers and leaders (particularly teamwork and influence) to enable deep, sustained and applied reflection. The CoP process enabled a reflection on process that scaffolded and supported different perspectives and drove reflection on transforming learning, teaching and curriculum in the school.

Concluding reflections

As HPS continues on the journey of transformation, the learning they undertake within the school and across the Community of Practice keeps iterating. What connects the new learning they choose is its impact on learning for students. They see in their classrooms a renewed focus on learner agency and self-regulation that is a direct product of an approach that values and engages deeply with learning dispositions and deepening student learning.

In their educators they have seen the evidence of an ongoing commitment to regular collaboration and reflection. They are hearing many more voices that have led to HPS being focused on the intrapersonal, interpersonal and cognitive needs of their learners – rather than 'coasting' on reliably high test scores. Underneath all of this is the shared endeavour that leads to increased opportunities for learners to develop and understand themselves and appreciate the dedication to learning throughout all of their lives, which brings us back to surfing and Snowy.

In the end Snowy McAlister's legacy is not only that he was the first or best at surfing. His lasting legacy was to build a focused and supportive community that glimpsed the possibility of surfing. His patient and thoughtful building of a community led to a sport that multitudes now enjoy recreationally and professionally. Similarly, those at HPS were not the first to glimpse the power of transforming learning. Like Snowy, it isn't individuals that necessarily make the difference but rather how collaborative, engaged and growth-focused collaboration can make deep and engaged learning possible. The growth of surfing as a movement required momentum. The same can be said for transformation in schools. Like surfing a wave, momentum comes through shared endeavour. In this way they can not only glimpse but also achieve the seemingly impossible to help students reach their potential and 'walk on water'.

Notes

1. J. Lave and E. Wenger, *Situated Learning: Legitimate Peripheral Participation* (Cambridge, MA: Cambridge University Press, 1991).
2. Lave and E. Wenger, *Situated Learning*.
3. M. Jefferson and M. Anderson, *Transforming Education: Reimagining Learning, Pedagogy and Curriculum* (London: Bloomsbury Publishing, 2021).
4. C. Day and C. Grice, *Investigating the Influence and Impact of Leading from the Middle: A School-Based Strategy for Middle Leaders in Schools* (Sydney: The University of Sydney, 2019).
5. Day and Grice, *Investigating the Influence and Impact of Leading from the Middle*.
6. Jefferson and Anderson, *Transforming Education*, 219.
7. J. Redden and C. J. Steiner, 'Fanatical Consumers: Towards a Framework for Research', *Journal of Consumer Marketing* 17, no. 4 (2000): 322–37.
8. Lave and E. Wenger, *Situated Learning*.
9. M. Jefferson and M. Anderson, *Transforming Schools: Creativity, Critical Reflection, Communication, Collaboration* (London: Bloomsbury Publishing, 2017), 137.
10. M. Alvesson and A. Spicer, *The Stupidity Paradox: The Power and Pitfalls of Functional Stupidity at Work* (London: Profile Books, 2016), 147.
11. E. Wenger, *Introduction to Communities of Practice: A Brief Overview of the Concept and its Uses* (Cambridge: Cambridge University Press, 2009). and E. Wenger-Trayner and B. Wenger-Trayner, *Learning to Make a Difference (Vol. 1: Value Creation in Social Learning Spaces)* (Cambridge: Cambridge University Press, 2020).
12. Jefferson and Anderson, *Transforming Schools*, 137.
13. Jefferson and Anderson, *Transforming Education*, 180.
14. B. M. Mercieca and J. McDonald, 'Leading and Sustaining Communities of Practice', in *Sustaining Communities of Practice with Early Career Teachers*, ed. J. McDonald & B. M. Mercieca (Singapore: Springer, 2021), 45–64.
15. Mercieca and J. McDonald, 'Leading and Sustaining Communities of Practice'.
16. A. F. Akinyemi, S. Rembe, J. Shumba, and T. M. Adewumi, 'Collaboration and Mutual Support as Processes Established by Communities of Practice to Improve Continuing Professional Teachers' Development in High Schools', *Cogent Education* 6, no. 1 (2019): 1685446, 2.
17. Akinyemi et al., 'Collaboration and Mutual Support as Processes Established by Communities of Practice to Improve Continuing Professional Teachers' Development in High Schools'.
18. Jefferson and Anderson, *Transforming Schools*.

19 Jefferson and Anderson, *Transforming Schools*, 129.
20 Jefferson and Anderson, *Transforming Education*.
21 Jefferson and Anderson, *Transforming Education*, 195.
22 Jefferson and Anderson, *Transforming Education*, 56.

References

Akinyemi, A. F., S. Rembe, J. Shumba, and T. M. Adewumi 2019. 'Collaboration and Mutual Support as Processes Established by Communities of Practice to Improve Continuing Professional Teachers' Development in High Schools'. *Cogent Education* 6(1): 1685446.

Alvesson, M. and A. Spicer 2016. *The Stupidity Paradox: The Power and Pitfalls of Functional Stupidity at Work*. London: Profile Books.

Carmichael, T. and M. Hadžikadić 2019. 'The Fundamentals of Complex Adaptive Systems'. In M. Hadžikadić & T. Carmichael (eds.), *Complex Adaptive Systems*, 1–16. Cham: Springer.

Day, C. and C. Grice 2019. *Investigating the Influence and Impact of Leading from the Middle: A School-based Strategy for Middle Leaders in Schools*. Sydney: The University of Sydney.

Jefferson, M. and M. Anderson 2017. *Transforming Schools: Creativity, Critical Reflection, Communication, Collaboration*. London: Bloomsbury.

Jefferson, M. and M. Anderson 2021. *Transforming Education: Reimagining Learning, Pedagogy and Curriculum*. Bloomsbury Publishing.

Koh, G. A. and H. Askell-Williams 2021. 'Sustainable School-improvement in Complex Adaptive Systems: A Scoping Review'. *Review of Education* 9(1): 281–314.

Magalhaes de Barros, A. P. R., E. Simmt, and M. V. Maltempi 2017. 'Understanding a Brazilian High School Blended Learning Environment From the Perspective of Complex Systems'. *Journal of Online Learning Research* 3: 73–101.

Mercieca, B. M. and J. McDonald 2021. 'Leading and Sustaining Communities of Practice'. In J. McDonald and B. M. Mercieca (eds.), *Sustaining Communities of Practice with Early Career Teachers*, 45–64. Singapore: Springer.

Wenger, E. 2009. *Introduction to Communities of Practice: A Brief Overview of the Concept and Its Uses*. Cambridge: Cambridge University Press.

Wenger-Trayner, E. and B. Wenger-Trayner 2020. *Learning to Make a Difference (Vol. 1: Value Creation in Social Learning Spaces*. Cambridge: Cambridge University Press.

How Schools Transform through Creative Disruption

Mitch Ulacco and Michael Anderson

6

Creative Disruption (p. 104)

Why is creativity required for school transformation? (p. 106)

Understanding Creative Disruption (p. 107)

Creative Disruption in education (p. 108)

Case study: Creative Disruption at St Eugene (p. 108)

A provocation for transformation (p. 109)

Making transformation a reality at St Eugene College (p. 110)
The Meerkat Strategy (p. 110)

Developing professional learning communities (p. 110)

The Festival of Positive Disruption (p. 113)

- The Festivals of Positive Disruption, September 2020 (p. 113)
- Teacher feedback on 2020 Festival of Positive Disruption (p. 115)
- The festival of Creative Disruption (p. 116)
- The Festival of Collaborative and Communicative Disruption, 2022 (p. 118)
- Where to from here? (p. 119)
- Concluding reflections (p. 119)

Creative Disruption

Derby, Tasmania, is a small town located in the north-east of Tasmania in Australia is a living example of creative change and how disruptions can allow for creativity to flourish. The area had been inhabited by the Palawa people for thousands of years. In the early 1800s, Europeans arrived and developed agriculture, farmed sheep and cattle and harvested timber for the expanding colony of Van Diemen's Land (later called Tasmania). The town like many others in that part of Tasmania suffered declines in primary industries until it became a shadow of its former self. Old industries degenerated leaving the opportunities for a creative response. Derby was facing the kind of disruption that had killed off so many towns before it and was destined to become a ghost town until the boom in mountain biking created a new prosperity for the tiny town. In the 1980s and 1990s, it established itself as a hub for the mountain biking.

Derby's rugged and mountainous terrain makes it a great location for mountain bike riders. The first mountain bike trails (see Figure 6.1) in Derby were built in the 1980s by local riders looking for a new and exciting way to explore the area. They used hand tools and grit to carve out trails through the dense bushland, and over time, these trails became known as the Blue Derby Pods. As the popularity of mountain biking grew, so did the number of trails in Derby. In the 1990s, the Derwent Valley Council began investing in more formalized trails to attract growing numbers of tourists to the region. The investment led to Derby rapidly becoming a magnet for mountain bikers from around the world attending annual events. The development and evolution of a mountain biking community were built on the heritage of

Figure 6.1 Mountain biking is now popular in Derby, Tasmania.

adventure sports in Tasmania. The new industry was also founded on the connection and understanding local people had of their economic context. The combination of these factors helped Derby respond to the decline of the old and create something novel to support the local economy.

Derby's transformation fits the model of Creative Disruption where new responses are sought for persistent problems. In Derby's case the disruption was caused by the decline of the local economy over time (agriculture, forestry, etc.) that led to the creative introduction of new economic activity (mountain biking, accommodation and adventure sports). In education the challenges are different, but the process of Creative Disruption can be applied usefully. Our current schooling system, for the most part, is not meeting the needs of our students.

As such transformation of learning, pedagogy and curriculum is required to ensure our students are gaining an education that is not a relic of a bygone era but rather is fit for their future and current needs. Creative Disruption in education draws on the relevant and useful learning and teaching practices of the past and generates ways to imagine, design and generate transformative action. This process can be collaborative, agentic and engaging for teachers, leaders and the school community. However, while the process may be engaging, it does, as we will see in the case study, disrupt and unsettle the status quo. Before we consider the case study, we would like to consider the role of creativity in school transformation.

Why is creativity required for school transformation?

We often associate creativity in schools with a capacity that can or should be taught in the classroom. The famous TED Talk 'Do schools kill creativity?' by Ken Robinson in 2006 focused significant discussion on how schools' squash young people's creativity. While Robinson's work has been critiqued[1] he did shine a light on student creativity. There is, however, a critical role for creativity in school transformation processes. As education researcher Linda Darling-Hammond explains, the transformation from old practices to collaborative and experiential learning is a form of creativity in itself:

> This spirit of creativity and innovation is visible throughout the schools, which are encouraged to engage both students and teachers in experiential and cooperative learning, action research, scientific investigations, entrepreneurial activities, and discussion and debate.[2]

The creativity required to make these shifts is often under recognized but there is significant imagination and innovation required to engage with these changes in school practices.

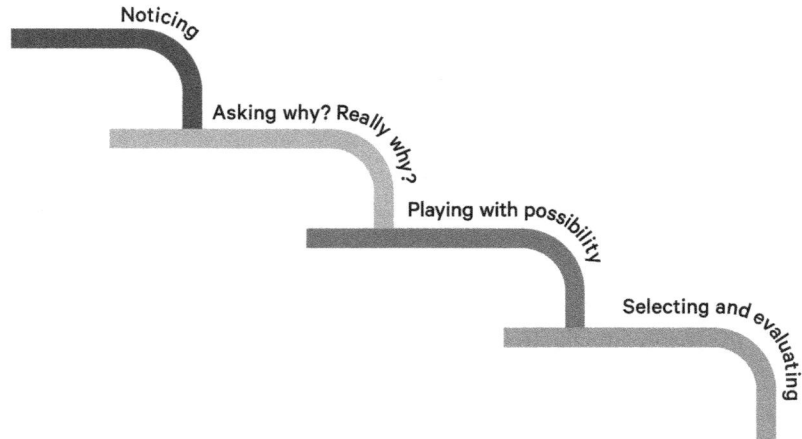

Figure 6.2 The Creativity Cascade.

Table 6.1 Application of the creativity cascade to school transformation

Noticing	Allows schools to identify and map their current practices. Noticing requires schools to 'make strange' their taken-for-granted beliefs. Noticing also asks schools to perceive their context deeply.
Asking why? Really why?	Allows schools to ask sometimes difficult questions about their school. Asking really why prompts schools to go beyond superficial or knee-jerk responses and dig deeper to gain a comprehensive and holistic understanding of why the school is the way it is.
Playing with possibility	This provides schools with ways to imagine their school differently. What are the possible ways forward to make a sustainable difference in the school.
Selecting and evaluating	This is where the first achievable plans move into tangible strategies. The possibilities are evaluated (sometimes by outsiders) to understand the nature and rate of the change. At this stage the school decides to make the possibilities into actions.

One of the ways 4C Transformative Learning and its school partners design transformation processes is around the Creativity Cascade (see Figure 6.2).[3]

The cascade has primarily been applied to classroom practice but the coherence maker is also relevant in school or organizational processes. Table 6.1 outlines the application of the Creativity Cascade in school transformation:

Once a school has considered the opportunities for transformation through the cascade, then a plan for the transformation approach is required. The school that features in the case study in this chapter decided after going through the cascade process that Creative Disruption was required.

Understanding Creative Disruption

According to French writer Jean Marie Dru,[4] Creative Disruption is the reconsideration or even breaking of conventions (i.e. the status quo) to accelerate movement to the future without cutting off or throwing away the past. In Derby's case the pressure for creative change came from a declining economy. In education the pressures emerged from the changes we see in the society and community around us. Ziaddin Sardar calls these forces Postnormality, contradiction, chaos and complexity,[5] and they make the need for Creative Disruption more acute to retain relevant and effective practices and promote imaginative responses to a complex present and future.

According to Ziauddin Sardar[6] the post-normal age is:

> characterised by uncertainty, rapid change, realignment of power, upheaval and chaotic behaviour. We live in an in-between period where old orthodoxies are dying, new ones have yet to be born, and very few things seem to make sense. Ours is a transitional age, a time without the confidence that we can return to any past we have known and with no confidence in any path to a desirable, attainable or sustainable future.

In the face of these uncertainties Creative Disruption provides a way for schools to meet the rapidly shifting needs of students as they navigate 'Postnormal Times'. To respond to these emerging realities, schools can choose to do nothing and maintain the status quo or they can attempt through creativity to respond to external disruptions. Before we discuss how they approached this transformation challenge let's define how the terms have been used and how they apply to schooling.

Creative Disruption in education

In the education sector, Creative Disruption can take many forms, such as the introduction of new technologies or pedagogical approaches that fundamentally change the way students learn and teachers teach. For us, Creative Disruption provides space for a critical reflection on past practices that allows educators to consider the research evidence and apply it to their context. Essentially this a space for critical reflection[7] where schools can:

1. Examine their assumptions about 'taken for granted' practices (Identifying Assumptions[8]);
2. Engage in a questioning of those assumptions (Why this? Why so?);
3. Contest, elaborate and adapt approaches for beneficial change (Contesting, Elaborating and Adapting); and then
4. Reimagine how practices might be recreated in a transforming school (Re-Solving).

The 'space for a critical reflection' sits between the past and the imagined future; the disorientation of strategic planning and the continued iterations of disruptions underpin a successful transformation of an existing learning culture, with students and teachers working together to co-create learning frameworks and practices that make reimagined learning possible. These aspirations sit at the foundation of The St Eugene Festivals of Positive Disruption that we describe in the case study. There are, however, challenges that face schools considering Creative Disruption as a pathway for transformation. While Creative Disruption can bring about positive changes in education, it also presents challenges for those invested in the status quo. The shock of disruption unsettles and challenges long-held and often-cherished beliefs about learning and this change can cause anxiety and fear. These anxieties were evident in our case study school, St Eugene College.

Case study: Creative Disruption at St Eugene

St Eugene College is a Prep-12 Catholic (ages 5–18) school north of Brisbane with a student population of 1,400, associated with Missionary Oblates of Mary Immaculate

Australia and part of Brisbane Catholic Education. Within the college there are four phases of learning:

- early years (P–2);
- junior years (3–6);
- middle years (7–9) and
- senior years (10–12).

Each phrase has a distinct focus but are all connected with the goal of achieving a seamless transition for students from Prep to Year 12.

A provocation for transformation

Marissa Dann (principal 2017–2021) was keen to examine how learning at St Eugene could move beyond a status quo. In response to that provocation the staff began to reimagine how they might better address the needs of the young people and the world they live in with its inherent chaos, contradictions and complexity. This led to the development of a college value about transformation. The value was expressed as 'to transform learning and ultimately schooling, staff needed to begin by transforming themselves'. This approach was inspired by and underpinned by the Alice Springs (Mparntwe) Education Declaration that argues

> Education has the power to transform lives. It supports young people to realise their potential by providing skills they need to participate in the economy and in society, and contributing to every aspect of their wellbeing.[9]

The school leadership team believed these principles could and should drive transformative change in the school.

The college leadership team believed any transformation or reimagining on a large scale was only possible if educators, as facilitators and as learners first transformed themselves, developing mindsets for transformation. This transformation mindset established an environment that was open to change and a willingness to explore ways of working and ways of learning beyond the industrial models. The aim was to develop and reimagine approaches to learning that equipped students with the dispositions that would support them as they navigate the complexities of their world.

In 2017, three staff attended a 4Cs Collaborative Network Day in Sydney to explore a partnership between the college and the organization (4CTL). The workshops were attended by 160 educational practitioners and facilitators including teachers, school leaders and students.

It was evident to the attendees from St Eugene that the community of learners at the network days were driven by the same passion and commitment to reimagine learning. The professional nature of sharing resources, connecting with like-minded professionals, the focus on teacher and student agency and voice and having students, staff and parents connected as learners, resonated with the college's vision and newly articulated transformative values. This encounter provided the impetus for the journey of reimagining schooling, inspired a climate of disruption and set the path to transforming learning at St Eugene College. The next step was to design a journey to transformation that met the specific needs of the school.

Making transformation a reality at St Eugene College

In our experience, any new framework or way of working may be met with scepticism from teachers. To achieve a mindset of transformation and for new learning to occur, the disruption had to come from the classroom teachers themselves. The college leadership team knew they could not implement this disruption using a top-down approach to change, understanding that it would most likely be met with resistance. They were also concerned that experienced teachers and facilitators might see this as another educational 'fad'. This tension continues today, however, with less resistance and more advocates of the transforming learning agenda. St Eugene has gradually seen more staff connecting with the transforming agenda and many teachers who were initially sceptical are beginning to engage.

To help overcome these tensions the school worked with those 'willing and able' to engage,[10] in the hope that others might notice the change and also engage. This is colloquially known as the Meerkat Strategy.

The Meerkat Strategy

The Meerkat Strategy is an approach to transformation that builds a Community of Practice from those interested in the possibilities and opportunities of beneficial and sustainable change. As this change occurs others who are not directly involved notice the activity. They hear students and parents discussing the 'new approaches' and, as meerkats often do, begin to peek over the metaphorical or actual fence to see what 'all the fuss' is about. The foundation of the strategy was designed by 4CTL to create early adopters. Those who engaged initially then developed local networks of emergent learning communities. These communities arose as interested onlookers became active in the transformation process.

Developing professional learning communities

Reimagining schooling at St Eugene required reimagining professional learning and integrating it throughout every activity at St Eugene. Just as Meerkats work in a 'mob', building communities, St Eugene wanted to work towards creating professional learning communities to build a transformed learning culture.

The role of the early adopters was to reimagine the 'teacher' not as the knowledge transmitter but rather as a facilitator and curator of learning. This reimagining positioned students as co-learners who could make choices and exercise agency over their learning by collaborating with the teacher and other students in the class. As the interested onlookers (meerkats) began to engage, the hope was they would see that the transformative work going was not faddish and had the potential to deepen and extend their own practice and the learning of their students.

The creation of Professional Learning Communities (PLCs) focused on transforming learning became embedded as a college-wide approach. This was a new approach for St Eugene. Traditionally, the school formed groups within subject- or stage-based departments. The PLC approach had a more explicit focus to reimagining the learner, learning and schooling.

Each PLC had a focus, and in collaboration each professional learning community made a commitment to achieve a desired outcome by 2022. For example:

- One group had a focus on the introduction of the Learning Disposition Wheel.[11] They explored how the wheel could unify curriculum and well-being;
- The leadership team explored how the wheel could support the planning of strategic initiatives and deepen the school executive's understanding of leadership;
- Another group explored the Wonder Web;
- The student voice group explored the agency in learning and teaching.

The purpose of these groups was to collaborate, find connections between the 4C frameworks (wheels, web and 4Cs, etc.) and forge a common language, strategies for moving forward in a supported networked way.

To enable this approach a group called STEGG (St Eugene Guiding Group) was established to manage the strategic implementation of the transforming agenda. This community had representatives from all areas of the college including: P-12 teachers, middle leaders and members of leadership. Its representative nature allowed staff to have a voice in the strategic planning of the learning agenda. In 2023, St Eugene plans to incorporate students within this group. By taking this approach, they hope to embrace student voice and continue to refine the partnership of learning through all relevant stakeholders within the college.

The explicit intent of the PLCs was to build teacher capacity as learners and facilitators of learning. PLCs were also to designed to increase teacher agency and begin the process of enhancing and refining the power of student voice and agency in the college. Each PLC member volunteered to be part of their chosen community, while purpose and intent was communicated to the staff. At this stage, not every staff member is in a transforming learning community. However, as the Meerkat Strategy continues to produce curiosity and grow in effectiveness, the college is exploring new and imaginative ways to create further professional learning communities that connect and extend the implementation of transforming learning at St Eugene College.

Figure 6.3 Meerkats are a metaphor in school transformation to engage the curious outsider.

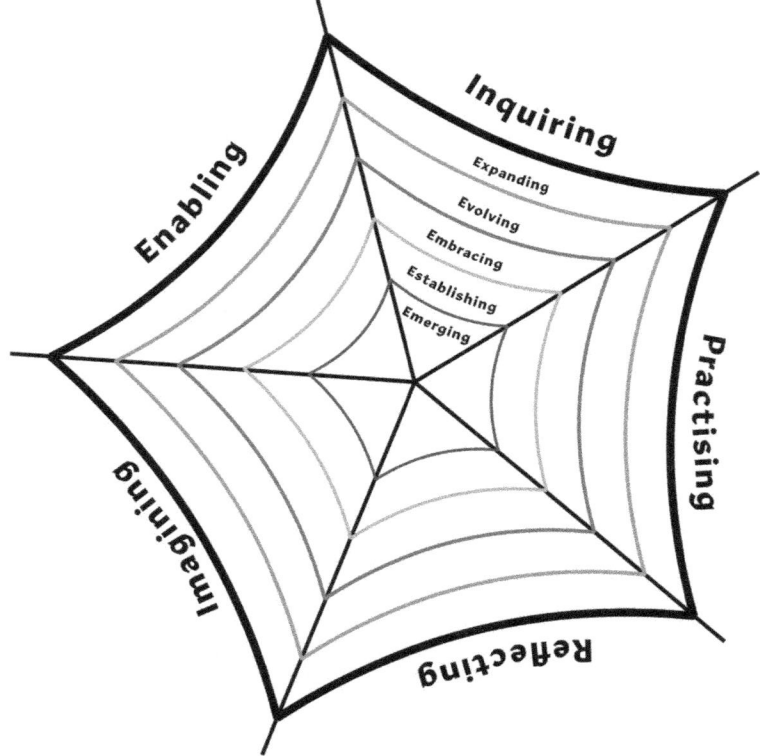

Figure 6.4 The Wonder Web.

The 2022 Professional Learning plan incorporated elements of Miranda Jefferson and Michael Anderson's approach.[12] Professional learning workshops, activities, staff meetings, leadership meetings considered a specific element of transformation including:

- 4Cs Coherence Makers[13] to understand and engage the 4Cs in learning;
- The Learning Disposition Wheel[14] to support explicit student focused development of learning capacities; or
- the WonderWeb (see Figure 6.3) to enrich and extend the learning and teaching culture at the school.

This approach ensured that all members of the learning community could begin to immerse themselves in transforming learning processes, procedures and practices. As the journey progressed, these strategies (Meerkat and Communities of Learners) contributed to the establishment of a transforming learning community. This community integrates curriculum, builds student achievement through learning dispositions[15] and builds an understanding of the 4Cs in learning and teaching. Another approach that built on these foundations was the development of the Festival of Positive Disruption.

The Festival of Positive Disruption

One key means of achieving the individual transformations needed to achieve St Eugene's vision for beneficial change, was to reimagine their annual professional learning day.[16] The leadership group decided that this transformative and collaborative work was a priority area in the college's professional learning plan. The arrival of the Covid-19 pandemic created an external disruption that prompted St Eugene to reimagine this day as a Festival of Learning.

The festival was designed to achieve three primary aims:

1. reframe, reshape and reimagine how effective and purposeful professional learning could be delivered,
2. acknowledge the skills, expertise and professionalism of the staff and
3. acknowledge that like students, staff have different and diverse needs, expectations and interests.

With these three aims the festivals were designed to maximize staff participation, build staff capacity in learning and teaching, enhance the relationship between staff in a P-12 and to increase staff agency. The first festival occurred in September 2020.

The Festivals of Positive Disruption, September 2020

This Festival was in the second week after the students and staff had returned from a five-week period of Covid-19 lockdown in Queensland. Staff morale was low even though many other places throughout Australia and the world endured more extended periods of lockdown and hardship. The continued threat of Covid-19 had now become part of the 'new normal' and while the students and staff had returned to the classroom, there was a sense of disconnectedness and a need to foster and nurture human connection.

With these challenges in mind, the focus of the positive disruption became staff mental health and well-being. In the past at these 'development days' staff would expect a full day of lecture and tutorial style professional development often led by external experts in various priority areas (pastoral care, religion, classroom management, etc). Often this limited the possibility of teacher agency and restricted any true collaboration or community building across the P-12 teaching community. This approach reinforced the status quo.

By contrast the Festival of Positive Disruption was developed by members of staff who were interested and committed to enhance the quality of professional learning and staff mental health and well-being. This included acknowledgement and valuing of the contribution staff had made during the lockdown period and the daily commitment they had made to the education of young people. It recognized their personal sacrifices during this period; the importance of mental health and well-being within the teaching profession and signalled the college's intention to work on communication, collaboration and creativity in their processes and practices across the school.

The programme was designed using the Learning Disposition Wheel.[17]

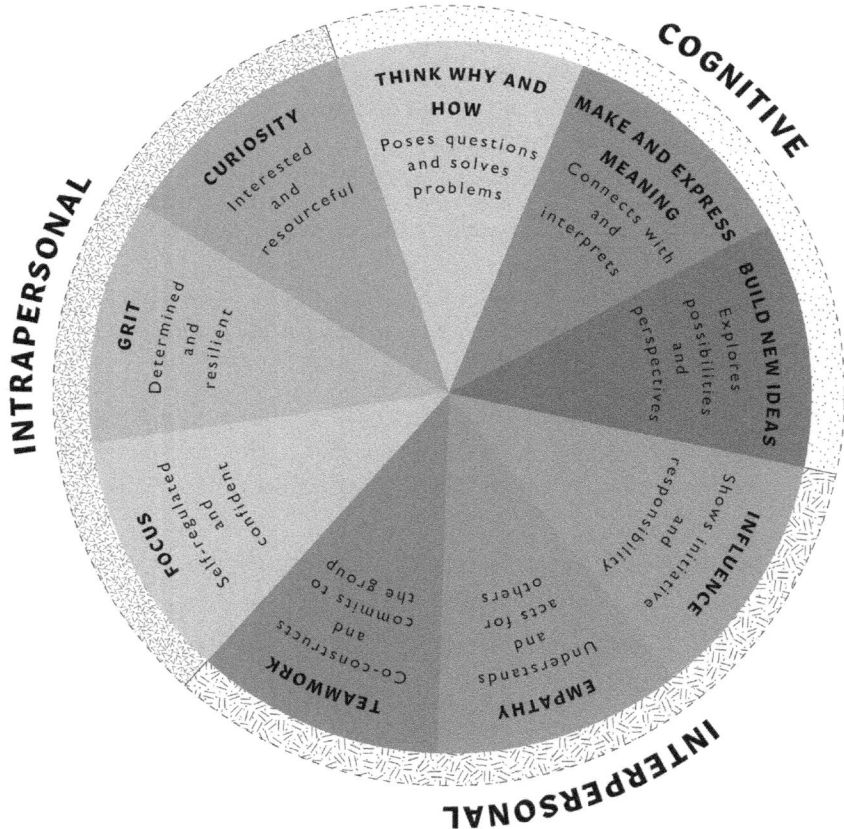

Figure 6.5 The Learning Disposition Wheel.

Consistent with the design of the wheel the event included cognitive, intrapersonal or interpersonal disposition development for staff. The design team created the day with this balance to allow teachers to engage with the areas they felt they most needed.

Prior to the day, staff were invited to select an individualized programme from a menu of events to meet their professional needs and personal mental health and well-being. They could choose to attend or participate in activities, on or off site, and engage in timed and untimed activities, including online webinars, online interactive workshops or create their own activities. This flexibility was well received by all staff. The staff feedback on the day justified many of the design decisions taken to increase teacher agency.

Teacher feedback on 2020 Festival of Positive Disruption

There is little doubt that upending years of 'status quo' teacher professional learning is a risk for schools. Entrenched practices in staff professional learning have created a kind of 'house style' that generates certain expectations. The approach taken by St Eugene prior to 2020 with a focus on lecture and tutorial approaches is not dissimilar from the kinds of 'Sage of the Stage' teaching approaches teachers have become used to in classrooms. It took courage to disrupt expectations and practice but the feedback from the teachers underscored the soundness of the risk inherent in this reimagined design. The response from teachers was overwhelmingly positive and the following responses highlight some of the common themes. One library school officer commented in their evaluation:

> The best PD ever – a real mental health day in my opinion – I had the best time – getting out of the library is a rarity these days to connect with anybody at college so I thoroughly enjoyed the experience and hope it is the start of many more days like this. Even though I didn't really understand the concept in the beginning – it ended up a fantastic day.

A Year 6 teacher identified the risk of approaching professional learning in this way but also recognized the benefits of disrupting traditional models of professional learning:

> This certainly ranks as a highlight in my experiences of professional learning, not necessarily due to the content (even though this in itself was delightful, varied and inspiring), but more so in the way it was delivered. It feels right. There is a huge risk with the approach we've adopted:
>
> - Will people attend?
> - Will people engage appropriately?
> - Will this meet the 'criteria'?

> There is tremendous empowerment and greater engagement in learning when learners are presented with choice, at least this is how I feel about it. In my view, this is deep learning. Everything I sampled on Friday has given me a thirst to dig deeper: How can I correct my topspin forehand?! How will I go about establishing a worm farm at home to accompany my composting? How can I utilise Breakout EDU as inspiration to challenge the way learning happens in my classroom? I haven't stopped thinking about it since. Isn't this the kind of curiosity that we want to instil in our students? I suppose the question is how? So, rather than the end, perhaps this is only the beginning.

The success of the festival inspired the college to maintain the 'disruption momentum' and decided that the next four festivals would be dedicated to each of the 4C coherence makers.[18] In 2021 creativity was the focus of the festival of Creative Disruption named after the process the school had been engaged with for several years.

The Festival of Creative Disruption

The next iteration of the festival was more streamlined and each of the workshops was focused and designed to address creativity and structured around the 3Ps (Pedagogy, Play and Performance). Mitch Ulacco co-author of this chapter and P-12 Head (Middle/Senior Years) explains the approach:

> Through the college's journey – play has been central to any workshop, learning they have undertaken. For us embodiment, experiential learning brings to life the Cs, the dispositions and underpins the success of the strategies we have worked with on this journey. From the 2020 festival feedback onwards staff adopted the three Ps – They said:

> 'it was great we could just play, have fun'.

> We wanted a focus on pedagogy and we wanted to challenge staff as learners but also their own pedagogical practices. We wanted to explore ways we could challenge traditional ways to deliver learning in and out of the classroom that engages learners. The performance was a vehicle for us to bring our community together – that concept of P-12, staff supporting each other, continued the support of staff wellbeing and mental health and continue to explore the world of building staff capacity and agency. It was also a play with and link to 4Cs. We now have the 4Cs and we can explore these via the 3Ps. This gave staff a structure of certainty, that sessions had a specific/targeted focus and outcome that supported participants who needed structure.

St Eugene wanted to understand through this festival how creativity could build confidence, capacity and agency in their teachers as facilitators and leaders of learning. The workshop leaders were encouraged to design their workshops using the Creativity Cascade to ensure there was a common language for creativity learning across the school.

Another design feature of the 2021 festival was the use of the Learning Disposition Wheel to identify and collect data on the dispositions staff were engaging with during the 2021 festival. This data revealed that the cognitive dispositions were less focused on by staff during the day and interpersonal dispositions were most focused on. These responses allowed the college to design the next phase of professional learning with a focus on the interconnectedness of the dispositions and the presence and role of the 4Cs in the wheel. The data provided a good understanding of the gaps in the learning and supported the ongoing design of future professional learning.

The Learning Disposition Wheel is used in classrooms at St Eugene but not at this point for teacher professional development. Using the LDW helped reinforce the applicability of learning dispositions to all learning and not just to student learning. In the 2021 festival St Eugene used the LDW as a data collection tool to understand the dispositions staff were developing through the professional learning in the festival. At the end of each professional learning workshop session, staff were asked to sign out via a QR code and record what dispositions teaching staff accessed during the workshop. This provided valuable pulse data[19] for the college leadership team to refine and iterate the transforming learning agenda and the professional learning plan for 2022.

The morning pedagogy workshops were developed by members of the professional learning communities. The middle session of the day was designed in response to the positive feedback from the event in 2020 where staff identified play and choice as critical to the effectiveness of the day. The final session was the highlight. Throughout the day, all staff (including administration, facilities and school officers) were placed in 'disposition groups'. Each group was led by a 4CTL facilitator to bring to life each group's understanding of the disposition they had been allocated. At the end of the day each group presented what they had learnt to the rest of the staff. This showcase reflected a community united in our transforming learning agenda. The session also demonstrated a continued focus on staff well-being, provided an opportunity to continue to build their capacity to learn and understand the dispositions.

The 2021 Festival of Creative Disruption created a future-focused vision where staff reimagined themselves as learners. Staff were openly discussing about reimaging learning in their classrooms and establishing a sense of curiosity of what a transformed schooling paradigm might look like. The success of the 2021 event was summed up by this comment from a Year 2 teacher. From her perspective the application of the coherence makers (4C and LDW) was key:

> The 'full' staff participation was beneficial and very effective I believe it becomes a part of all teacher's repertoire and language. Watching the groups perform and showcase their learning at the end of the day – it was really refreshing to see the 'buy in' from the staff.

The continued success of the festivals ensure that the college leadership team had to again reimagine what the focus of the 2022 festival.

The Festival of Collaborative and Communicative Disruption, 2022

The 2022 festival focused on how teachers at St Eugene could 'join the dots' to create a coherent approach deep and transformative learning'. The leadership team decided to connect the coherence makers of Collaboration Circles and the Communication Crystal to embed collaboration and communication into classroom practice.

Building on the previous festival the staff expected the event to have the following qualities:

- collaboratively connecting the P-12 community
- fun
- challenge them as a learners
- practical to ensure it influence their own pedagogical practices.

It was evident to the leadership team that the staff were now embracing a culture of reimagining learning for themselves to improve their capacity as facilitators of learning in their classroom. The next question for St Eugene was how they build on this culture to encourage and drive further transformation and cultural change.

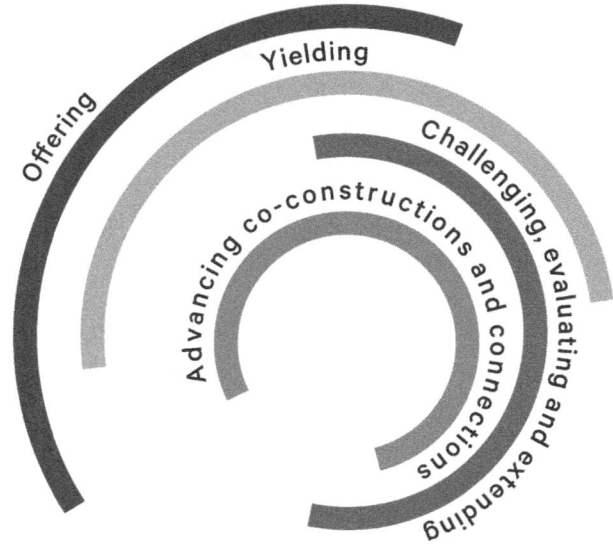

Figure 6.6 Collaboration Circles.

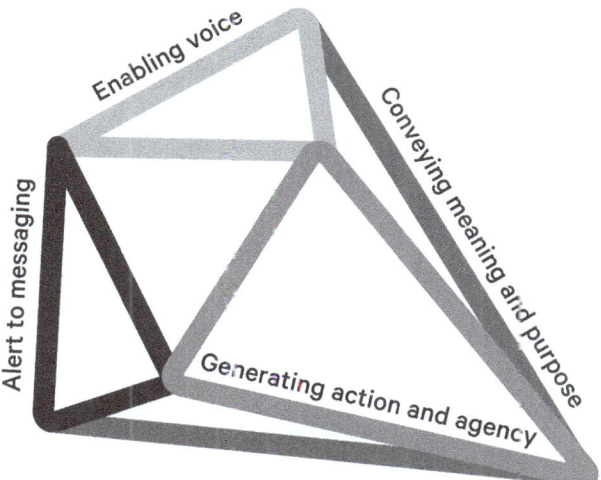

Figure 6.7 Communication Crystal.

Where to from here?

One of the great challenges the leadership team identified in transforming learning agenda for teachers is that there appears to be no endpoint or point of success. There is no point where St Eugene feels it can say, 'we have transformed ourselves, our learners and schooling'. The key to success will be when teachers no longer expect an endpoint. When they understand that a culture of transforming learning is a lifelong experience that continues to evolve through each iteration constantly working towards challenging learners to explore and build new possibilities and be agents of change. The festivals of disruption have laid the foundations for that shift in teacher understanding.

The festivals have also created the environment and the opportunities for all school staff to become agents of change. They have been challenged to re-evaluate themselves as learners, reconsider their role as facilitators of learning as they begin to reimagine learning and schooling beyond the status quo. It is through this reimagining that teachers develop the essential skills, knowledge and wisdom to influence and reshape learning. In the view of the St Eugene leadership team it is a moral imperative for all schools to provide students the opportunity to become great humans by developing skills, dispositions that matter and the capabilities to become successful learners beyond school.

Concluding reflections

We began this chapter with a discussion of the town of Derby in Tasmania that has seen Creative Disruption up close. Old industries have left space for new opportunities to revive the town through creative iterations making it a success story in regional Australia. Derby's experience with the growth in mountain biking demonstrated the value of Creative Disruption to communities. In St Eugene case study, the school leadership team crafted a creative professional learning process in collaboration with staff to ensure 'engagement' and 'buy in'. This school's experience suggests the 'how' of school transformation occurs when the 'status quo' is disrupted to provide space for critical reflection on teaching and learning, curriculum, values and other aspects of the school's culture. The festival and other professional learning strategies that they employed provide an example of a school who are serious about student agency, transformative practice, play and student and teacher voice in learning. The Creative Disruption that St Eugene takes seriously is the need to reimagine schooling for a world that is changing rapidly.

Notes

1. M. Karwowski, 'School Does Not Kill Creativity', *European Psychologist*, 2021.
2. L. Darling-Hammond, *The Flat World and Education: How America's Commitment to Equity Will Determine Our Future* (New York: Teachers College Press, 2015), 6.
3. M. Jefferson and M. Anderson, *Transforming Schools: Creativity, Critical Reflection, Communication, Collaboration* (Bloomsbury Publishing, 2017).
4. J. M. Dru, *The Ways to New: 15 Paths to Disruptive Innovation* (Hoboken, NJ: John Wiley & Sons, 2015).
5. Z. Sardar, 'Welcome to Postnormal Times', *Futures* 42, no. 5 (2010): 435–44.
6. Sardar, 'Welcome to Postnormal Times'.
7. M. Jefferson and M. Anderson, *Transforming Education: Reimagining Learning, Pedagogy and Curriculum* (London: Bloomsbury Publishing, 2021).
8. The bracketed terms are from Jefferson and Anderson's Critical Reflection Crucible coherence maker (Jefferson and Anderson, *Transforming Education*).
9. Council of Australian Governments Education Council, 'Alice Springs (Mparntwe) Education Declaration', 2019, http://www.educationcouncil.edu.au/site/DefaultSite/filesystem/documents/Reports%20and%20publications/Alice%20Springs%20(Mparntwe)%20Education%20Declaration.pdf.
10. Jefferson and Anderson, *Transforming Education*.
11. Jefferson and Anderson, *Transforming Schools*.
12. Jefferson and Anderson, *Transforming Schools*.
13. Jefferson and Anderson, *Transforming Schools*.
14. Jefferson and Anderson, *Transforming Schools*, 39.
15. Jefferson and Anderson, *Transforming Schools*.
16. Professional Learning Days are staff professional learning and are usually at the end or the beginning of school holidays. They are often called pupil free days as students are not present at school.

17 Jefferson and Anderson, *Transforming Schools*.
18 Jefferson and Anderson, *Transforming Schools*.
19 Pulse data is collected at regular intervals over a period of time. It is often used in educational research to track changes or trends in various aspects of the education system, such as teacher professional learning, student achievement, teacher effectiveness and school climate.

References

Baumol, W. J. 2002. *The Free-Market Innovation Machine: Analyzing the Growth Miracle of Capitalism*. Princeton, NJ: Princeton University Press.
Council, E. 2019. *Alice Springs (Mparntwe) Education Declaration*. Education Services Australia.
Darling-Hammond, L. 2006. *Powerful Teacher Education: Lessons From Exemplary Programs*. San Francisco, CA: John Wiley & Sons.
Darling-Hammond, L. 2015. *The Flat World and Education: How America's Commitment to Equity Will Determine our Future*. Teachers College Press.
Dru, J.M. 2015. *The Ways to new: 15 Paths to Disruptive Innovation*. John Wiley & Sons.
Fullan, M. 2007. *The new Meaning of Educational Change*. Teachers College Press.
Jefferson, M. and M. Anderson 2017. *Transforming Schools: Creativity, Critical Reflection, Communication, Collaboration*. Bloomsbury Publishing.
Jefferson, M. and M. Anderson, 2021. *Transforming Education: Reimagining Learning, Pedagogy and Curriculum*. Bloomsbury Publishing.
Joyce, B. and B. Showers 2005. *Student Achievement Through Staff Development*. Alexandria, VA: Association for Supervision and Curriculum Development.
Karwowski, M. 2022. 'School Does Not Kill Creativity'. *European Psychologist* 27(3): 263–75.
Sardar, Z. 2010. 'Welcome to Postnormal Times'. *Futures* 42(5): 435–44.
Schumpeter, J. 1942. *Capitalism, Sociatism and Democracy*. Harper & Brothers.

Time to Be Seen

Transforming Learning through Community Engagement for Children with Special Educational Needs Using Drama and Technology

Paul Sutton, Max Dean and Margaret Jones

7

The partnership (p. 126)

Origins of the project (p. 127)

Structure (p. 129)

The Covid-19 pandemic (p. 131)

What is the legacy of the project? (p. 133)

The art – and science – of combination (p. 134)

Technology – in multiple modes and manifestations – is regularly used to support and enhance the life experience of disabled people. From wheelchairs to prosthetics, screen readers to hearing aids, technological innovations have been developed to augment the capacities and lives of disabled people, facilitating often transformational improvements to people's lives. A similar drive for innovation has fuelled the development of a huge range of new educational software solutions, designed to support the school-based learning of children with learning disabilities, or who might be identified as being neurodiverse.

For example, Tingting Windy Wang and Rick Garner[1] have catalogued the ways internet-based technologies in the flipped art classroom can enable more effective learning for disabled students, citing how their disabilities 'can make lectures ineffective because of problems in maintaining attention, discrimination in note taking'.[2] Fuglestad has described her work using iPad and tablet technologies to enhance instruction and art production in visual art teaching in special education.[3]

Such pedagogical practices largely focus on repurposing existing, mainstream software for adaptive use in SEND (Special Educational Needs and Disabilities) contexts. This is not uncommon in education, where a scarcity of resources often necessitates invention through adaptation. However, other technologies start from a position of direct innovation, facilitating often transformational improvements to people's lives, seeking to address an access need through a bespoke technological solution. For example, Eyegaze is an eye operated communication and access device which uses sophisticated image processing software to analyse and determine when and where the user is looking at a computer screen. It enables students to interact with the computer by where they are looking, enabling them to write emails or documents, control applications or their environment (lights, sound, etc.), browse the web or generate speech. For students with Visual Impairments (VI) apps such as Seeing AI, developed by Microsoft, use visual recognition through smartphone cameras to provide an audio description of people, objects and landscapes in the immediate vicinity of the user.

These innovations are of course welcome, transforming the learning experience for many disabled students. However, many such technological innovations proceed from medically or scientifically oriented paradigms of the potential of technology in learning. Terry Mayes talks of the emergence of 'educational neuroscience' describing, for example how processes of cognitive analysis through brain imaging can inform digital innovations.[4] However welcome these pedagogic insights and technological adaptions might be, they most frequently frame the question of accessibility and learning through what is commonly known as the Medical Model of Disability. As the name suggests, the term proceeds from a medical diagnosis of what is 'wrong' with a person and works to 'cure' or correct an individual's disability, restoring them to what non-disabled people describe as 'full' health. In schools this might by to use technology to augment the human condition, helping to 'raise up' disabled students' capacities to engage in lectures, note taking and other standardized learning activities.

Tim Webb, co-founder of Oily Cart Theatre Company and author of *Sensory Theatre*, observed such tendencies in the educational expectations of schools when developing their pioneering model of inclusive theatre making:

> Terms like PMLD [Profound and Multiple Learning Disability] and ASC [Autism Spectrum Condition] have their uses in determining the curriculum, allocating educational resources and indeed providing a shorthand for schools, families and theatre companies to negotiate with one another. . .these terms are reductive, sometimes even pejorative and they tell us more about what people cannot do than what they can.

In the UK, children with learning disabilities still pursue the same National Curriculum as their non-disabled peers: it is a common standard for all, regardless of how inappropriate its content or cognitive expectations might be. The subtext is that disabled students just need to get better at learning what everyone else is learning and that technology is there to help them.

The social model of disability challenges these widely held conceptions of disability. It proposes that it is society itself that disables people, creating buildings that are inaccessible and services that proceed from a set of assumptions about our sensory or intellectual capacities. The Social Model argues these are not challenges individual needs to overcome alone; they are socially built biases that need to be resolved by society itself.

Oily Cart's work is emblematic of this paradigm. Shaping and describing a practice that proceeds from an inclusive descriptor 'the kinaesthetic, interactive and close-up'[5] rather than an excluding definition of who that audience is, or what they cannot do. Grove and Harwood's work in 'storysharing' proceeds from similar principles, but in the discipline of storytelling with SEND, advancing from notions of 'respect, attunement, responsivity and valuing of all forms of communication'.[6]

What both these creative approaches share with their technological counterparts is what W. Brian Arthur describes in his Theory of Technology as the process by which 'Individual technologies are constructed or put together – combined – from components or subsystems at hand . . . each component of technology is in itself a miniature technology'.

So, for example, the combination of telephony technologies, originally developed by Alexander Graham Bell, with satellite navigation systems pioneered in the 1970s and computing software can today give every smartphone the capacity to generate turn-by-turn interactive maps. Each technological component rests on the capacities of the others. Nothing stands alone.

This is an account of a three-year project that embodies these principles in technological, creative and pedagogic innovation as well as its underpinning values and ethos. It is a collaboration between UK-based applied theatre and digital technology company C&T and Fort Royal Community Primary School, which caters for children with a range of multiple, complex physical and learning disabilities in the city of Worcester, England. The collaboration was driven by shared motivation to not only create new educational software solutions fusing drama and experiential learning with digital technologies but also to use this hybrid practice to challenge preconceptions of disability in the wider Worcester community. The project focused on using C&T's drama/digital online learning platform Prospero to facilitate the design, testing and deployment of new interdisciplinary creative educational applications, designed to enrich the lives of the school's students and the local community.

The chapter takes the form of a structured dialogue between C&T's Artistic Director Dr Paul Sutton, Dr Max Dean, C&T's Creative Director and Margaret Jones, the coordinator of the project in Fort Royal. It begins with a discussion of the partnership between Fort Royal and C&T.

The partnership

Margaret: Fort Royal is a school for children with disabilities. It serves an area of approximately 15 miles: the entire city of Worcester with approximately 120,000 residents. The school was originally built for 140 children but at this moment in time we have 230 students, aged 3–11 years of age, illustrating the surge in demand for such services in recent years. Children join us via our Nursery Assessment Unit, from which children move through the reception class into the main school.

I came to the school after working in the voluntary sector running a charity in Worcester, first as a teaching assistant, but after a while the head teacher created a role for me as a grants and fundraising manager, a job I have done for the last ten years. Over this period it became very apparent to me that the school simply didn't have enough money to provide the educational services and resources things that the children needed. Staff were constantly coming to me and asking if I could raise some money for, for example, new sensory equipment, or a bike to support a particular child who might have a particular physical need, or the Eye Gaze technology, which supports children with very limited mobility, tracking their eye movements on a computer screen, enabling them to engage in conversation and writing. My role became to support this expanding provision.

Paul: C&T was founded as a Theatre-in-Education company in 1988, serving Worcestershire schools as well as a range of youth and community projects. We got to know Margaret in those very early days when we were both part of the Worcester Play Council, a voluntary group working to support holiday play schemes and improvements to local children's playgrounds. Margaret was always a force of nature, advocating for improvements in provision for some of the city's most disadvantaged young people, so it was no surprise that years later we reconnected, this time with Margaret working at Fort Royal.

C&T's work within SEND goes back to those early years, when we would tour specialized Theatre-in-Education programmes into Worcester's special schools alongside collaborative youth performance projects bringing together children with special educational needs and young people in mainstream schools at our local repertory theatre, The Swan. We also worked extensively on projects with learning disabled actors with director Richard Hayhow, who later founded and leads Open Theatre Company in Coventry.

As our work began to mix digital media with applied theatre practices we began to explore how the two could be fused to create inclusive services and provision for learning disabled people as well as in mainstream schools. For example, early iterations of our LivingNewspaper.net online documentary drama project included a three-year touring programme serving neurodiverse participants living in isolated village communities in rural Herefordshire, alongside work in primary and secondary schools in the UK and internationally.

Over the last five years this fusion of digital and drama has been driven by the development of our own in-house digital creativity platform called Prospero.

Prospero is a web-based Online Distance Learning (ODL) platform. It is rooted in the drama methodologies that informed our work. From the early days working with Margaret, it was also an interdisciplinary tool, offering functionality that facilitates learning across artforms and pedagogies. It integrates applied theatre methods with virtual and augmented reality, smartphones, tablets, artificial intelligence, motion tracking and GPS into immersive learning experiences. It enables arts-based, collaborative blended learning in real spaces, places and classrooms.

Prospero has enabled C&T to partner with education and cultural organizations who struggle with digital inclusion and engaging young people through tech. It's a effectively a digital toolkit from which anyone can build their own creative learning resources and share these online. This means people can reach new audiences at scale and distance, in ways that resonate with young people and that challenge the digital divide.

Given this motivation to challenge the digital divide it became increasingly clear to us that we needed to turn full circle and connect with that sector of our community that had so much informed our early work with learning disabled people.

Origins of the project

Margaret: The project was born out of a desire to support the learning of children with complex needs, behavioural problems, autism and children with life-threatening illnesses, so that, rather than using the traditional educational tools, we could open up a whole new world for them, empowering them to become more actively involved in the wider community. This was our starting point at Fort Royal.

Building a sense of community is difficult for us. The majority of our children come to school via special transport because of their disabilities, so unlike mainstream schools we don't have that cohesive group of parents gathering twice a day at the school gates. Families don't very often get together socially, so it's very difficult to build relationships between staff and the school. This is compounded by the fact that children with disabilities are still viewed by a lot of people as being difficult to engage with. If people have no direct personal experience with disabled people they are often quite frightened about what to say to them or how to approach them, so I've always felt that we need to work breakdown those barriers. One of my main jobs is to work with external partners in the wider community, welcoming them into school and actually showing the general public if you like what a vibrant happy place our school can be. That's where conversations about our collaboration with C&T began.

Max: Initially there was a prolonged dialogue between Fort Royal, C&T and the UK's National Lottery Community Fund, who developed an early interest in supporting our partnership. In a sense we were trying to find the sweet spot between Fort Royal's needs, C&T's interests and skill set and the priorities of the fund.

Disabled people's treatment in the UK is getting worse, according to a highly critical report from the Equality and Human Rights Commission (EHRC). The EHRC's 'Progress on Disability Rights in the UK' is an independent report on the UK's compliance with the UN Convention on the Rights of Persons with Disabilities. This reports states that 'the picture emerging from the most recent evidence about disabled people's lives remains deeply concerning'. The United Nations' Equality and Human Rights Commission recently reported to the UN Committee on Disability Rights that in the UK 'more and more disabled people are finding it difficult to live independently, be included, and participate in their communities on an equal basis'.[7] More disabled people live in poverty than non-disabled people, and more are bullied in schools. Forty per cent of disabled people do not feel valued by society; according to research by Scope, half feel excluded and only 42 per cent feel the UK is a good place for disabled people to live.[8] Our partnership is formed out of a shared conviction that these prejudices and attitudes need to be challenged at the earliest point: through the lives and opportunities made available to children and young people.

There seemed to be a rich vein of possibilities in how the school might better connect with the wider Worcester community, thereby challenging preconceptions about learning disabled people. The school felt that we needed to make connections back to the National Curriculum they were required to teach, but we all arrived at a structure where we felt we could achieve both. It wasn't about 'either/or' but about 'and'. For C&T this chimed not only with our long-standing commitment to arts education but also in how technology could play its part in promoting awareness in the community of the social model of disability and how we all have a role to play in its promotion and adoption. Hence the project title 'Time to Be Seen'. These conversations helped us develop three themes for exploration. First, how could our digital platform be used as a tool for inclusion for learning and physically disabled children? Second, how could Prospero's affordances be used as a mechanism to advance the cause of the social model of disability in the wider Worcester community? Finally, was it possible to design virtual and physical spaces where the processes of community consultation and curriculum priorities could meaningfully intersect?

Paul: In a sense we were aspiring to square the circle between the educational needs of children with SEND and actively promoting the social model of disability to the wider Worcester community through the particularities of Fort Royal's needs. In that sense the project was almost a meta-project: trying to be true to its own content while modelling a bigger set of social justice values. I think we were trying to hone Prospero's ability to be an educational software service for both teachers and students at Fort Royal with C&T's values as a socially engaged team of applied theatre practitioners. Normally these differing priorities might be seen as oppositional, or mutually exclusive, but for us there seemed to be a potential new model for positioning Prospero as an ally to both 'causes'. Allyship as a concept is more commonly associated with large organizations or institutions positioning themselves to support marginalized groups. I think we were trying to position our software almost as an abstracted form of third-party social justice activism, rather than purely as a set of priorities intrinsic to C&T. We saw this as having exciting potential for future partnerships and collaborations.

Structure

Paul: We developed what you might call a templated structure for the project. By this I mean a repeating cycle of conceptualization, planning, consultation, development and delivery for our activities. This template was applied to a three-year rolling programme, cycling through nine discreet projects. These roughly corresponded to school terms. So typically, first, C&T and Fort Royal would identify a cross-curricular theme that would have resonance with the wider community. We would then organize a public consultation event, using Open Space Technology methods where members of school staff and members of wider Worcester would come together to find ways in which both could contribute to learning materials that could be deployed in and out of school, bringing both communities together. C&T would then develop these learning resources in Prospero. Finally, teachers in school would deploy these resources in classrooms for children to engage with. As digital resources, unlike other forms of arts intervention, these materials would remain available to Fort Royal beyond its first deployment, building an online catalogue of rich, immersive arts experiences that school could draw on for years to come.

Max: One of our early projects took a cross-curricular approach to the teaching of the theme of 'Skyscrapers and Subways'. Although the school had a number of predetermined teaching schemes that related to the English National Curriculum, for our project this theme provoked questions for us as to how we – and Prospero – could open up previously inaccessible urban environments in Worcester to disabled people.

Our initial consultation event brought together diverse representatives from across the city, everything from local housing associations to Worcester's medieval cathedral. There were very generous offers to open up spaces and resources to the school to enable the development of work. The key seemed not to just take up these offers for school visits – which we did, and these were tremendously valuable in their own right – but it seemed logical to also try to position Prospero as a software service as an ally to the work of these new partners, so as to maximize their valuable offers.

To do this we then moved to develop a set of classroom process-drama activities that took full advantage of these possibilities. Using Prospero's full range of capabilities, we developed a participatory narrative adapted from Roald Dahl's *James and the Giant Peach*. By positioning three Prospero-controlled tablet computers and the classroom's interactive whiteboard as if each were a compass point in the room, we were able to cascade an immersive storytelling adventure around the four corners of the space. Each screen displayed different prompts and activities for students to playfully engage with. This was a real innovation for the school, and it was brilliant to see how the students self-managed this learning experience for themselves, as they controlled the devices and tasks for themselves with minimal support from the teachers. However, we were also able to use this drama structure to integrate the content we had created with our community partners – for example, 360 immersive videos captured from the high tower of Worcester Cathedral. Immersive technology has been recognized as particularly effective in developing a sense of presence since immersive audio, augmented reality and virtual reality create distinct experiences by merging the physical world with a digital or simulated reality. As videogame pedagogy theorist Karl Kapp explains 'immersive games have the visual and temporal-specific relations to provide a strong, rich association between what you're doing and your long-term memory ... the ability to recall elements of the game, the game board or the game environment, and what was done to solve the problem'.[9] This recognition of the pedagogical potential of immersive technology is reinforced by Gordon Callega's research exploring how the interface a player has with a digital experience influences their sense of presence. Callega argues that the more physically linked a player is with the digital world they are inhabiting, the greater their sense of presence. Callega demonstrates this on his 'continuum of control' which at one end has what he terms 'symbolic control' which includes interfaces such as keyboards or console controllers which have no direct relationship between the action performed on the input device and the in-game response, while at the other end of the continuum lies 'symbiotic control', where actual player actions are mimetically mapped onto those of the game character, for example through gesture control. As he puts it: 'the most intimate link between a player and even the most unlikely looking avatar is movement' because it represents the 'locus of the players exertion of agency within the game environment'.[10] While there is much to critique in terms of Callega's blanket support for immersive technology as an interface, the widespread recognition of immersive technology being a powerful way to engender player engagement made it an enticing prospect to experiment with. By weaving 360 immersive video into fragments of Dahl's original narrative the whole process-drama became a playful adventure that located the children both at the centre of imaginary spaces but also simultaneously in virtual/real spaces in their home city.

Margaret: They could look at their city from a different angle and in 360 degrees all around they could identify landmarks that they could see when they looked down. This was just the most amazing thing.

Paul: And we had succeeded in not only building drama-based interactive digital learning resources, but we had taken some of what might be regarded as Worcester's most traditional organizations and spaces with us, changing their mindsets towards disabled people and validating this change in their minds through their direct involvement in the project process.

The Covid-19 pandemic

Margaret: Less than a year into the project the Covid-19 pandemic hit. Like everybody else, we were horror struck. Our children are fairly isolated at the best of times. Being at home is already a challenge for the parents of these children. They need complex regulation, routines and programmes they need to follow, and this was taken away. Staff worked tremendously hard. For example, we emptied all the sensory rooms and staff took a selection of things to families to use at home then regularly rotated these. It was incredibly hard to make sure that all of those children had got different things to do.

Paul: While in the performing arts sector Covid-19 was immensely challenging, we were perhaps less disadvantaged than most. Having already developed our own digital learning platform we were now able to take full advantage of these digital capacities for what everyone was calling 'the new normal'. Yes, we had to reconfigure how we *Time to Be Seen* would work, but I would like to feel we played an important part in helping Fort Royal to mitigate the impact of the pandemic. So, we continued to undertake public consultations, moving them online, engaged with numerous community groups and created banks of digital resources. Everything from interactive walks around the River Severn, using learning disabled actors to retell Greek myths, through to immersive explorations of ancient Egyptian tombs. Also, with the school's physical closure, we were able to gain access to previously unavailable spaces, enabling us to physically embed some new Prospero innovations into the structure of the school itself.

Margaret: For example, the school has a hydrotherapy pool. It is a very warm, safe space where the children can go down with team members of the physiotherapy department. The use it for exercise so, for example, children who use wheelchairs can be hoisted into the pool and then work to strengthen their muscles and limbs. For some of our children who are perhaps severely autistic or who have challenging behaviours it can be a space that is calming. If they are particularly anxious or suffering from severe anxiety it gives them the space in the quiet to calm down and be themselves.

Max: Fort Royal identified that the percentage of new attendees at the school with severe disabilities is increasing. These children's conditions mean they often have severely limited movement, speech and/or cognitive abilities. Many of these pupils are at their most responsive and intellectually engaged when in the school's hydrotherapy pool. This obviously raised difficulties for teachers to fully make use of this moment of engagement for these pupils. We wanted to develop an intuitive interface that would be usable in the context for teachers to design and create their own educational experiences.

We believed we could use the principles of Self-Determination Theory (SDT) as a rubric to design an interactive motion capture interface to enable active participation and engagement in challenges and narrative adventures with this particular demographic. We chose this method for assessing the levels of engagement for participants since both C&T and Fort Royal agreed with its central tenet that 'When people are intrinsically motivated, they engage in an activity because the activity itself is interesting, enjoyable, and congruent with their selves'.[11]

Edward Deci and Richard Ryan argue that SDT motivation arises based on an individual's three basic social-cognitive needs: First, a feeling of competence in the task they are undertaking; this is because people 'seek challenges that are optimal for their capacities and to persistently attempt to maintain and enhance those skills and capacities through activity'.[12] Second, a feeling of autonomy or control of their own behaviour: 'the tendency to work toward inner coherence and integration among regulatory demands and goals'.[13] Finally, relatedness refers to 'a sense of belonging both with other individuals and with one's community'.[14] Since this demographic was limited verbally but could make their intentions understood when moving in the hydrotherapy pool, movement within this space became the semiotic interface we needed to enable through Prospero to make these participants feel competent, autonomous and able to achieve goals. We subsequently developed a motion tracking functionality that meant using the camera on a smartphone or tablet Prospero could observe gestures and movements. When Prospero recognized a particular movement or body shape it could react to this, triggering video, media or narrative choices. This meant that a carefully positioned tablet computer, directed towards the pool area could interact with a child's directional movements in the pool.

For example, we developed an interactive water-based adventure story in Prospero. A tablet computer was positioned at one end of the pool running the Prospero online adventure, with a linked projector displaying its image on a large, facing wall. At certain points in the action, Prospero asked the child in the pool to direct the developing story in a particular way: did they want to go deep-sea diving or explore coastal caves? By gently moving from one side of the pool or the other the child could make a choice, which Prospero would track through the tablet's camera and thus trigger a divergence in the narrative to match their motion-based choice. This enabled many process-drama techniques and activities to be facilitated through a digitally gamified interface.

Fabian Groh has argued that all of the characteristics of SDT can be achieved in digital gaming experiences through 'the power of meaningful narratives, stories and fantasy, providing a relatable experience to the players'.[15] This is supported by Valentijn Visch et al. who argue in their research on persuasive game design that 'an individual is driven by the same motivational needs in the real world and game worlds'.[16] Chin-Lung Hsu and His-Peng Lu's research into flow experiences in those playing online games further argue that this drive for competence is increased when the activity itself is self-rewarding.[17] By hybridizing the pedagogic approaches of live co-created storytelling with the digital game interface of motion detection we were able to create interactive narratives that the most severely disabled members of Fort Royal could not only experience themselves but through their own engagement become cocreators of.

Paul: Theatrically, the approach was influenced by Oily Cart's and National Theatre Wales's *Splish Splash*, which pioneered (literally) immersive theatre for audiences of autistic children, those with profound and multiple learning disabilities and deaf-blind; working in swimming pools and combining lighting, sound and a number of interactive boxes. It was never an objective to create a digitized version of this incredible work, but it certainly seemed to us that Prospero could offer additional ways, through motion tracking, of sensorily engaging participants beyond the highly effective tactile methods developed by Oily Cart.

What is the legacy of the project?

Paul: I think there are three dimensions to the legacy. First, there are the resources themselves. Of course, one of the key qualities of most performative arts-education interventions is their ephemerality. Prospero's ability to digitize these performative experiences means they are repeatable. Fort Royal now has ongoing access to all the resources we created over the entire three years of the project, which they can easily deploy again and again.

Second, through the process of engagement with C&T and Prospero, Fort Royal's staff are now trained and equipped to create their own resources in Prospero. For us, this is the route to a sustainable form of practice. If teachers can design, build and deploy their own interactive lessons quickly and easily, we hopefully have developed a route to a form of practice that can have long-term benefit and efficacy. What's more, it opens up the possibilities of sharing these practices more widely. Any school with internet access has the potential to deploy these resources, enabling a growing Community of Practice.

Finally, there are the innovations that the project has enabled us to build into Prospero itself. For example, the motion tracking features we developed for the hydrotherapy pool will go on to benefit other users of Prospero. When it comes to software innovations, one of the litmus tests for us is scalability. If something works in one location, it should work in others.

This has proved perfectly true for motion tracking. It has already been deployed by a special school in Brooklyn in New York City. There, students with a range of physical and learning disabilities integrated the technology into a live performance context, with the software responding to choices and decisions made as part of a story about cleaning up Coney Island's beaches from litter and waste. It's this ability to repurpose the platform for a variety of contexts, mediated purposes and audiences that has so much potential.

Margaret: For Fort Royal, the project brought together groups of people who had never worked with each other or us before, helping us to engage with the local community and help develop and empower the children with special education and physical needs here in Worcester. Paul and Max helped us break down those barriers with innovative uses of drama and technology and gave our children new learning opportunities. It enabled them to learn together in school and to open up to the wider community. It gave staff and pupils an opportunity to be at the forefront of inspiring best practice and think to the future.

The art – and science – of combination

The narrative of this conversation mirrors the flow of the project's cyclical iterative development processes: a repeating cycle of identified need, community consultation, digital and creative pedagogic development and implementation. This cycle, despite Covid-related interruptions, formed a spiral, iteratively progressing towards more ambitious and complex interventions and deployments. The subsequent building on the developments of the previous.

In a sense, this flow mirrors Arthur's thesis in the *Nature of Technology*: 'in the real world a technology is rarely fixed. It constantly changes its architecture, adapts and reconfigures as purpose change and improvements occur'[18]. In *Time to Be Seen*, the 'real world' realities faced by many disabled people became the prism through which the partnership's creative, pedagogic and technological modes could by reconfigured in line with need and aspiration. In many ways this process is implicit to the Prospero platform itself. As a web-based technology, it is positioned to be able to adapt, change and grow in line with new demands, building on the technological innovations of those in other fields. For example, at the time of writing ChatGPT, a third-party chatbot artificial intelligence system is being tested for potential integration into Prospero.

At Fort Royal School, this iterative process continues too. Following *Time to Be Seen*, the UK's Youth Music Trailblazer's scheme is funding a research and development music education programme, using the Prospero motion detection software, first developed for the school's hydrotherapy pool. This software is now being used to frame a disabled student as a virtual orchestra's conductor/composer. Standing in front of a configured computer and sound system, each gesture, movement and action of the participant is tracked by Prospero and interpreted as musical notation, generating unique sounds and music compositions. Working with award-winning theatre and opera composer Martin Ward, this new iteration of the values, pedagogy and creativity of Time to Be Seen continues to illustrate the potential of digital technology in transformational arts-based learning for disabled people.

Notes

1. T. Windy Wang and R. Garner, 'Exploring the Possibilities and Effectiveness of Flipped Classroom', in *Exploring Digital Technologies for Art-based Special Education*, ed. R. L. Garner (New York: Routledge, 2019), 91.
2. Windy Wang and Garner, 'Exploring the Possibilities and Effectiveness of Flipped Classroom'.
3. T. Fuglestad, 'The Educational Implications of Godzilla, Ghosts and Aliens', in *Exploring Digital Technologies for Art-based Special Education*, ed. R. L. Garner (New York: Routledge, 2019), 39.
4. T. Webb, *Sensory Theatre* (New York: Routledge, 2023).
5. Webb, *Sensory Theatre*.
6. N. Gove and J. Harwood, "Storysharing" Personal Narratives for Identity and Community', in *Storytelling Special Needs and Disabilities*, ed. N. Grove (New York: Routledge, 2022).
7. Equality and Human Rights Commission, *Progress on Disability Rights in the UK* [PDF file], n.d., https://www.equalityhumanrights.com/sites/default/files/progress_on_disability_rights_in_the_uk.pdf; R. Verma, 'Disability Rights Facing "Serious Regression" Says Equality Watchdog', *EachOther*, 9 October 2018, Retrieved 15 July 2021, from https://eachother.org.uk/disability-rights-facing-serious-regression-says-equality-watchdog/.
8. SCOPE, 'Accessibility and Disability: UK Research and Statistics', n.d., Retrieved 11 July 2021, from https://business.scope.org.uk/article/accessibility-and-disability-facts-and-figures.
9. K. M. Kapp, *The Gamification of Learning and Instruction: Game Based Methods and Strategies for Training and Education* (San Francisco, CA: Pfeiffer, 2012), 68.
10. G. Callega, *In-Game: From Immersion to Incorporation* (Cambridge, MA: MIT Press, 2011), 61.
11. A. Uysal and I. G. Yildirim, 'Self-Determination Theory in Digital Games', in *Gamer Psychology and Behaviour*, ed. B. Bostan (Cham: Springer, 2016), 125–36.
12. Edward L. Deci and Richard M. Ryan, 'Overview of Self Determination Theory: An Organismic Dialectical Perspective', in *Handbook of Self Determination Research*, ed. R. M. Ryan (Rochester, NY: University of Rochester Press, 2004), 7.
13. Deci and Ryan, 'Overview of Self Determination Theory', 7–33.
14. Deci and Ryan, 'Overview of Self Determination Theory', 7–33.

15 F. Groh, 'Gamification: State of the Art Definition and Utilisation', in *Proceedings of the 4th Seminar on research Trends in Media Informatics* (n.d.), 39–45, https://d-nb.info/1020022604/34.

16 V. Visch, N. Vegt, H. Anderiesen, and K. van der Kooij, 'Persuasive Game Design: A Model and it's Definitions', in *Proceedings of the CHI Workshop Designing Gamification: Creating Gameful and Playful Experiences*, Paris, France, 27 April–2 May 2013 (New York: ACM, 2013), 2.

17 C.-L. Hsu and H.-P. Lu, 'Why Do People Play On-Line Games? An Extended TAM with Social Influences and Flow Experience', *Information and Management* 41, no. 7 (2004): 853–68.

18 Ibid., W. B. Aruther, *The Nature of Technology: What It Is and How It Evolves*. (London: Penguin, 2010), 41.

References

Aruther, W. B. 2010. *The Nature of Technology: What It Is and How It Evolves*. London: Penguin.

Callega, G. 2011. *In-Game: From Immersion to Incorporation*. Cambridge, MA : MIT Press, 61.

Deci, E. L. and R. M. Ryan 2004. 'Overview of Self-Determination Theory: An Organismic Dialectical Perspective'. In R. M. Ryan (ed.), *Handbook of Self-Determination Research*, 7–33. University of Rochester Press.

Equality and Human Rights Commission n.d. *Progress on Disability Rights in the UK* [PDF file]. https://www.equalityhumanrights.com/sites/default/files/progress_on_disability_rights_in_the_uk.pdf.

Fuglestad, T. 2019. 'The Educational Implications of Godzilla, Ghosts, and Aliens'. In R. L. Garner (ed.), *Exploring Digital Technologies for Art-based Special Education*, 39. New York: Routledge.

Gove, N. and J. Harwood 2022. '"Storysharing" Personal Narratives for Identity and Community'. In N. Grove (ed.), *Storytelling Special Needs and Disabilities*, 159–67. New York: Routledge.

Groh, F. n.d. 'Gamification: State of the Art Definition and Utilization'. In *Proceedings of the 4th Seminar on Research Trends in Media Informatics*, 39–45. https://d-nb.info/1020022604/34.

Hsu, C.-L. and H.-P. Lu 2004. 'Why Do People Play On-Line Games? An Extended TAM With Social Influences and Flow Experience'. *Information and Management* 41(7): 853–68.

Kapp, K. M. 2012. *The Gamification of Learning and Instruction: Game-Based Methods and Strategies for Training and Education*. Pfeiffer, 68.

SCOPE n.d. *Accessibility and Disability: UK Research and Statistics*. Retrieved 11 July, 2021, from https://business.scope.org.uk/article/accessibility-and-disability-facts-and-figures.

Uysal, A. and I. G. Yildirim 2016. 'Self-Determination Theory in Digital Games'. In B. Bostan (ed.), *Gamer Psychology and Behaviour*, 125–36. Springer.

Verma, R. 2018. 'Disability Rights Facing "serious Regression" Says Equality Watchdog'. *EachOther*, 9 October. Retrieved 15 July, 2021, from https://eachother.org.uk/disability-rights-facing-serious-regression-says-equality-watchdog/.

Visch, V., N. Vegt, H. Anderiesen, and K. van der Kooij 2013. 'Persuasive Game Design: A Model and its Definitions'. In *Proceedings of the CHI Workshop Designing Gamification: Creating Gameful and Playful Experiences*, Paris, France, 27 April–2 May, 2. ACM.

Wang, T. W. and R. Garner 2019. 'Exploring the Possibilities and Effectiveness of Flipped Classroom'. In R. L. Garner (ed.), *Exploring Digital Technologies for Art-based Special Education*, 91. New York: Routledge.

Webb, T. 2023. *Sensory Theatre*. New York: Routledge.

Windy Wang, T. and R. Garner 2019. 'Exploring the Possibilities and Effectiveness of Flipped Classroom'. In R. L. Garner (ed.), *Exploring Digital Technologies for Art-based Special Education*, 91. New York: Routledge.

Transforming Assessment
Assessing the 'Unassessable'

Debbie Hunter and Miranda Jefferson

8

First flight: Taking aim, letting go and propelling forward with pedagogy (p. 142)

Landing: Where to next in transformation? (p. 143)
Formative assessment (p. 144)

Second flight, pulling back and taking aim: How to tackle assessment? (p. 145)
Views on assessment and learning (p. 145)
Learning continuum rubrics for the Learning Disposition Wheel (p. 146)

The Wonder Web: A coherence maker (p. 149)

Letting go: Insights gained from the teacher action inquiry (p. 150)
1. A metalanguage for learning encourages a growth mindset (p. 154)
2. Student self- and peer-assessment encourages the development of learning dispositions (p. 155)

3. Shared teacher dialogue framed by the learning continuums contributes to powerful teacher learning (p. 156)

4. The learning continuums were most valuable as tools for reflection and assessment for learning (p. 156)

5. Pedagogy, learning and assessment have to be reimagined for self-regulating students (p. 157)

Propelling forward: Using assessment *for* learning (p. 158)

Why does a child want to let go of a balsa wood aeroplane using a slingshot of elastic rubber? (see Figure 8.1) Because they are being assessed on it? Or because they are curious about what will happen when they let it go? Are they curious about what it feels like? How it will fly? How far it will go? Where it might land? In many schools, learning is being driven by assessment and not what interests students or what interests teachers about students. Curiosity is simply the urge to know more, and it is a powerful motivator for learning. Curiosity is characterized by the joy of discovery, the motivation to seek answers about the unknown and to engage with activities that are personally meaningful.[1] Evidence tells us that students learn when they are curious, and yet curiosity is little recognized in learning and assessment.[2] Opportunities for students and teachers to express curiosity wanes in schools because other things get it in the way.[3] One of things that can get in the way of fostering curiosity is how learning is assessed.

According to developmental psychology researcher Susan Engel, an inhibitor to developing curiosity in schools is the emphasis on mastery and finishing tasks rather than inquiry and discovering tasks. As a result, most assessments in schools measure mastery and achievement, not inquiry and curiosity. The teaching and learning in schools is guided by the set 'script' of mastery and assessment, and is unable to respond to the curiosity, interest and self-regulation of students and teachers. In this chapter we explore how dispositions for learning like curiosity and inquiry can be assessed and how the way learning is assessed can foster self-regulatory motivation to learn.

Using a case study we examine how to assess what has been long been considered unassessable: learning dispositions and 4C capabilities. Across OECD[4] member countries, learning dispositions and capabilities such as curiosity, creativity and collaboration, have been considered difficult to assess. In 2009, an OECD working paper *21st Century Skills and Competencies for New Millennium Learners in OECD Countries*[5] found that most countries have written competencies into their curriculums but were yet to give guidance on how to assess them. In the report the OECD asked, 'What types of assessment are appropriate for the monitoring and evaluation of

Figure 8.1 What motivates a child to fly a balsa wood aeroplane?

twenty-first-century skills and competencies? How can they be developed?' There are initiatives in the OECD and other educational bodies[6] that are beginning to answer these questions. We explore how twenty-first- century skills and competencies can be assessed and how the way we assess is in a profound interrelationship with how these competencies are taught and learnt.

Our case study school, Oatley Public School embarked on a school transformation journey and in a year made enormous, positive gains in transforming pedagogy towards student agency and self-regulation. They work with a professional learning organization (4C Transformative Learning[7]) and use the Learning Disposition Wheel (see Figure 8.2) and 4C coherence makers (from Jefferson and Anderson's research and practice in *Transforming Schools* and *Transforming Education*) to inform and frame many of their new approaches to pedagogy. A team of teachers at Oatley were curious about how they could measure and evaluate the changed learning behaviours they saw in their students. They wondered why they should assess learning dispositions and capabilities and what assessment should look like in a more student-centred, learner-empowered and 'teacher as collaborator' classroom? The focus of this case study is the teachers' experience responding to these questions through an action inquiry. We use the balsa aeroplane slingshot as a metaphor to structure the 'taking aim, letting go, propelling forward and landing' of Oatley's transformative experiences. Oatley Primary School's action inquiry provides a rich insight into what really happens on the ground when developing assessment innovation in a school. Before discussing their inquiry into assessment, we begin the Oatley story by briefly describing their first 'balsa wood aeroplane flight' to transform pedagogy and learning.

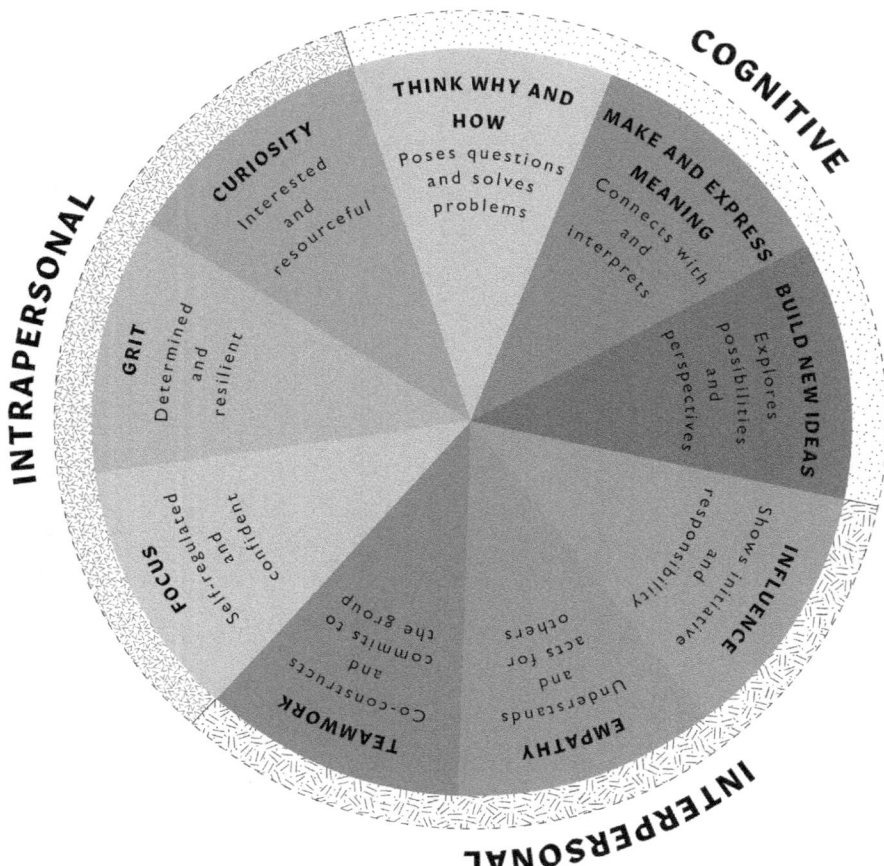

Figure 8.2 The Learning Disposition Wheel describes the dispositions for deeper learning. The research underpinning the wheel is discussed in Jefferson and Anderson's Transforming Education (2021). It was developed from the National Research Council's 2012 report, 'Education for Life and Work: Developing Transferable Knowledge and Skills in the 21st Century', and is informed by Self-Determination Theory (Ryan and Deci, 1985, 2000).

First flight: Taking aim, letting go and propelling forward with pedagogy

Oatley Public is a government-funded school where the students come from a multicultural, middle-to-high income community. The community takes pride in education, and the students achieve high results targeted and measured by state and federal educational bodies. However, teachers at Oatley noticed students were not risk takers, that they lacked resilience when things became challenging, and that they only liked to work independently. There was an embedded culture of students producing independent written work that teachers assess in relation to curriculum outcomes. The teachers felt they had a teacher-centred procedural, pedagogical approach to curriculum delivery and assessment. The attitude of student compliance was 'I will do what I think the teacher wants'. There was a growing realization among teachers that students were not demonstrating the dispositions of grit, building new ideas and teamwork in the Learning Disposition Wheel (see Figure 8.2). In a broader sense the teachers believed they weren't creating learning experiences to develop the 4C capabilities (creativity, collaboration, communication or critical reflection) in their students.

The teachers 'took aim' to address their pedagogy through professional learning in the strategies and processes of a 4C approach, using the Learning Disposition Wheel[8] and 4C coherence makers[9] as pedagogical tools. After a year of 'letting go and propelling forward' in shared professional learning and changed pedagogical practice, the teachers revealed (through collaborative reflections, in individual reflection logs and evaluation school surveys) they were seeing their students differently. Students who previously might not have contributed frequently to lessons were gaining confidence to express themselves and participate in discussions. Students were demonstrating positive changes in their learning, particularly in taking risks and knowing how to work with others. Teachers were realizing they could curate pedagogy that focused on the learner and the learning, not the teacher and the teaching. They recognized that creating a culture of making and accepting mistakes empowered the learners (and themselves) to explore new thinking and new ways of doing things. Integrating subjects across the curriculum was also creating more authentic experiences for students to develop the skills of collaboration, communication, creativity and critical reflection.

A year into their transforming pedagogy journey, Oatley Public School 'landed' their slingshot aeroplane and evaluated their 'trajectory' so far. Students had greater voice and were beginning to self-regulate and work with others in their learning. Teachers were influencing each other through critical reflection and sharing innovative practice, and the 4C capabilities and learning dispositions were beginning to underpin the learning framework at the school. Now that Oatley had embarked on their first 'transformative aeroplane' voyage, they had to decide where they needed to go next.

Landing: Where to next in transformation?

The team at Oatley examined feedback from student and teacher focus groups and student surveys about the introduced learning and practices. These practices are essentially experiential and embodied, and develop skills in learning dispositions through creativity (exploring possibilities), critical reflection (identifying assumptions), communication (enabling voice and agency) and collaboration (co-constructing a shared endeavour).[10] The summative data from student responses was that they:

a) reflected that the Learning Disposition Wheel (LDW) was invaluable;
b) wanted to learn more and in greater depth about LDW learning;

c) could connect their learning about the LDW to life skills;
d) wanted to apply new LDW learning strategies after learning about the importance of dispositions; and
e) found the cognitive dispositions as the most challenging to understand.

Students voiced that relating learning experiences to real life situations was instrumental to a deeper understanding of their learning. Some students expressed they needed to develop more understanding of learning dispositions with comments such as:

- *'I didn't get it.'*
- *'I need to see more examples of this learning.'*
- *'I just need to talk about it more.'*
- *'I need more time to get it.'*
- *'You could have more challenges explaining why we need to have these dispositions in our lives.'*

In response to student reflections and teacher observations, the team at Oatley proposed that assessment and feedback may deepen students and teachers understanding of dispositions in learning. The team was seeing the development of self-regulation in their learners through pedagogical change, and wondered how they could measure behavioural change in students through a form of assessment. They initiated an action inquiry that hypothesized student agency and learning growth may be enhanced through formative assessment, which is also known as assessment *for* learning.

Formative assessment

Defining formative assessment is controversial. Some view it as a diagnostic test and interim assessment, and others consider it not as a test but as a process.[11] This dichotomy is an over-simplification as both approaches can be useful depending on what the purpose of the assessment is for. However, assessment as a measure of achievement and not a process for learning dominates the teaching and learning experience.[12] This form of interim assessment, often fed back to students as a score or grade, signals to students and teachers that only learning that is assessed in this way is worth engaging with.[13] In this sense, assessment is not a process *for* learning but a form of summative assessment that measures a student's attainment and achievement in meeting certain standards and requirements. Instead, formative assessment as a process is feedback used by learners to authentically further their learning growth.

In their action inquiry, a team of Oatley teachers considered how they would explore, and potentially use assessment for transforming and evaluating learning in their context. Once again, Oatley had to pull back their 'transformation aeroplane slingshot' to explore the role of assessment in the development of learning dispositions and self-regulation of students.

Second flight, pulling back and taking aim: How to tackle assessment?

As the Oatley team considered how to assess learning dispositions and 4C capabilities, they began to wonder 'what is the purpose of assessment?' The changes they had made with pedagogy, changed learning and changed learners, but what did it mean for assessment? They realized assessment practices at the school (both summative and formative) were mostly used to describe a student's merit in attaining curriculum knowledge, as opposed to the student's identity as a learner. But how should assessment be treated when dealing with a learner's identity and how they see themselves? What impact could assessment have on the student's self-regulatory motivation to learn?

The teachers also recognized that an individual teacher was often the sole judge of a student's attainment and feedback for both summative and formative assessment. The perspective and experience of other teachers weren't considered, and critically the student's perspective was not recognized in assessment. The feedback from assessment was mostly one-way from the teacher to the student. There was also the assumption that when assessing the learning of students that the teaching was 'perfect'. They asked themselves:

- How could assessment encompass the role the teacher plays in building learning capacity and growth in students?;
- What learning opportunities do teachers provide for students and how do those conditions impact assessment?; and critically,
- What is the role of the self-regulated student in building and assessing their own learning growth?

The teachers at Oatley were not only grappling with how to assess the Learning Wheel dispositions and 4C capabilities, but also what assessment should look like in a more student-centred, learner-empowered and 'teacher as collaborator' classroom?

Views on assessment and learning

Assessment in learning is an integral concept to education[14] but understanding assessment depends on how you view and define its purpose. Education researcher, Richard Elmore brings into sharp focus the issues of learning and assessment in his 2019 research paper, *The Future of Learning and the Future of Assessment*.[15] He describes two very different conceptions of learning and assessment. The first describes a historically entrenched systemic and institutionalized approach to assessment which values the role of attainment, custody and control of students and their learning. The second focuses on redefining learning and assessment as capabilities to build individual agency so that learners have control of and make judgements about their learning. Here Elmore summarizes these two conceptions of learning, schooling and assessment:

Learning 1:

Learning is the ability to recall and deploy information and algorithms accurately and appropriately.

Schooling is the mechanism by which we organize social and status consistent with this definition of learning.

Assessment is the means by which we define, measure, evaluate, and confer 'merit' consistent with this definition of learning.

Learning 2:

Learning is the ability to consciously modify understandings, beliefs, and actions in response to evidence, experience, and reflection.

Schooling is one of many environments in which humans develop the capability to exercise judgement and control over what they learn, how they learn, what they intend to do with what they have learned.

Assessment is the means by which individuals receive useful information about the development of their capabilities as learners over time.[16]

The team at Oatley was developing the Learning 2 approach but they realized they were in a larger policy and political system that perpetuates the Learning 1 concept and that is a tension they would need to navigate. The shift from Learning 1 to 2 illustrates how changes in pedagogy and learning necessitate changes in how teachers engage with students through assessment. At Oatley, the changes to pedagogy in their classroom were developing self-regulated, agentic learners with skills to direct and make judgements about their own learning. How would this affect their approach to assessing learning dispositions? To explore this question, the Oatley team began an action inquiry focusing on how learners responded to individual and collective (class) interventions in developing one disposition in the Learning Disposition Wheel. The chosen disposition was *grit* (determination and resilience) as this was the most relevant to the learners' needs (further impacted by the Covid pandemic and learning from home). They undertook the action inquiry with a Community of Practice of schools who were also interested in the assessment of dispositions.

Learning continuum rubrics for the Learning Disposition Wheel

Learning continuum rubrics had been developed for all the Learning Wheel dispositions through research and development by the organization 4C Transformative Learning (4CTL) with another school[17] in the Community of Practice. Learning continuums or progressions are defined as 'descriptions of successfully more sophisticated ways of reasoning within a context domain'.[18] The LDW rubrics are continuums in the domain of developing dispositions for learning and can be applied to any area of the curriculum, or to behaviours beyond the classroom. Learning progressions according to measurement researchers Shepard, Penuel and Pellegrino[19] must be validated and grounded in a theory of learning, and the LDW progressions are grounded in sociocultural and cognitive learning theories discussed in Jefferson and Anderson's *Transforming Education*.[20] The theory of learning that underpins the LDW supports self-regulation, which can be defined as learners cognitively, motivationally and behaviourally promoting their own learning.[21]

The action inquiry used the learning continuum rubric for grit (see Figure 8.3) as a basis for teachers to notice in detail three to five students in their classes. Teachers implemented their chosen actions, and gathered evidence and resources that addressed the inquiry question, 'What is *grit* and how can it be developed and assessed?' This question was framed within a larger inquiry question, 'How can we embed deeper learning through the teaching and assessment of student's learning dispositions?' When the teachers initially engaged with the rubric, their understanding of grit as a disposition was challenged and deepened. They assumed that grit was only about being resilient, rather than proactively seeking out challenges. They also became aware that grit involved employing strategies to navigate challenges and set goals in learning. This had implications for their approach to teaching and learning in grit.

Teachers in the Community of Practice also had more general responses to the learning continuum that were the:

- E scale (emerging, establishing, embracing, evolving, expanding) suggested a positive and growth mindset.[22]
- E scale suggested a circular or spiral perspective of learning and development, it was not linear.
- progression did not generalize the disposition to all aspects of a student's learning but addressed the disposition to specific areas of learning in or beyond the classroom.
- progression was generic to any age group including adult learners.

The teachers realized they needed to develop student friendly and age specific language for learners, such as 'I can do . . . ' statements. The language of the learning continuum also highlighted that student reflections, and both student and teacher observations were necessary to use the rubric. The Community of Practice discussed how developing student's dispositions depended on the type of learning experiences teachers provided in the classroom. They recognized that a teacher's pedagogical approach had an impact on the development of grit as described in the learning progression. A coherence maker, the Wonder Web (see Figure 8.4) was introduced to support teachers in exploring and examining their teaching of grit (and any area of the curriculum).

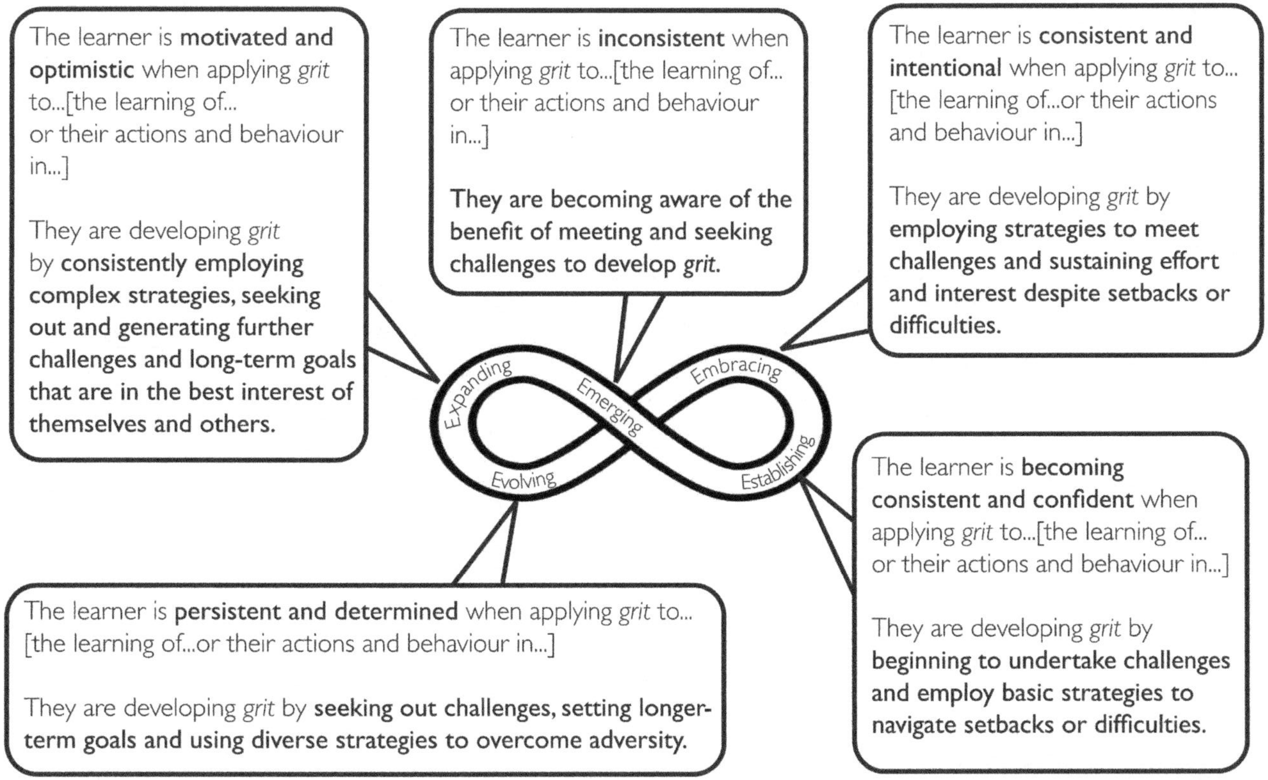

The learner is **inconsistent** when applying grit to...[the learning of... or their actions and behaviour in...]

They are becoming aware of the benefit of meeting and seeking challenges to develop grit.

The learner is **consistent and intentional** when applying grit to... [the learning of...or their actions and behaviour in...]

They are developing grit by employing strategies to meet challenges and sustaining effort and interest despite setbacks or difficulties.

The learner is becoming **consistent and confident** when applying grit to...[the learning of... or their actions and behaviour in...]

They are developing grit by beginning to undertake challenges and employ basic strategies to navigate setbacks or difficulties.

The learner is **motivated and optimistic** when applying grit to...[the learning of... or their actions and behaviour in...]

They are developing grit by consistently employing complex strategies, seeking out and generating further challenges and long-term goals that are in the best interest of themselves and others.

The learner is **persistent and determined** when applying grit to... [the learning of...or their actions and behaviour in...]

They are developing grit by seeking out challenges, setting longer-term goals and using diverse strategies to overcome adversity.

Embracing / Establishing / Emerging / Evolving / Expanding

Figure 8.3 Grit is being determined in seeking out and persevering with challenges, and resilient when navigating setbacks or difficulties.

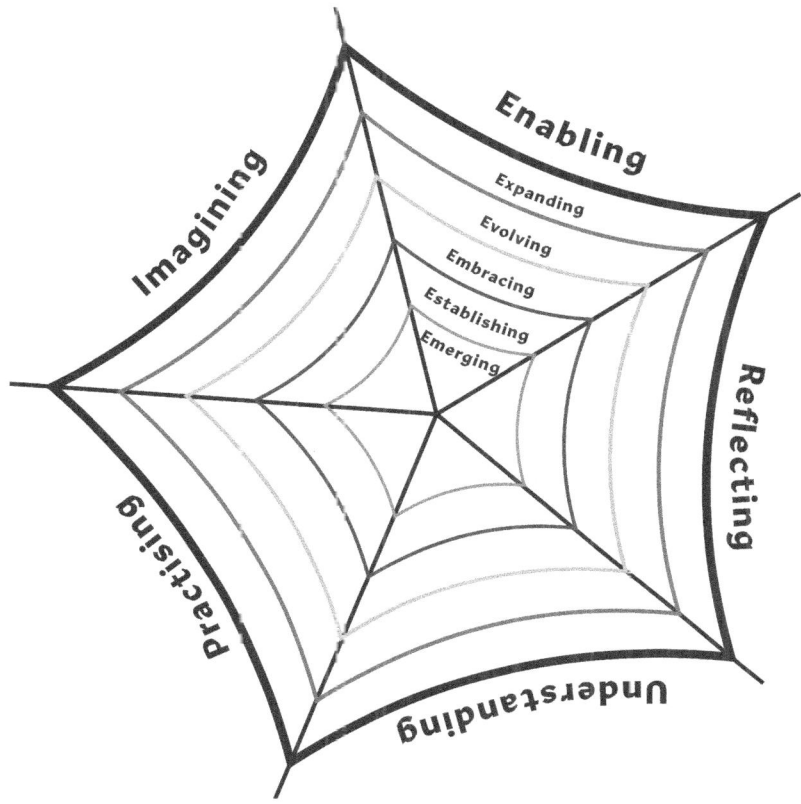

Figure 8.4 The Wonder Web.

The Wonder Web: A coherence maker

The Wonder Web was created to assist teachers and students in being metacognitive when creating and undertaking learning experiences. The metaphor of the 'web' is used to explore the flexibility, strength, connections, rebuilding and expansion evident in learning experiences. The Wonder Web is a synthesis of research from Blooms Taxonomy,[23] Self-Determination Theory[24] and Generative Learning Strategies,[25] and around the outside of the Web are verbs to describe how students may be engaging with their learning. The Wonder Web allows teachers to ask, how are students having opportunities to experience:

- *inquiring* in why they are learning what they are learning;
- *practising* the what and the how of their learning;
- *reflecting* on the why, what and how of their learning;
- *imagining* other ways of using and applying the learning; and
- *enabling* others or teaching others in the learning.

The E scale (emerging, establishing, embracing, evolving, expanding) within the Web is for teachers to consider how well they are creating experiences for students to inquire, practise, reflect, imagine and enable others in the learning of grit, or any area of learning. The Oatley team worked with the Wonder Web to frame their teaching and programming, allowing them to 'let go' and interrogate the learning progression and assessment through their action inquiry.

Letting go: Insights gained from the teacher action inquiry

Before discussing the overarching themes that emerged from the Oatley team's action inquiry, below we use some example observations and reflections from Oatley to create a picture of what happened on the ground in classrooms. Table 8.1 provides an example of a teacher using the Wonder Web to frame one learning activity focused on grit and the building of a tower. In Table 8.2, three students

Table 8.1 An example of a teacher using the Wonder Web to frame a learning focused on grit and the building of a tower

Inquiring: *As a class we discussed what grit is. We then shared times in learning where 'grit has been needed'. The challenge guidelines were then explained, with students understanding that they may need some grit to be successful in this challenge.*
Practicing: *Students were provided with time to discuss a plan on how they were going to use the materials provided to build their tower. They then engaged in the activity, working together to build their Tower.*
Enabling: *We identified different points throughout the learning process to stop work and have specific groups share what they were doing. This was to assist students in other groups who were struggling to come up with ideas or experiencing difficulty. We asked students to share 'what they had decided to do' and 'why'. We also had students reflect on how they work together as a team, as many struggled with this. This was an opportunity for students to learn from their peers.*
Reflecting: *Once the challenge ended there were varying outcomes for each group. Students again reflected on 'how did you use grit today' and 'were there any other dispositions used?' This was interesting as it became very evident that another disposition, teamwork was a key factor in the success of this challenge.*
Imagining: *At the end we connected this to learning in the classroom – 'Sometimes you are going to find work in the classroom very challenging, just like today. Which is why it is so important that we talk about the feelings we might have which help us to understand we need to use our "grit" so we know when we might need it.'*

Table 8.2 Three students and their teacher reflect on the development of grit in a particular area of learning

Student K
Student reflection on their grit: Grit is keeping on trying and not giving up. My group didn't use my idea and the Tower failed. I was frustrated so I gave up. I needed grit for my group to listen to me.
Teacher observation and reflection with grit rubric: Each member of the group has their own ideas and none were willing to compromise. I placed Student K as emerging on the grit progression. She has an awareness and understanding of grit but was unable to employ basic strategies to navigate setbacks and difficulties.
Teacher future action: I will facilitate more active communication among group members and possibly be more deliberate in group formation. I will highlight some of the instances where grit is required and have them pre-determine the challenges they might face in learning prior to the task commencing.
Student reflection on developing grit: I am getting better at sharing my ideas with my group. I am helping more and showing grit when it doesn't work.
Teacher reflection on student developing grit: Scaffolding the lesson so that Student K had to think of her own ideas in response to the problem, draw a design, share her ideas with the group, then combine ideas to decide on the final design allowed her to make valuable contributions. She maintained more interest in the task, trialling different materials when some didn't work, employing 'grit' more consciously at these times. Working in a pair was also a better group structure for her. She did however lose interest towards the end of the task once a few failed attempts occurred. She has improved in her ability more consciously employ basic strategies to navigate setbacks however continued focus is required to build her capacity to persevere for a more sustained length of time.
Student B
Student reflection on their grit: I used grit when the tower didn't work and kept going.
Teacher observations and reflection with grit rubric: Throughout the challenge Student B happily sat back peeling sticky tape and made little contribution to the group. She did not appear bothered by this and was happy not putting herself out there. Her response that she had shown grit in the reflection, but I believe was repeating what other students had said. I have placed Student B as emerging due to her inability to seek out any challenge throughout the task.

(Continued)

Table 8.2 (Continued)

Teacher future action:	
I need to facilitate opportunities for equal voice and equal contribution in the STEM tasks. I need to work with Student B's group and build her self-confidence, allowing her to see her contributions are valued.	
Student reflection on developing grit:	
I am starting to show grit in maths when I find things hard. I am proud of myself for showing grit and learning things.	
Teacher reflection on student developing grit:	
Student B has had a grit 'break through' across the last few weeks. She finds many areas of the curriculum challenging and has low self-confidence. When working in Maths she was finding a particular concept challenging to master. I provided her with some one-on-one support to go through the processes required in order to be successful. She then attempted the task again and was able to work out the answer. She was very excited that she had used 'grit' and not given up and now understood it. It is these teaching moments that were critically in allowing her to 'feel' the success of grit which I believe will assist her when moving forward. This then allowed her to approach the next STEM task with a new found confidence. She continues to require support when working in a group as she intuitively just allows others to take over and doesn't seek challenge at these times.	
Student E	
Student reflection on their grit:	
I was really frustrated building the tower as people contributed nothing and I was left to think of ideas. I had to use a lot of grit at different times. I am happy and proud.	
Teacher reflection with grit rubric:	
Student E feels a lot of emotion in learning and has very high expectations of himself, and when anything is seen as a challenge where there might be a winner, he has in the past given up before starting. Through the challenge Student E's level of frustration with his group was at an all time high. After trying a few different ways and trying to rally his team to contribute, he burst into tears. A quick group 'check in' gave Student E some space and a new idea to work with. Through all the ups and downs with his group, they constructed a tower. Student E probably showed the greatest grit in the class throughout the challenge. I have placed him in embracing on the grit rubric due to his ability to seek out challenge and employ strategies to meet the challenges despite the setbacks and difficulties he experienced.	
Teacher future action:	
In opportunities to practice grit use his success story to remind him of the benefits of using grit when learning.	

(Continued)

Table 8.2 (Continued)

> **Student reflection on developing grit:**
> *I enjoyed the task and liked working with my friend. I used grit when our bridge wouldn't stand up and kept falling down. We kept on trying though.*
>
> **Teacher reflection on student developing grit:**
> *Student E appeared less frustrated and more confident when approaching the next STEM tasks. Reminded of his success and the strategies employed in previous tasks set him up for success with a positive mindset. He navigated setbacks during the task well, refining their design and trying new things. However, when it came to each group sharing their responses to the challenge, he became agitated by those he perceived as being more successful than him. When it came to presenting, he was reluctant to share. Student E requires continued focus on developing a growth mindset and viewing learning from others as being a positive, not a competition.*

reflect on their use of grit in a particular task, and this is accompanied by a teacher reflection of the students' grit in relation to the rubric. This is followed with ideas for future action by the teacher for that individual student. There is also a description of the student's development or lack of development of grit over time by the teacher and the student.

The teacher in the example we provide had programmed learning for the whole class cohort focusing on grit over 10 weeks in a STEM inquiry-based learning project that involved a research partnership with Sydney Metro (a new, fully automated rapid transit system for the city). The teacher's class programme for grit involved themes such as, 'what does grit mean to you?', and 'defining grit' and 'I can . . . statements' such as 'I can persevere with challenging tasks', 'I can set goals to improve in areas of need and follow through with them' and 'I can advocate for myself in stressful situations' etc. All these themes were explored with students through varied experiential and embodied activities and through the larger STEM inquiry task.

From the action inquiries undertaken across the Community of Practice of schools, teachers developed a wealth of ideas, strategies and resources to share with each other in the teaching and learning of grit. Specific to their learning about the disposition of grit, teachers discovered that some of their 'high achieving' students were not seeking out challenges or setting more difficult goals. In these cases, the students were regurgitating similar and formulaic responses to tasks and showing little grit as they found the learning of little challenge cognitively. Whereas other students who struggled with learning, such as in literacy or numeracy for example, were developing strategies and goals to overcome their challenges and demonstrating far more grit. These findings were a revelation to the teachers, and it profoundly impacted how they understood and observed their students.

In relation to more general findings about pedagogy and formative assessment, the Oatley team's action inquiry (which began to examine other disposition rubrics, other than grit) revealed the following five major themes:

1. A metalanguage for learning encourages a growth mindset.
2. Student self- and peer-assessment encourages the development of learning dispositions.
3. Shared teacher dialogue framed by the learning continuums contributes to powerful teacher learning.
4. The learning continuums were most valuable as a tool for reflection and assessment *for* learning.
5. Pedagogy, learning and assessment have to be reimagined for self-regulating students.

We will explore each of these emergent themes from Oatley's inquiry and discuss the wider research surrounding their observations. The first theme was how metalanguage (developed using the LDW and continuum rubrics) encouraged a growth mindset in learners.

1. A metalanguage for learning encourages a growth mindset

For the Oatley teachers, their inquiry affirmed that the authentic and embedded use of cognitive, intra- and inter-personal metalanguage developed from the LDW rubrics supported students' positive beliefs in learning and a growth mindset. The psychology of a growth mindset[26] (as opposed to a fixed mindset) explains how learners can use feedback to direct and motivate their future learning efforts. A learner with a fixed mindset uses feedback to reaffirm or refute how they see themselves as learners. A fixed mindset views learning challenges as unnecessary or a risk where they may experience feelings of failure. Feedback depends on the learner believing in the potentiality of their own growth and productively using feedback. Feedback is essential to learning; however, it is not always effective as it is not necessarily received by students in the desired way. An individual's disposition affects the reception to feedback, and therefore the development of self-regulation and a growth-oriented learner identity is critical to feedback being effective as assessment *for* learning.[27]

A metalanguage for learning supports learners to make sense of and develop insight into their identity as a learner.[28] However, if metalanguage used by students is performative (used to please the teacher) or used by teachers as a commodity (used as a grading or point system to motivate students) there are scarce authentic learner insights or encouragement of self-regulatory behaviour.[29] The use of a metalanguage for dispositions is only authentic when it supports students to develop a learning orientation that enables self-regulation. According to evaluation methodology researcher Lorrie Shepard, most growth mindset learning approaches in schools are short-duration interventions separate to other programming. They are largely ineffective because they are not integrated throughout the classroom and school's culture of learning. Shepard argues that 'A better approach is not to conceive of separate motivational therapies but rather to develop a classroom culture focused on learning, where trajectories for development of academic, intrapersonal and interpersonal capabilities are integrated and mutually supportive. This means, for example, resisting grading practices and normative comparisons that by definition make only some children winners.'[30]

At Oatley, developing a metalanguage was instrumental to creating a learner's growth mindset and for developing authentic formative assessment in a mutually supportive classroom environment. The teaching and learning of dispositions were integrated into curriculum programming, and the metalanguage was used in self- and peer-assessment for reflection and feedback to teachers and students.

2. Student self- and peer-assessment encourages the development of learning dispositions

The teachers at Oatley noticed the significant role that self-assessment and peer-assessment play in the development of self-regulation. They realized student involvement in assessment *for* learning requires skills in self-regulation, but self-regulation is built through assessment *for* learning. The effectiveness of assessment for all learning depends on students' capacity to self-regulate. Lorrie Shepard explains that developing self-regulation and formative assessment requires a range of pedagogical processes and a classroom culture of trust and mutual respect between students and teachers. She says:

> Formative assessment strategies include explicit sharing of learning goals and criteria for judging quality work, questioning and other classroom routines that make thinking visible, explicit feedback plus informal feedback through hearing other students' ideas, and peer- and self-assessment. These techniques are critical for providing information and for shifting the nature of classroom interactions, but they are insufficient by themselves if there is not a commensurate change in the social meaning of evaluation. Deep learning can only be supported in a cultural context of trust and respect where students are willing to reveal what they currently understand with full confidence that talking about ideas will surely lead to new learning.[31]

The Oatley teachers realized that self- and peer-assessment as reflective feedback relies on self-regulation and a classroom culture of trust and respect. They recognized that these components are interconnected, and necessary for deeper learning. They learnt through the inquiry that their understanding of assessment was shifting because of the growth of self-regulation in their students.

Developing self-regulation through student goal setting, self-assessment and peer-assessment is still little practiced or understood in many schools, particularly secondary schools.[32] This may be because high stakes testing at the end of secondary school creates a culture of assessment that is mostly summative. Or authentic formative assessment may not be understood as it involves reimagining pedagogy in classrooms. Assessment researcher, Ruth Dann describes how assessment *as* learning (AaL) is more complex than most teachers realize. She argues, 'AaL' is the complex interplay of assessment, teaching and learning which holds at its core the notion that pupils must understand their own learning progress and goals through a range of processes which are themselves cognitive events. Implicit is the need for pupils to be active in both learning and assessment.[33] This complex interplay between assessment, teaching and learning, and students' active involvement became apparent to the teachers at Oatley through their inquiry. They shared their many observations about students through professional learning dialogue where they reflected and challenged their learnings together as a team.[34]

3. Shared teacher dialogue framed by the learning continuums contributes to powerful teacher learning

For the Oatley teachers the team discussions they had about students using the learning dispositions rubrics were invaluable. The discussions with others provided them with other perspectives in understanding their learners and exploring possibilities as future actions to support those learners. As a frame, the LDW continuum rubrics deepened the teachers' insights into learner identity and motivation. Evidence shows that shared teacher discourse communities or communities of practice support teacher learning and in turn student learning.[35] Structures and time dedicated to collaborative professional learning in classroom practice, particularly framed as an inquiry, are an investment in developing teacher and student growth.[36] It is a model of professional learning that the Oatley team will continue and develop at their school.

Learning continuums (developed through rigorous theory and practice) can provide substantiative insights into students thinking and behaviours in learning.[37] The teachers believed the effect of the rubrics was primarily in deepening their conversations about knowing their learners and developing pedagogy and strategies for student self-regulation. They were intrigued by the subtle differences between teachers interpreting the rubric in relation to students, but it also revealed how the differing perspectives in their inquiry team brought about greater understanding and consensus when discussing students. The value for the teachers was in using the rubrics to frame their professional learning discussions when considering future action for and with their students. The learning continuums as a reflection and pedagogical tool were deepening understanding and action for teachers and students in developing dispositions for learning.

4. The learning continuums were most valuable as tools for reflection and assessment for learning

The action inquiry at Oatley highlighted that the LDW learning continuums had greater potency as a tool for pedagogy and assessment *for* learning, rather than as a summative or evaluative measure of a student's capacities. It revealed to them that using the rubric to measure and score students could negatively affect students' learning growth and detract from using the rubric as an effective reflection and feedback tool. This is a view held by assessment researchers who argue that learning progressions should be used for formative assessment and instructional purposes, and that using them for grading can harm rather than enhance learning.[38] This is because scoring can affect the development of students' self-regulatory motivation and their use of feedback. Even for reporting to parents, explanations and examples of student milestones are far more informative for parents as feedback to support their children's growth. However, these formative assessment practices are often in contradiction to large-scale assessment practices and school evaluations by systems that often value scoring as reward and punishment accountability. These large-scale assessment processes can sabotage school classroom approaches to deep, self-regulated student learning.[39]

Researchers Shepard, Penuel and Davidson argue that it is better to design learning continuums from the 'bottom up' in schools.[40] They explain that when assessment processes are developed in the practice of schools there is greater coherence between curriculum, pedagogy, assessment and teacher learning. Learning progressions such as the Learning Disposition Wheel rubrics should be iterated and developed in schools to inform ongoing teacher practice and learning. Critically, in schools like Oatley that value self-regulation, the learner can have an active stake and involvement in developing the assessment of their learning. This idea changed how the teachers viewed the relationship between pedagogy, learning and assessment.

5. Pedagogy, learning and assessment have to be reimagined for self-regulating students

The action inquiry by the teachers illustrated to them the interconnectedness of pedagogy and assessment in developing student self-regulation. However, it did raise the question: is formative assessment really pedagogy, not assessment? Assessment researcher Gavin T. L. Brown argues that assessment *for* learning does not satisfy the methodology of reliability (consistency) and validity (accuracy) in assessment measures.[41] He explains that formative assessment is fundamentally pedagogy as it focuses on 'teachers engaging with learners in co-constructing new knowledge and in that moment-to-moment process teachers interactively adjust their teaching, prompts, activities, groupings, questions, and feedback in response to the ideas, skills, or knowledge exhibited by students'.[42] Brown argues, however, that involving students in their learning goals, evaluating themselves and their peers, and being involved in feedback processes are potentially powerful teaching techniques, but he believes they do not involve the validity and reliability of assessment as judgement.

From another viewpoint, Ruth Dann argues that assessment is intertwined with pedagogy and learning in deeply complex ways, particularly in classrooms where students are encouraged to understand and take ownership of their own learning. She argues that the significant 'assessment judgments' are the ones students are encouraged to make to further their own learning, rather than the assessment judgements of teachers. Dann says, 'If teachers are to further pupil learning, they need to recognise and explore the ways in which pupils control their own "learning gaps" rather than make assumptions that they (teachers) control them.'[43] Student self-regulation in learning shifts pedagogy and our understanding of assessment, as it blurs the boundaries between assessment, teaching and learning. In the paradigm of self-regulated learning in the classroom, assessment becomes authentically a part of pedagogy and learning. The Oatley inquiry team discovered through the action inquiry that assessment is in a complex relationship with how we learn. This had implications for how they 'propelled forward' in transforming assessment.

Propelling forward: Using assessment *for* learning

The Oatley inquiry team had discovered that the relationship between learning, assessment and teaching is complex. They believed an inquiry approach with the whole staff would help to navigate this complexity and continue to develop understandings of dispositions, assessment and agency in their school community. The learning for the team was that dispositions are 'assessable' but that when developing self-regulation in classrooms, assessment must be understood as formative and authentic to a growth mindset in the learner. Their view is that assessment of learning becomes most powerful as a process of self- and peer-reflection, and teacher reflection.

Oatley's experience prompts other schools pursuing the assessment of dispositions and capabilities to ask:

- How is assessing dispositions developing a growth mindset?
- How is assessing dispositions a shared dialogue? (with students, between teachers)
- What is the role of pedagogy in and for assessment of dispositions?
- How is assessment being used for learning growth in students and teachers?

At Oatley they discovered that understanding learners and learning through substantive, reflective dialogue is a process of assessment. Dispositions can be assessed but the motivation and purpose of assessment must foster growth in learners. How we assess in schools has a huge impact on how students create their 'individual autobiography as a learner'.[44] The Oatley team is aware that assessment should grow dispositions and capabilities and that using them as reporting and evaluation tools like conventional scores or grades would be detrimental to that growth.

This understanding of assessment and learning from Oatley's inquiry is interesting to frame through the disposition of curiosity and H.I Hill's work on the 'zone of curiosity'.[45] The zone of curiosity explains how learners in this zone, 'of their own volition, are motivated to put themselves into conditions of uncertainty, novelty and difficulty because the process of learning is pleasurable and rewarding'.[46] Either side of the 'zone of curiosity' sits the 'zone of relaxation' and the 'zone of anxiety' (see

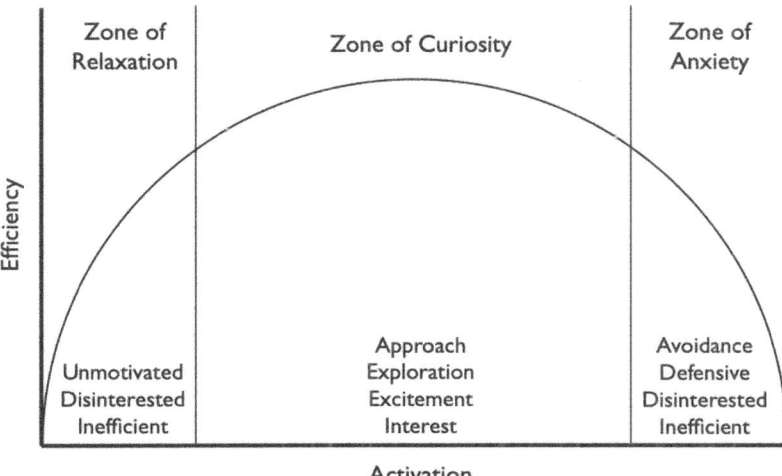

Figure 8.5 In this diagram, D. I. Hill (1982) explains the curvilinear relationship between activation levels and the effectiveness of learning. The 'sweet spot' is the 'zone of curiosity' which involves uncertainty, novelty and difficulties, but leads to learning that is pleasurable and rewarding.

Figure 8.5) and in these zones learning does not flourish. If teachers can develop a zone of curiosity in their classroom environment and in individual learners, students can develop dispositions for self-motivated learning.[47] Curiosity is influenced by social and individual factors[48] and is enhanced when individuals can engage in activities that are meaningful to them.[49] According to Ruth Dann, 'Assessment in this context may not so much need to focus on understanding what children know but understand learners' dispositions and willingness to learn. Formative assessment, which seeks to inform the learning process so that learning can develop, must give some acknowledgement to drivers for learning.'[50] This is what formative assessment is fundamentally for. It is to ask, what is driving learning and what is needed to drive the learning towards curiosity and self-regulated motivation?

In the Oatley story of transforming pedagogy and assessment, the teachers' professional learning experiences can also be explored through the lens of the zone of curiosity. The team at Oatley is driving their learning through curiosity and passion, as well as creating a zone of curiosity throughout the school culture. Transforming all the complex aspects of schooling takes time and is a forever changing and challenging process, and it can't happen unless teachers are curious and motivated to learn. Like their students, the teachers at Oatley are developing their own learning dispositions to reimagine and transform their school. To transform is to challenge assumptions, question deeply held beliefs about professional practices and change our frame of reference through reflection and action. Oatley Primary School is propelling forward by exploring assessment, the learning dispositions and the 4C capabilities with curiosity, critical reflection and active practice. In their transformation story, they will 'land their balsa aeroplane' – they will reflect, reassess and reimagine, and 'pull back and take aim' again with their next flight in transformation.

Like transformation in schools, assessment should not only be considered the 'landing' phase of learning achievement. Assessment should encompass the 'pulling back, taking aim and propelling forward' of the learning process. For Oatley, authentic formative assessment of dispositions and capabilities is a learning process that can contribute to developing agency in their students and teachers. The teachers at Oatley Primary School have learnt through their action inquiry that to develop twenty-first-century skills through learning dispositions and the 4Cs – pedagogy, learning and assessment must be viewed differently to transform and realize what is possible in schools.

Notes

1. P. Shah, H. M. Weeks, B. Richards, and N. Kaciroti, 'Early Childhood Curiosity and Kindergarten Reading and Math Academic Achievement', *Pediatric Research* 84 (2018): 380–6.
2. Susan Engel, 'Children's Need to Know: Curiosity in Schools', *Harvard Educational Review* 81, no. 4 (2011): 625–784; *The Hungry Mind: The Origins of Curiosity in Childhood* (Cambridge, MA: Harvard University Press, 2015).
3. Engel, 'Children's Need to Know'; *The Hungry Mind*.
4. Organisation for Economic Co-operation and Development.
5. K. Ananiadou and M. Claro, *21st Century Skills and Competences for New Millennium Learners in OECD Countries*. OECD Education Working Papers, no. 41 (OECD Publishing (NJ1), 2009).
6. Ananiadou and Claro, *21st Century Skills and Competences for New Millennium Learners in OECD Countries*.
   OECD is currently working on assessment and rubrics for creativity and critical thinking https://read.oecd-ilibrary.org/education/fostering-students-creativity-and-critical-thinking_62212c37-en#page20 Educational Research and Innovation Fostering Students' Creativity and Critical Thinking What it Means in School (2019).
   An example is the Victorian government's Dept of Ed using the work of researcher Guy Claxton https://www.education.vic.gov.au/school/teachers/teachingresources/practice/improve/Pages/eitassessattitudes.aspx.
7. 4C Transformative Learning is an organization that works in long-term partnerships with schools to transform learning, teaching and leading. Their work is based on the research and practice discussed in M. Jefferson and M. Anderson, *Transforming Schools: Creativity, Critical Reflection, Communication, Collaboration* (Bloomsbury Publishing, 2017), and M. Jefferson and M. Anderson, *Transforming Education: Reimagining Learning, Pedagogy and Curriculum* (Bloomsbury Publishing, 2021). Their website is https://www.4ctransformativelearning.org.
8. OECD is currently working on assessment and rubrics for creativity and critical thinking https://read.oecd-ilibrary.org/education/fostering-students-creativity-and-critical-thinking_62212c37-en#page20 Educational Research and Innovation Fostering Students' Creativity and Critical Thinking What it Means in School (2019).

An example is the Victorian government's Dept of Ed using the work of researcher Guy Claxton https://www.education.vic.gov.au/school/teachers/teachingresources/practice/improve/Pages/eitassessattitudes.aspx.

9. Jefferson and Anderson, *Transforming Schools*.
10. Examples of these practices are described in Jefferson and Anderson, *Transforming Schools*, and Jefferson and Anderson, *Transforming Education*.
11. R. E. Bennett, 'Formative Assessment: A Critical Review', *Assessment in Education: Principles, Policy, and Practices* 18, no. 1 (2011): 5–25.
12. L. A. Shepard, W. R. Penuel, and J. W. Pellegrino, 'Using Learning and Motivation Theories to Coherently Link Formative Assessment, Grading Practices, and Large-Scale Assessment', *Educational Measurement: Issues and Practice* 37, no. 1 (2018): 21–34.
13. H. Torrance, 'Assessment as Learning? How the Use of Explicit Learning Objectives, Assessment Criteria and Feedback in Post-Secondary Education and Training Can Come to Dominate Learning', *Assessment in Education* 14, no. 3 (2007): 281–94; 'Formative Assessment at the Crossroads: Conformative, Deformative and Transformative Assessment', *Oxford Review of Education* 38, no. 3 (2012): 323–42.
14. B. Bernstein, 'Class and Pedagogies: Visible and Invisible', *Educational Studies* 1, no. 1 (1975): 23–41.
15. R. F. Elmore, 'The Future of Learning and the Future of Assessment', *ECNU Review of Education* 2, no. 3 (2019): 328–41.
16. Elmore, 'The Future of Learning and the Future of Assessment', 333.
17. Acknowledgement of HPS in the development of the disposition rubrics with the professional learning organization. 4CTL.
18. C. L. Smith, M. Wiser, C. W. Anderson, and J. Krajcik, 'Implications of Research on Children's Learning for Standards and Assessment: A Proposed Learning Progression for Matter and the Atomic-Molecular Theory', *Measurement: Interdisciplinary Research and Perspectives*, 2006.
19. Shepard et al., 'Using Learning and Motivation Theories to Coherently Link Formative Assessment, Grading Practices'.
20. Jefferson and Anderson, *Transforming Schools*.
21. B. J. Zimmerman, 'A Social Cognitive View of Self-Regulated Academic Learning', *Journal of Educational Psychology* 81, no. 3 (1989): 329.
22. C. S. Dweck, *Mindset: The New Psychology of Success* (New York: Ballentine Books, 2007).
23. L. W. Anderson and D. R. Krathwohl (eds.), *A Taxonomy for Learning, Teaching, and Assessing: A Revision of Bloom's Taxonomy of Educational Objectives* (Complete edition) (New York: Longman, 2001).
24. R. M. Ryan and E. L. Deci, 'Brick by Brick: The Origins, Development, and Future of Self-Determination Theory', in Elliot, A. J. (Ed.), *Advances in Motivation Science* 6 (2019): 111–56.
25. L. Fiorelli and R. E. Mayer, *Learning as a Generative Activity: Eight Learning Strategies that Promote Understanding* (New York: Cambridge University Press, 2015).

26 Dweck, *Mindset*.
27 R. Dann, 'Assessment as Learning: Blurring the Boundaries of Assessment and Learning for Theory, Policy and Practice', *Assessment in Education: Principles, Policy & Practice* 21, no. 2 (2014): 149–66.
28 Dann, 'Assessment as Learning'.
29 L. A. Shepard, 'Classroom Assessment to Support Teaching and Learning', *The ANNALS of the American Academy of Political and Social Science* 683, no. 1 (2019): 183–200.
30 Shepard, 'Classroom Assessment to Support Teaching and Learning', 9.
31 Shepard, 'Classroom Assessment to Support Teaching and Learning', 14.
32 Shepard, 'Classroom Assessment to Support Teaching and Learning'.
33 Shepard, 'Classroom Assessment to Support Teaching and Learning'.
34 Professional learning dialogue for the Oatley teachers happened formally with facilitators from 4CTL, with their principal, mentor and with each other, and there were also many informal sharing of practice and learnings.
35 L. Darling-Hammond and N. Richardson, 'Research Review/Teacher Learning: What Matters', *Educational Leadership* 66, no. 5 (2009): 46–53.
36 H. Timperley, L. Kaser, and J. Halbert, *A Framework for Transforming Learning in Schools: Innovation and the Spiral of Inquiry*. Centre for Strategic Education Seminar Series Paper No. 234, April. Melbourne, VIC, 2014.
37 L. A. Shepard, 'Learning Progressions as Tools for Assessment and Learning', *Applied Measurement in Education* 31, no. 2 (2018): 165–74.
38 Shepard, 'Learning Progressions as Tools for Assessment and Learning'.
39 Shepard, 'Learning Progressions as Tools for Assessment and Learning'.
40 Shepard, 'Learning Progressions as Tools for Assessment and Learning'.
41 G. T. Brown, 'Is Assessment for Learning Really Assessment?', *Frontiers in Education* 4 (2019): 64. Frontiers Media SA.
42 Brown, 'Is Assessment for Learning Really Assessment?', 4.
43 Dann, 'Assessment as Learning', 162.
44 Term used by Elmore, 'The Future of Learning and the Future of Assessment'.
45 H. I. Day, 'Curiosity and the Interested Explorer', *Performance & Instruction*, 1982.
46 Day, 'Curiosity and the Interested Explorer', 20.
47 Shah et al., 'Early Childhood Curiosity and Kindergarten Reading and Math Academic Achievement'.
48 Jefferson and Anderson, *Transforming Education*; S. Buckingham Shum and R. Deakin Crick, 'Learning Dispositions and Transferable Competencies: Pedagogy, Modelling and Learning Analytics', in *Proceedings of the 2nd International Conference on Learning Analytics & Knowledge*, 29 April–2 May, 2012, Vancouver, British Columbia, Canada.
49 A. E. Black and E. L. Deci, 'The Effects of Instructors' Autonomy Support and Students' Autonomous Motivation on Learning Organic Chemistry: A Self-Determination Theory Perspective', *Science Education* 84, no. 6 (2000): 740–56.
50 Dann, 'Assessment as Learning', 158.

References

Ananiadou, K. and M. Claro 2009. *21St Century Skills and Competences for new Millennium Learners in OECD Countries*. OECD Education Working Papers, no. 41. OECD Publishing (NJ1).

Anderson, L. W. and D. R. Krathwohl (eds.) 2001. *A Taxonomy for Learning, Teaching, and Assessing: A Revision of Bloom's Taxonomy of Educational Objectives*, Complete edition. New York: Longman.

Bennett, R. E. 2011. 'Formative Assessment: A Critical Review'. *Assessment in Education: Principles, Policy, and Practices* 18(1): 5–25.

Bernstein, B. 1975. 'Class and Pedagogies: Visible and Invisible'. *Educational Studies* 1(1): 23–41.

Black, A. E. and E. L. Deci 2000. 'The Effects of Instructors' Autonomy Support and Students' Autonomous Motivation on Learning Organic Chemistry: A Self-determination Theory Perspective'. *Science Education* 84(6): 740–56.

Brown, G. T. 2019. 'Is Assessment for Learning Really Assessment?'. *Frontiers in Education* 4: 64. Frontiers Media SA.

Dann, R. 2014. 'Assessment as Learning: Blurring the Boundaries of Assessment and Learning for Theory, Policy and Practice'. *Assessment in Education: Principles, Policy & Practice* 21(2): 149–66.

Darling-Hammond, L. and N. Richardson 2009. 'Research Review/teacher Learning: What Matters'. *Educational Leadership* 66(5): 46–53.

Day, H. I. 1982. 'Curiosity and the Interested Explorer'. *Performance & Instruction* 21(4) (May): 19–22.

Dweck, C. S. 2007. *Mindset: The New Psychology of Success*. New York: Ballentine Books.

Elmore, R. F. 2019. 'The Future of Learning and the Future of Assessment'. *ECNU Review of Education* 2(3): 328–41.

Engel, Susan 2011. 'Children's Need to Know: Curiosity in Schools'. *Harvard Educational Review* 81(4): 625–784.

Engel, Susan 2015. *The Hungry Mind: The Origins of Curiosity in Childhood*. Harvard University Press.

Fiorelli, L. and R. E. Mayer 2015. *Learning as a Generative Activity: Eight Learning Strategies That Promote Understanding*. New York: Cambridge University Press.

Jefferson, M. and M. Anderson 2017. *Transforming Schools: Creativity, Critical Reflection, Communication, Collaboration*. Bloomsbury Publishing.

Jefferson, M. and M. Anderson 2021. *Transforming Education: Reimagining Learning, Pedagogy, and Curriculum*. Bloomsbury Publishing.

Ryan, R. M. and E. L. Deci 2019. 'Brick by Brick: The Origins, Development, and Future of Self-Determination Theory'. In Elliot, A. J. (ed.), *Advances in Motivation Science* 6: 111–56.

Shah, P., H. M. Weeks, B. Richards, and N. Kaciroti 2018. 'Early Childhood Curiosity and Kindergarten Reading and Math Academic Achievement'. *Pediatric Research* 84: 380–6.

Shepard, L. A. 2018. 'Learning Progressions as Tools for Assessment and Learning'. *Applied Measurement in Education* 31(2): 165–74.

Shepard, L. A. 2019. 'Classroom Assessment to Support Teaching and Learning'. *The ANNALS of the American Academy of Political and Social Science* 683(1): 183–200.

Smith, C. L., M. Wiser, C. W. Anderson, and J. Krajcik 2006. 'Implications of Research on Children's Learning for Standards and Assessment: A Proposed Learning Progression for Matter and the Atomic-Molecular Theory'. *Measurement: Interdisciplinary Research and Perspectives* 4(1): 1–98.

Timperley, H., L. Kaser, and J. Halbert 2014. *A Framework for Transforming Learning in Schools: Innovation and the Spiral of Inquiry*. Centre for Strategic Education Seminar Series Paper No. 234, April. Melbourne, VIC.

Torrance, H. 2007. 'Assessment as Learning? How the use of Explicit Learning Objectives, Assessment Criteria, and Feedback in Post-secondary Education and Training can Come to Dominate Learning'. *Assessment in Education* 14(3): 281–94.

Torrance, H. 2012. 'Formative Assessment at the Crossroads: Conformative, Deformative, and Transformative Assessment'. *Oxford Review of Education* 38(3): 323–42.

Transforming Teacher Education
The Power of Praxis and Inquiry

Alison Rourke and Kelly Freebody

9

Making connections (p. 166)

Critically framing teacher education: Problematizing the status quo (p. 166)

Teacher learning and the case for praxis (p. 167)

A model: Spirals of Inquiry (p. 169)

A case study: Alison's School (p. 171)
About the school (p. 171)
The need to reimagine professional learning (p. 172)
What was the process? (p. 173)

Inquiry and the 4Cs (p. 176)

Conclusion (p. 177)

This chapter explores how we approach initial teacher education and ongoing professional learning as a critical element in the work of teachers, schools and systems. In it, we aim to critically frame opportunities and challenges in teacher learning and make a case for a *praxis* approach to understanding the work of teachers. We draw on the 4Cs to explore an example of teacher learning to consider how inquiry is a catalyst for unlearning teacher accountability by making space for continual, hopeful inquiry and development of the work of schools and individual teachers in an increasingly demanding time. At a time when policy agenda in education are often considered to be constraining, rather than supporting, teachers' work[1] and the sociopolitical context of the early 2020s is exhausting teachers' bodies and minds,[2] we believe continued hopeful inquiry to how we do our work is more critical than ever.

Making connections

In the field of education there is a stubborn rhetoric of disconnection between initial teacher education and the classroom. Additionally, ongoing debates about teacher learning and how teachers consolidate four years of learning in the abstract university lecture halls to become a 'classroom ready' teacher position pre-service teachers and early-career teachers as problematic, and unprepared for the workforce. Much of this rhetoric considers the extent to which initial teacher education is failing its mandate to prepare the profession adequately. However, as a teacher educator and school principal writing and thinking together, we have been amazed at the symbiotic ideas about what we should celebrate, problematize and change about our work supporting teacher education and teacher professional learning. In this chapter, we unpack these discussions, using Alison's school as a case study, we draw on a *Spirals of Inquiry* approach to consider how we develop and grow our knowledge and skills in teaching throughout our careers. Unpacking the practices of a particular school allows us to draw connections with and between theory and knowledge in ways that speak to the praxis of our field.

Critically framing teacher education: Problematizing the status quo

The role of the teacher in schools, systems and society has changed significantly in the last fifty years. While some aspects of teachers' work are unchanging, many teachers have reported increased accountability, increased reporting mechanisms and a narrowing of curriculum. Some scholars have claimed that education reforms influenced by neoliberalism have led to an 'ideological disempowerment' of teachers. Neoliberal agendas in education are also considered influential in the intensification of teachers work, driven by complacency and compliance. This leads to the work of teachers becoming more about paperwork than people-work. While many consider the need for increased accountability of teachers and schools in the public interest, in the field of education, this change is sometimes considered detrimental to teacher-student relationships, student creativity and teacher well-being.

While there are debates about the value and necessity of these changes, we wonder if an unintended consequence of neoliberal influences that result in the increasingly demanding and 'public-facing' nature of teachers' work has resulted in a danger for teachers in being perceived as vulnerable or weak. To be 'accountable' to such a demanding role, working in a complex system, during a chaotic time, teachers must appear strong, organized, productive and successful. They are required to have answers rather than questions and provide documented evidence of their ability to 'value add' on and for their students. While in our experience most teachers *are* strong, organized, productive and successful, we also worry that the need to constantly appear so runs contrary to the process of learning, collaboration, dialogue and creativity.

Good teaching requires teachers to be continuously inquiring into their work, reflecting on what has and, crucially, has *not* worked. It requires a willingness to experiment and make mistakes. To support teachers, school leaders need to provide collegial spaces where teachers can have conversations and express doubts and concerns, rather than give answers or provide solutions. In many ways, it seems we need to unlearn, and then reframe, what it means to be accountable. Current 'accountability rhetoric', informed by neoliberalism, places the focus on the teacher themselves – what they have or have not achieved, what they need to improve, what they should be celebrating. Recent research has demonstrated how this focus is harmful to teachers professional identities and impacts teacher commitment, well-being, agency and effectiveness. In our experience, the best professional learning conversations instead focus on the *work* of teaching and the experience and development of teachers *and* students. We believe that for schools to be places where these conversations can take place, a model needs to be put in place, practised and embodied by the school leadership and the teaching community.

Teacher learning and the case for praxis

In this chapter, we take a *praxis* approach to understanding the everyday work of teachers and as an approach to teacher education. In *Transforming Schools*, Jefferson and Anderson discuss the tendency for concepts such as creativity to be 'aerosol words' – ideas that are sprayed around and smell good but are impossible to see, touch or grasp in any tangible sense. In many ways educational theory operates in a similar way – easy to discuss but difficult to enact or observe in practice. On the other hand, considering teaching practice without a theoretical underpinning can reduce teaching to a series of actions and moments (getting through the fifty-minute class), failing to consider how broader social or pedagogical purposes connect, and therefore neglect the complexity and dynamism of the work. *Praxis* connects these things and allows us to consider the way they interact to build understanding and knowledge about the how and why of good teaching practice.

The origin of the word *praxis* comes from Greek *prattien* which means 'to act' or 'to do' and it is commonly defined as action or practice. This origin has merged into a definition that considers what it means to practice an art or science, or to transform an idea into action. This attends to a relationship between a theory, skill or idea, and a subsequent action; practice that is informed by theory. In many fields and intellectual traditions, *praxis* is a specialist term with particular and often slightly different meanings. Marxist theory considers praxis to be action that transforms the social world in some way. In the field of education there are nuanced ways of understanding *praxis*. It is often simply understood as theory combined with practice. A potentially more cyclical view considers it practice informed by theory, which then re-informs further theory. In this chapter we draw on the definition provided by Kemmis and Smith in their 2008 volume *Enabling Praxis*:

> It is action that is morally-committed, and oriented and informed by traditions in a field. It is the kind of action people are engaged in when they think about what their action will mean in the world. Praxis is what people do when they take into account all the circumstances and exigencies that confront them at a particular moment and then, taking the broadest view they can of what it is best to do, they act.

There are several aspects of this definition that are salient in discussions about teacher learning and inquiry. First, it is not only concerned with educational knowledge and theory (although that is present) but encourages a broader view to consider current understandings and beliefs in the field about what we do and why. Second, it speaks to the 'in-the-moment-ness' of much teaching practice. Teachers are faced with moments and are required to act. While planning is key in teacher practice, the teaching itself is experienced by students and teachers 'in the moment'. Kelly has previously written that she considers this to be one of the key challenges in teaching:

> The ideas are so big – discipline content areas, cross-curriculum priorities, social and educational inclusion, pedagogy, social justice – and the stakes are so high – the education of future generations, the good of the community, the wellbeing of children. The reality of the classroom, however, is that these big, important, community- and life-building things happen in the tiniest moments. Decisions about activities, comments left on essays, responses to questions, reactions to behaviour and so on. And so, to do their jobs 'well' teachers need to make a series of split-second decisions, lesson plans, late night book-marking, and teaching moments that can meaningfully feed into a broader praxis of social justice in education.

In our opinion, for 'good' teaching to occur there needs to be thoughtful and deliberate connections between the big ideas of teaching and the everyday moments of the classroom. This makes reflection, both in action and on action important for developing the intellectual, social, moral and practical resources that teachers have to draw on as they engage in teaching. A view of teacher learning that incorporates these ideas is best described as developing teacher *praxis*.

One of the central concerns of this chapter is considering how teachers inquire about teaching, to develop their understanding of their work. Knowledge about teaching, like all other knowledge ' . . . emerges only through invention and re-invention, through the restless, impatient, continuing, hopeful inquiry human beings pursue in the world, with the world, and with each other'.[3] When considering what inquiry is, and why it matters, we could respond with statistics about teacher retention or student achievement; making the case that teachers who engage in inquiry into their teaching achieve better results. However, for us, Freire's reflections identify the features of inquiry that make it indispensable for teacher learning. It is **restless**, it seeks change and movement, to be working with people to advance; it is **impatient**, because it speaks to the urgency of our desire to meet the needs of the children in our care; it is **continuing**, as we are learning new things and each year brings new students, new contexts and new ideas; and it is **hopeful**. Hope is in key idea in the philosophy of critical pedagogy and central to the 4Cs approach. Rather than optimism or faith, hope is critical about things that can and should change, but resolute in the belief that things *can* change. A hopeful outlook considers society to be unfinished 'a challenge rather than a hopeless limitation'.

In many ways inquiry makes sense as a central praxis in teacher learning. Teaching itself, particularly when effective, can be considered as 'a process of ongoing inquiry into, and evaluation of practice'.[4] Teacher learning, therefore, should enable consideration of practice to unfold over time, and should also consider 'all the ways teacher inquiry practices and processes may be helping or hindering professional learning in education settings and addressing areas for improvement'.[5]

In this chapter, we discuss one model for inquiry into teaching practice, the *Spirals of Inquiry* model. We use this example to discuss the challenges and opportunities associated with working with teachers to develop praxis, to unlearn and then reframe accountability and to adopt a hopeful approach where they are able to consider their themselves and their work as 'in progress'.

A model: Spirals of Inquiry

The central philosophy of the Spirals of Inquiry (SoI) approach to teacher learning is that at no stage in their career, do teachers stop learning to be teachers. It rejects the fixed mindset that sees teachers as 'done' with their education at graduation. A fixed mindset about teachers and teaching, coupled with institutional neoliberal logic of individual responsibility, can lead to a focus on teaching as 'sorting' – organizing instruction, recording summative assessment results, and responding to external pressures to be accountable through data. Instead, a SoI approach

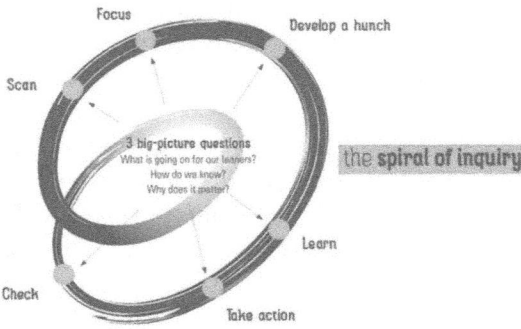

Figure 9.1 The Spirals of Inquiry.

considers teaching as a learning process – learning about the needs of students, learning and experimenting, collaborative approaches, and a focus on internalized commitment and responsibility. The process of Spirals of Inquiry shares many traits with action research approaches to teacher learning, in that it consists of a cyclical process of discovery, inquiry, action and evidence. Unlike many forms of action research, however SoI has a constant focus on what is happening for the learners. The focus on the experiences of learners, rather than the actions of teachers, provides teachers space and time to unlearn the teacher-centred accountability discourses and re-focus on their commitment to their learners, and the joy that this brings.

Joy might be a strange word to see written in a chapter about teacher learning, but there is ample evidence (both anecdotal and empirical) to suggest that many teachers begin their teaching career with a sense of enjoyment, passion and idealism and that this is lost under the strain of managing the competing demands of students, schools, parents and systems. The focus on learners, rather than individual teachers, can bring teaching teams together as a collaborative, supportive, network with a shared purpose .

The SoI approach has six intersecting phases (see Figure 9.1), which result in a continual feedback loop, which can be considered as complimentary to the creativity and critical reflection coherence makers developed by Jefferson and Anderson's 4Cs approach :

1. Scanning – using rich information and discussion to consider what is really going on currently in the school/classroom. This aligns with the need for *noticing* as the instigator of creativity and *identifying assumptions* as the beginning of a process of critical reflection.
2. Focusing – considering and deciding where to concentrate professional time and energies for this inquiry.
3. Developing a hunch – unpacking the focus and asking 'what is leading to the present situation and, just as important, how we – the professionals – are contributing to that situation' This phase develops creativity process through *asking why, really why*? And critical reflection by asking *why this? Why so?*

4. Engaging in new professional learning – considering what we need to learn to do in order to make the sorts of change we would like? Phase 4 supports the development of creativity by *playing with possibility*.
5. Taking new action – Deciding what we need to do differently and what practices we will put in place. Time and support is critical in this phase. After asking 'why?' engaging in critical reflection requires contestation, elaboration and adaptation. Phase 5 encourages teachers to do this through active decision-making about their practice.
6. Checking that a big enough difference has been made, and then re-engaging to consider what is next. This final phase supports the final steps in both creativity and critical reflection coherence makers, *selecting and evaluating* and *resolving*.

These stages are all informed by asking the same three questions:

- 'What is going on for our learners?'
- 'How do we know?' and
- 'Why does this matter?'

The questions maintain three key ideas throughout the process. First, it keeps the focus of inquiry on the learners. Second, it ensures that there is an orientation to data and evidence, rather than assumptions. This does not necessarily mean the process must be quantitative, or 'empirical', but rather that the conversations consider how we interpret the vast and diverse information we have access to as teachers. Finally, it reminds the team that what they are doing matters. This helps us see the ways professional learning helps us creating change that makes a difference to your students, rather than for the sake of reporting/accountability to systems.

A case study: Alison's School

About the school

Fairy Meadow Demonstration School (FMDS) is a unique environment that provides contemporary education to 400 children in NSW Australia. The school has five support classes for children with disabilities, a preschool and thirteen mainstream classes. The rich diversity of the population sees 30 per cent of children from language backgrounds other than English and 10 per cent of students identify as Aboriginal or Torres Strait Islander.

As one of only five demonstration schools in the state, Fairy Meadow has established strong links with the University of Wollongong. The school currently hosts two Bachelor of Education subjects, where pre-service teachers work in the school alongside in-service teachers. Integrating theory and practice within initial teacher education is not only an effective way to incorporate real-world experience for pre-service teachers, but it increases their engagement in the course. Having the pre-service teachers working on site at FMDS allows for an integration of theory and practice, where university learning is connected and cyclical; pre-service teachers bring their ideas into the school and then bring their experiences back to the university classroom to inform their ongoing development of ideas. Pre-service teacher feedback from a recent review of the programme Eady, Green & Capocchiano provided evidence that the pre-service teachers found this particularly helpful and enjoyable, one commented: '*Being able to go into FMDS and not only learn through tutorials, online modules and lectures, but also through being in the classroom and school setting*'. The professional partnership also aides our in-school inquiry sessions by providing FMDS with links to university partners as critical friends, and access to information about emerging research and leading educational reform practices.

The need to reimagine professional learning

During the development of the Strategic Improvement Plan in 2019, teaching staff at FMDS said they found professional learning in its current state to be repetitive and unrelated to classroom practice. They sought something that was not only relevant, but also ongoing, rather than one-off, and that impacted the learning of the students in the classroom. Having worked in schools where Spirals of Inquiry were embedded in practice, the leadership team embarked on a process that focused on inquiry, rather than professional learning that focused on transmitting knowledge from Point A (the professional learning leader's head) to Point B (the teacher's head). The staff wanted learning that would be rigorous, restless and involve student voice to make the learning impactful and relevant to the learners. Research into high-impact professional learning opportunities led to the work of Halbert and Kaser[6] and the decision was made to implement the Spiral of Inquiry model.

Fairy Meadow Demonstration School restructured the Professional Learning to meet the needs of a diverse and mostly experienced team. During the External Validation process – a process that provides opportunities for schools to discuss judgements about current practice and the evidence that underpins these judgements, it became evident that professional learning already targeted school priorities, the needs of students in the school, and the achievement of professional goals. However, what it failed to meet was the needs of the teachers or provide them with opportunities to be active participants in the professional learning process. As school leaders at FMDS, we needed to support teachers and executive staff to identify what was happening with and for their students in the classroom, and then critically reflect on what we learnt about their own teaching needs from this data.

As teachers we are often formally and informally held accountable. During the transformation process and through Spirals of Inquiry, teachers are asked to 'unlearn accountability'. The purpose of the process steers away from judging the teacher or their progress lies and instead focuses on the evidence from our student learners, our own learning and the creativity of the action. This aligns with a growth, rather than fixed mindset, one that considers us to be always developing as teachers. A deliberate process of unlearning, coupled with transformative learning processes, allows theory to become practice and accountability to be seen as an attention to what's happening now and why is it happening, rather than who is to 'blame'. Teachers develop ownership of situations that they are involved in and therefore consider their role in what happens next. As Perry and McWilliam[7] state:

> The capacity of skilled teachers to be responsive to classroom dynamics, to allow students and themselves to experiment and take risks, must not be buried in an exclusive drive to respond to systemic accountabilities. Accountability is an essential component of the professional repertoire of contemporary school leaders. However, the responsibility to engage with the social as well as the systemic can be lost when accountabilities are the only leadership imperative.

The reimagining of the professional learning model used at FMDS provided a platform for teachers to be collaborative, creative and critical thinkers who took risks and experimented with possibilities.

What was the process?

As we discussed earlier in the chapter, the times we are currently teaching in are chaotic on the ground and highly regulated from above. This makes negotiating changes to teacher knowledge and student learning a complex task. Timperley, Kaser and Halbert warn that when that change is more complex educators can:

> slow down in order to speed up. In these complex situations, some actions may be premature, and we need to bring collective thinking to the table before leaping in. That is what the inquiry spiral is all about. Otherwise, we can get into unproductive cycles of experimentation, disillusionment and abandonment, only to jump to the next thing that may or may not work.[8]

The common frustrations that teachers experience with teacher inquiry can arise from the lack of support that they receive to deeply understand the teaching through an inquiry framework, and then to put that understanding into practice. At FMDS the Spirals of Inquiry framework supported complex pedagogical change, providing the time to think about what we did, the results of what we just did and what we need to do in the future.

School leaders led staff in the creation of their individual Performance and Development Plans (PDPs), supporting them in setting professional learning goals based on system and school priorities (as identified in school plan) as well as personal teaching and career aspirations. At the same time, we began professional learning with the 4C Transformative Learning (4CTL) organization as regular, ongoing workshops with leadership teams and explored the work as a community of schools across Wollongong. The workshops occurred in school hours and after school hours, with time in between sessions to explore new ideas and strategies. We took a deep dive into learning dispositions and the pedagogical tools that supported the transformation of classroom practice and engaged in Collaborative Classroom Visits (CCV's) and Deep Noticing and Action (DNA)[9] as a critical reflection of our practices. CCV's were undertaken by a team of school leaders (not hierarchical leaders but leaders of learning) and often students visiting each other's classrooms to observe and reflect on the learning taking place. Each classroom visit was five to ten minutes and focused only on the hunch, the part of the Spiral of Inquiry that needs testing. At the end of the visit, the host teacher and the team leave the classroom to reflect on the learning and generate action require. This was developed by the DNA – a guided reflection used to stimulate discussion between teachers and students and co-construct a shared reflection of the experience of the learners in the classroom. What began to unfold for us, was a clear and powerful link between what we were doing in our inquiry sessions and the work of our partnership with 4CTL.

Spiral of Inquiry sessions were organized in stage teams, for example Year 3 and 4 teachers, every three weeks. Time was strictly quarantined; dedicated to answering the questions, making the change and focusing on the change. Critically, the focus of the sessions moved away from accountability and refocused onto vulnerability. Everyone entered the Spiral of Inquiry with the same status. The principal, executive staff, classroom teachers, support teachers and professional educators had equal status and contributed equally. The movement away from power and hierarchy made this process so appealing to our early-career teachers. Their voice had equal prominence in the inquiry, there was no leader in the process.

Each phase of the spiral reminded us of where we need to go next, we also found the phases in the framework do not necessarily occur in order. That didn't matter, the inquiry spiral was continuous and continuing, allowed us to take time to discover new things about ourselves and our learners. What mattered most to us was that we found ways to understand what is going on for our learners, and that we use this information to make decisions on what new learning we will do. Focusing the inquiry this way allowed us to challenge our assumptions about what might be happening and constantly check our progress along the way. In essence, we developed an adaptive expertise mindset, making the Spiral of Inquiry a transformative way of reimagining and learning.

Scanning: What is going on for our learners?: We collected available internal and external student data such as national tests, standardized assessments or formative assessments. We also collected student voice in the form of short videos where students were asked to answer key questions pertinent to the focus of the Spiral of Inquiry such as; Where are you going with your learning in reading? Why does this learning matter? How's it going? Where to next? The deep dive into data is to explore our first question: What is going on for our learners? Together as a team, we unpacked both internally and externally collected student data and we investigated the video and data evidence. This collection of raw data supported the scanning phase of the Spiral of Inquiry. In this model of inquiry, scanning is an essential part of the framework. It allowed us to understand what learners were experiencing and consider where to go next to support future student learning. Initial scans got us on the path of looking for a hunch that could be followed, scanning continued throughout our whole inquiry journey.

Focusing: What is going to give you the biggest impact?: The conversations around the data created feelings of restlessness that often placed us in vulnerable situations that were uncomfortable and without immediate explanation leading us into a new world of opportunity as we sought to explore what we saw and heard from our students. These conversations then generated a sense of hopefulness, creativity and critical thinking as we explored the possibilities of where to focus next.

Developing a hunch: What's leading to this situation?: Having the opportunity to articulate and discuss our deeply held beliefs and assumptions about our practices, provided us with the chance to consider different options while checking our assumptions for accuracy before moving ahead. In this phase we are curious about other people's thinking and open to listening to ideas and the views of others, ensuring that we are able to test our hunches.

Learning: What do we need to learn?: Often one of the most exciting phases of the inquiry is considering what learning and, at times, unlearning needs to occur to make meaningful changes to teaching practices. During the learning phase, we often engage with professional readings to inform the action we will take. Understanding new ways of doing things better that can be sustained and supported over time, requires focused professional learning.

Taking Action: What can we do differently to make enough of a change?: The action phase is about real change, not just talk. It is a deep dive into the new learning. At FMDS we acknowledged that team members may be feeling vulnerable about trying new approaches and tried to make the risks less risky by emphasizing the qualities of a growth mindset, including the capacity to learn from failures as well as successes.[10] Changing practice is both confronting and exciting. Learning together and now acting on that learning makes the learning visible and evidence of impact accessible.

Checking: Have we made enough of a difference?: The purpose of a shared inquiry is to make a difference to the learning of our students. Gathering evidence of impact during this phase to ensure we are making a great enough difference, can include records of assessment, video snapshots of student voice and student work samples. 'Change does not always equal improvement or transformation. There may be instances where teachers change what they are doing only to find out that not much has changed for their learners. New action arising from an inquiry spiral can only be considered "good" if learner outcomes and experiences have changed for the better'.[11]

Central to the approach was the power of *yet* as an antidote to deficit thinking and teaching. As we are all growing and learning, we are not obliged to know all, be all, and achieve all. When we notice things we want to change, or find things we have not done, we can remind ourselves that we cannot do it/have not done it *yet*. This allowed us to be vulnerable and truthful. It also put pressure on the executive to ensure we were providing the time, resources and support for the team to act upon their hunches. These processes, built on inquiry and a willing riskiness through the simple act of allowing ourselves not to know *yet*, helped bring the joy and love of learning for staff and were paramount to the success of our change in school culture. Spirals of Inquiry became the final piece of the initial puzzle as we invested our financial resources towards our greatest asset – our staff.

Inquiry is not about a packaged solution in search of a problem. The issues we face are complex, so they require adaptive approaches. Most of the significant learning challenges at a school will require experimentation, new discoveries and shifts in some established practices. Routines polished over years of use will be challenged and will change.[12] At Fairy Meadow Demonstration School, we are undergoing transformation. It is a slow and challenging process but one that allows for curiosity and creativity to flourish. Professional learning communities like Spirals of Inquiry allow for agency, teacher and student voice, and leadership to be a developing cultural practice that keeps everyone on an 'level playing field'. Our strong links with other schools and the University of Wollongong allow us to build partnerships that bring research, knowledge, support and the facilitation of teacher education into our practices.

Each Spiral of Inquiry leads to another. Built on each other, these small changes not only allow a community of learners to build confidence but also leads to more sustained change. This is how transformation happens. Using the SoI approach not only changes the practice of teachers, but also students and schools. Change 'is likely to happen if young people are learning in engaging and innovative settings where curiosity – for everyone – is a way of life'.[13] Working in this inquiry space is serious work that makes a difference to increasing students' achievement and improving school outcomes.

Inquiry and the 4Cs

While the case study we have discussed in this chapter focuses on the Spirals of Inquiry as an example of praxis, the work is influenced and has a significant crossover with the 4Cs approach to transforming learning developed by Jefferson and Anderson.[14] SoI is easily incorporated into a 4Cs approach not just philosophically but as a practical way of working in schools. The SoI phases align with the creativity and critical reflection coherence makers, and the work is built on understanding and developing good communication and collaborative practices in schools. Both maintain a focus on the learner and learning, through the informing questions in a SoI approach, and through the Learning Disposition Wheel in the 4Cs.

Essentially, in this chapter the crux of our argument has centred around how developing an inquiry approach to teacher learning can assist teachers and schools to unlearn and reframe accountability. Inquiry, when done well, fosters praxis. It requires us to make meaning by connecting what is happening with what we know, and how we might learn more to make change. It is therefore connected to the past (theory we have already learnt and experiences we've already had), the present (what is happening and how we know) and the future (can I imagine how this could be better, what do I need to learn next?). It makes our work visible to ourselves and others, and it is active, which provides us with agency. It allows us to consider our work as emerging, rather than static, and therefore provides us with hopeful perspectives that are oriented to change. Taken together, we believe this makes the work of teaching not only more purposeful and successful, but also more joyful.

The 4Cs, as outlined by Jefferson and Anderson and in this volume are not only core for teachers work in classrooms but also play a large role in how we understand effective teacher education. Feedback from the staff at FMDS prior to their adoption of the Spirals of Inquiry approach indicated that they found professional learning transmissive, disconnected and focused on agenda set by others. Inquiry process, by contrast was deeply collaborative, it required us to connect with each other, listen, offer, yield to the offers of others, create, plan, test and evaluate together. Central to the process was a focus on communication. This was not just communication with others in the inquiry process, but with our students in classrooms, our school community and the field more broadly, connecting and communicating with educators working elsewhere. Inquiry only happens when there is critical reflection about that connects the past and present to wonder about what is happening, why it is happening and why it matters. Creativity is required to play with possibilities, to imagine change and to select and evaluate potential next steps.

Beyond the need for each 'C' individually, an inquiry approach to teacher learning helps to develop explicit understandings of learning processes that allow spaces for creativity, collaboration, communication and critical reflection to occur almost simultaneously. The explicit nature of this understanding is key. Teachers need to understand not just what their students learn, but also how they learn. They need to experience teaching and learning and then reflect on and inquire about these experiences before they can enact them in their own classroom. 'Students and teachers need to have the capacity to learn by doing (experience), reflect deeply on those experiences (critical reflection) and then build inquiry to drive further learning through action'. To achieve this, however, we feel we need to 'unlearn' and then redesign current professional learning practice to focus on inquiry, collaboration, imagination and hopefulness.

Conclusion

As a school principal and teacher educator we believe that school and system transformation are critical. FMDS links with University of Wollongong aims to provide a collaboration and communication link between pre-service and in-service teacher education but it still has a long way to go to build transformative learning in pre-service teacher education. Similarly, while we know there are many wonderful things happening in classrooms all over Australia (and indeed, the world) we also know that there is much that needs to change.

In their book *Transforming Education* Jefferson and Anderson argue that 'transformation happens when schools fundamentally reimagine values, learning, pedagogy, curriculum, teacher education and leadership' and that 'when nurtured and developed collaboratively, will make a material difference for this generation of learners and many that will follow'. In this chapter we have extended on this claim to suggest that, to reimagine and nurture our profession and our work, we need to unlearn and reframe accountability. To focus on teaching and learning, rather than teachers and teacher quality, and to enact praxis through inquiry. Teacher education is critical to this process of transformation, and inquiry is critical to effective teacher education. As leaders of schools and universities we need to enable a more agentic, inquiry-based, transformative learning environments for in-service and pre-service teachers. The reframing we advocate for in this chapter can span the divide between learning contexts – teacher education instructions, schools and teachers' classrooms – to create a new way of responding to the complex and dynamic challenge of teaching and learning in these increasingly demanding times.

Notes

1. Scott Fitzgerald et al., 'Intensification of Teachers' Work Under Devolution: A "Tsunami' of Paperwork," *Journal of Industrial Relations* 61, no. 5 (2019), https://doi.org/10.1177/0022185618801396, https://journals.sagepub.com/doi/abs/10.1177/0022185618801396.
2. Joanne R. Beames, Helen Christensen, and Aliza Werner-Seidler, 'School Teachers: The Forgotten Frontline Workers of COVID-19,' *Australasian Psychiatry* 29, no. 4 (2021): 420–2.
3. P. Freire, *Pedagogy of the Oppressed* (New York: Continuum, 1970), 72.
4. J. Parr and H. Timperley, 'Multiple "Black Boxes": Inquiry into Learning within a Professional Development Project', *Improving Schools* 13 (2010): 158–71, p. 10, https://doi.org/10.1177/1365480210375349.
5. Rebbecca Sweeney, 'Six ways to Support the Implementation of the Spiral of Inquiry: Lessons from New Zealand', https://telp.educ.ubc.ca/spiral-of-inquiry-lessons-from-new-zealand/
6. J. Halbert and L. Kaser, *Spirals of Inquiry for Equity and Quality* (Vancouver: BCPVPA Press, 2013), Further information, www.bcpvpa.bc.ca/node/108.
7. L. A. Perry and E. McWilliam, 'Accountability, Responsibility and School Leadership', *The Journal of Educational Enquiry* 7, no. 1 (2007).
8. H. Timperley, L. Kaser, and J. Halbert, *A Framework for Transforming Learning in Schools: Innovation and the Spiral of Inquiry*. Centre for Strategic Education, Seminar Series Paper No. 234 (April 2014).

9. M. Jefferson and M. Anderson, *Transforming Education: Reimagining Learning, Pedagogy and Curriculum* (London: Bloomsbury, 2021).
10. L. Kaser and J. Halbert, *The Spiral Playbook*. c21canada.org, 2017.
11. J. Halbert and L. Kaser, 'A Focus on Equity and Excellence in Networks of Inquiry', *The Queensland Principal*, 21 September 2019, 23.
12. J. Halbert and L. Kaser, *Spirals of Inquiry for Equity and Quality* (Vancouver, BC: BC Principals and Vice Principals Association, 2013).
13. Timperley, Kaser, and Halbert, *A Framework for Transforming Learning in Schools*.
14. M. Jefferson and M. Anderson, *Transforming Schools: Creativity, Critical Reflection, Communication, Collaboration* (London: Bloomsbury, 2017).

References

Acton, Renae and Patti Glasgow 2015. 'Teacher Wellbeing in Neoliberal Contexts: A Review of the Literature'. *The Australian Journal of Teacher Education* 40(8): 99–114. https://doi.org/10.14221/ajte.2015v40n8.6.

Bahr, Nanette Margaret and Suzanne Mellor 2016. *Building Quality in Teaching and Teacher Education*. Australian Education Review, 61. Camberwell, VIC: Australian Council for Educational Research.

Beames, Joanne R., Helen Christensen, and Aliza Werner-Seidler 2021. 'School Teachers: The Forgotten Frontline Workers of Covid-19'. *Australasian Psychiatry* 29(4): 420–2.

Cochran-Smith, Marilyn, Elizabeth Stringer Keefe, and Molly Cummings Carney 2018. 'Teacher Educators as Reformers: Competing Agendas'. *European Journal of Teacher Education* 41(5): 572–90.

Fitzgerald, Scott, Susan McGrath-Champ, Meghan Stacey, Rachel Wilson, and Mihajla Gavin 2019. 'Intensification of Teachers' Work Under Devolution: A "Tsunami" of Paperwork'. *Journal of Industrial Relations* 61(5): 613–36. https://doi.org/10.1177/0022185618801396. https://journals.sagepub.com/doi/abs/10.1177/0022185618801396.

Freebody, Kelly 2019. *Frameworks for Social Justice in Teacher Education: Moments of Restless Sympathy*. Cham: Springer International Publishing, 225–42.

Freire, Paulo 1970. *Pedagogy of the Oppressed*. New York: Continuum.

Freire, Paulo 1974. *Education for Critical Consciousness*. London: Sheed and Ward.

Freire, Paulo, Myra Bergman Ramos, and Donald Macedo 2014. *Pedagogy of the Oppressed*. Thirtieth anniversary edition. New York: Bloomsbury.

Gavin, Mihajla, Susan McGrath-Champ, Rachel Wilson, Scott Fitzgerald, and Meghan Stacey 2021. 'Teacher Workload in Australia: National Reports of Intensification and Its Threats to Democracy'. In Stewart Riddle, Amanda Heffernan, and David Bright (eds.), *New Perspectives on Education for Democracy*, 110–23. Routledge.

Guenther, Amy R. 2021. '"It Should Be Helping Me Improve, Not Telling Me I'm a Bad Teacher": The Influence of Accountability-Focused Evaluations on Teachers' Professional Identities'. *Teaching and Teacher Education* 108: 103511. https://doi.org/10.1016/j.tate.2021.103511.

Halbert, Judy and Linda Kaser 2013. *Spirals of Inquiry*. Vancouver, BC: BC Principals and Vice Principals Association.

Halbert, Judy and Linda Kaser 2019. 'A Focus on Equity and Excellence in Networks of Inquiry', *The Queensland Principal*, September 21, 23.

Jefferson, Miranda 2017. *Transforming Schools: Creativity, Critical Reflection, Communication, Collaboration*. Edited by Michael Anderson. London: Bloomsbury Academic, an imprint of Bloomsbury Publishing Plc.

Jefferson, Miranda and Michael Anderson 2017. *Transforming Schools: Creativity, Critical Reflection, Communication, Collaboration*. Edited by Michael Anderson. London: Bloomsbury Academic, an imprint of Bloomsbury Publishing Plc.

Jefferson, Miranda and Michael Anderson 2021. *Transforming Education: Reimagining Learning, Pedagogy and Curriculum*. London: Bloomsbury Publishing Plc.

Kemmis, Stephen and Tracey J. Smith 2008. *Enabling Praxis: A Challenges for Education*. Pedagogy, Education and Praxis 1. Rotterdam: Sense Publishers.

Mockler, Nicole 2018. 'Early Career Teachers in Australia: A Critical Policy Historiography'. *Journal of Education Policy* 33(2): 262–78. https://doi.org/10.1080/02680939.2017.1332785.

Kaser, L. and J. Halbert 2017. 'The Spiral Playbook'. 2017. Canadians for 21st Century Learning and Innvoation, accessed 2 May 2022, http://c21canada.org/playbook/.

Tsang, Kwok Kuen and Qingyan Qin 2020. 'Ideological Disempowerment as an Effect of Neoliberalism on Teachers'. *Power and Education* 12(2): 204–12. https://doi.org/10.1177/1757743820932603.

Vedder-Weiss, Dana, Nadav Ehrenfeld, Michal Ram-Menashe, and Itay Pollak 2018. 'Productive Framing of Pedagogical Failure: How Teacher Framings Can Facilitate or Impede Learning From Problems of Practice'. *Thinking Skills and Creativity* 30: 31–41. https://doi.org/10.1016/j.tsc.2018.01.002.

Conclusion
The Threads of Transformation: Finding the Patterns

Miranda Jefferson and Michael Anderson

- The courage to transform (p. 182)
- Learning to transform (p. 184)
- Processes and structures to transform (p. 185)
- 4C capabilities to transform (p. 186)

As we foreshadowed in Chapter 1, the case studies cannot be generalized to your school. Your school is unique. The power of the case studies is in how they may resonate with your context and how they may challenge you or inspire you with what is possible. Your school, like all the stories in this book, are like squares in a patchwork quilt. Each square in a patchwork quilt is distinctive but put together they make up a pattern (see Figure 10.1). There are patterns created from the unique case studies in this book, from which you can ponder how your school may begin to transform or continue to transform.

The pattern that emerges from the case studies guides us to some of the threads that support our understanding of how to transform schools. Sociologist Norman Denzin and research methodologist Yvonna Lincoln use quilt making to explain how a qualitative researcher stiches, edits and puts slices of reality together to bring about a unity or pattern when interpreting experiences.[1] The case study experiences in these

Figure 10.1 The case studies in this book are like squares in a patchwork quilt, each story is unique but together they create patterns or threads for us to learn from.

chapters create the complex bricolage of a patchwork quilt, and from that patchwork, our reflections of the stories reveal to us these threads:

- Courage is required in transforming anything in schools.
- There must be deep and ongoing professional learning to sustain and evolve transformation, innovation or even improvement in schools.
- Schools depending on their context, approach the transformation of processes and structures differently.
- Relentlessly focusing on capabilities such as creativity, critical reflection, communication and collaboration empowers a school's culture to continue to change.

We will discuss these interwoven threads throughout the case studies as features of how to transform schools.

The courage to transform

In the case study *Pedagogies and Politics: Drawing on the 4Cs – Normal Pig*, the teachers were brave in exploring a new pedagogical approach in their classroom, antithetical to the way things were done at their school. The same is illustrated in the case study *Connections, Creative Chaos and Vulnerability: Reflections of*

Transformative Praxis. Courage is determination, resilience and grit and without it there is no drive or action to transform schools or classrooms. American poet and civil rights activist Maya Angelou said, 'Courage is the most important of all the virtues, because without courage you can't practice any other virtue consistently. You can practice any virtue erratically, but nothing consistently without courage.'[2] Doing things erratically does not sustain change in schools. It is the consistency of courage that shifts the status quo and the stasis that pervades the institutionalized cultures or habitus of schools.

Transformation can only be led by courageous and collaborative leadership, not transformational 'hero' leaders as the chapter *Transforming Leading Through Coherence* points out. Courageous and collaborative leadership is evident across the case studies, but particularly emerges in the voice of the school principal in *Transforming Pedagogy: How to Take the Jump*. Courageous leadership is to take the jump, it is to walk the talk, not talk the walk. To lead transformation, leaders must want to be transformed, to see things differently and to do things differently. Outsourcing change in schools is not a feature of these case studies.

Gary Pisano, an expert in business innovation and strategy, describes in *Creative Construction: The DNA of Sustained Innovation*[3] how leadership is critical to building a culture of innovation and transformation. His research in business organizations resonates with what we see in schools aspiring to change through innovation and transformation. First, strong leadership should take direct ownership of the innovation challenge and role model the capabilities and processes required for change to happen. By walking the talk, leaders' model and take responsibility for the risk-taking and experimentation required of innovation and transformation. The story in the case study *How Schools Transform Through Creative Disruption* illustrates how such a culture of experimentation and challenge can be modelled by teacher leaders.

Pisano also argues leadership must incubate and protect the innovators or transformers, so that the template for a transformative culture can emerge and develop in an organization. In all the case studies, there are groups of teachers and leaders who are encouraged to try, experiment, iterate and learn how their classroom or professional learning may be transformed. School leadership supports these groups and considers how these transformers and innovators can positively influence people, processes and structures towards change in their schools. Without the best team, without collaboration, without a clear sense of direction and without courage, transformation in schools is impossible. The chapter *Transforming Learning as Walking on Water* illustrates the necessity of leading with a collaborative team that has strategic direction and courage.

School leadership for innovation and improvement has the courage and drive to look to the long term but achieve milestones in the short term by strategically 'chunking' transformation. Transformation, innovation and even school improvement are both a marathon and an accumulation of sprints. It takes years to transform and sustain cultural shifts in schools and classrooms. None of the case studies are stories of overnight success. There are different speeds, focuses and places where transformation happens, evolves or indeed reverses in the schools. We acknowledge the courage these teachers and leaders have, to sustain focus, energy and determination to change and challenge what is best for their students in their context. And they cannot do this without learning – constantly.

Learning to transform

Aspirations for deep, authentic and ongoing professional learning and classroom learning are common to all the case studies. The individual leaders and teacher's voices we hear in the chapters are learners that are curious, inquiring and resourceful. Learning inspires them to take action, to learn from their actions and to let their actions inform their learning. The cycle of learning as formalized praxis comes to life in the case studies, *Transforming Teacher Education: The Power of Praxis and Inquiry* and *Transforming Assessment: Assessing the 'Unassessable'*. Authentic and habitual learning that involves classroom and leadership practice with research and teacher reflection is the 'superpower' of transforming what happens in schools.

Education policy and change researcher Richard Elmore criticizes education system's and their policies (and indeed his own earlier policies) that conflate 'implementation of best practice at scale' with the concept of 'learning'. He argues that the terms 'implementation', 'best practice' and 'at scale' misconceives how human beings actually learn, develop, adapt and change.

> 'implementation' is something you do when you already know what to do; 'learning' is something you do when you don't yet know what to do. The casual way policy-focused people use the term obscures this critical distinction. The knowledge of what to do has to reside not in the mind of some distant policy wonk or academic, but in the deep muscle-memory of the actual doer. When we are asking teachers and school leaders to do things they don't (yet) know how to do, we are not asking them to 'implement' something, we are asking them to learn, think, and form their identities in different ways.[4]

Professional learning should just be that – learning that involves what we don't already know, that makes us think and forms who we are in a new way. Like learning for our students, professional learning for teachers and leaders should be:

- *deep and generative* (able to be applied to other contexts and situations).
- *lifelong* (dispositional and capability focused for the acquisition of new and ongoing learning).
- *developmental* (affecting teacher and leader identity and how they see themselves) and
- *responsive to diversity* (of school contexts and people within that context).[5]

These are features and aspirations of all the professional learning in the case studies.

However, according to Elmore, powerful learning environments where human beings continually change their understandings and actions through evidence, experience and knowledge are rare. His observations of powerful learning in schools and systems may enhance our understanding of the patterns in how and when transformation works.

The learning characteristics Elmore identifies in outlier schools and systems that manage real and effective change are:

- *The principle of transparency*: the ideas for learning are open, accessible and explicit for teachers and students alike, although they will be operating at different levels and capacities.
- *The pursuit of divergent thinking within a well-defined practice*: neither the adults nor the young people know the answers in learning.
- *The pursuit of intentional surprise*: transformation (and learning) is messy with fits and starts in the vague pursuit of discovery.
- *The pursuit of intentional design*: a school's learning theory should develop the design of a learning environment.

These ideas are challenging, sophisticated and demanding for schools and systems, and they demonstrate the complexity and difficulty of any school change. Every school's context also makes the challenge unique, and that is reflected in the case studies and whether their focus is on transforming processes or structures or both.

Processes and structures to transform

Processes are actions like learning, teaching, reflecting, collaborating and assessing. Structures are the arrangement and organization of something. For example, structure is how professional learning, leadership or curriculum are organized in schools, or how learning environments or timetables are arranged. In the case studies we observe varied processual and structural shifts strategically driven by leaders and teachers in their unique cultural context. Conceptualizing transformation through processes and structures is useful for understanding contextual differences between schools and their approach to change. Processes and structures are also a useful frame to reflect and determine what may be appropriate in your context, at what time.

Processes and structures are both significant in effecting change.[6] In some settings at certain times, schools change structures without changing processes, and some change processes without changing structures, and some do both. There is evidence of both processual and structural change in the case study, *Time to Be Seen: Transforming Learning through Community Engagement for Children with Special Needs Using Drama and Technology*.

To consider how process or structural adjustments may work in your school, it is constructive to apply Pisano's matrix or 'landscape map' for organizational

Table 10.1 A matrix for the innovation and transformation of processes and structures in schools adapted from Gary Pisano's *Creative Construction: The DNA of Sustained Innovation* (2019)

Requires new structures	**DISRUPTIVE** Different structures Same processes	**ARCHITECTURAL** Different processes Different structures
Leverages existing structures	**ROUTINE** Same processes Same structures	**RADICAL** Different processes Same structures
	Leverages existing processes	Requires new processes

innovation.[7] He describes innovation as either routine, disruptive, radical or architectural. Table 10.1 is an adaption of Pisano's research to explain how changes in processes or structures may affect schools. The matrix assists schools to recognize that they can't do everything at once and it clarifies what priorities are needed for schools at what time as they navigate the complexity of making change. Sometimes schools will leverage existing structures or processes to create new structures or processes (Table 10.1).

Strategy is critical for teachers and leaders to achieve change in schools, but without a culture for innovation or improvement, strategy cannot achieve anything. Capabilities empower people to innovate and improve their practice, and collectively people with capabilities influence the culture of organizations. This is why the 4Cs – creativity, critical reflection, communication and collaboration – are vital to any sustained influence in a school culture for innovation and transformation.

4C capabilities to transform

The capability approach pioneered by Amartya Sen and Martha Nussbaum[8] explains how through the development of capabilities, people have real freedoms to achieve their well-being through their potential 'to do' and 'to be'. For instance, you can give schools resources like new classrooms, furniture and technology, but it is how these resources are used that converts them into human functioning and flourishing. Access to skills and knowledge in capabilities is what empowers people to use the resources they have. Capabilities have been recognized as critical to education, and this is illustrated by the OECD (the Organisation for Economic Cooperation and Development) Learning Framework 2030.[9] In the Framework they argue that to navigate the volatility, complexity and uncertainty of social and economic life,

> Students will need to apply their knowledge in unknown and evolving
> circumstances. For this, they will need a broad range of skills, including cognitive

and meta-cognitive skills (eg. critical thinking, creative thinking, learning to learn and self-regulation); social and emotional skills (eg. empathy, self-efficacy and collaboration); and practical and physical skills (eg. using new information and communication technology devices).

The use of this broader range of knowledge and skills will be mediated by attitudes and values (eg. motivations, trust, respect for diversity and virtue).[10]

The OECD's vision for education resonates with the aspirations of all the case studies in this book but their stories are more than aspirations. They describe the 'how' of trying to transform their classrooms and schools, and in those stories there are 4C capabilities being used to empower learners, teachers and leaders to learn and transform their way of 'doing' and 'being'.

How these schools transform is in how the capabilities of creativity, critical reflection, communication and collaboration support a culture of transformation, innovation and improvement. 4C capabilities must not just be words in curriculum documents and lofty aspirations of educational policy. They must be practiced skills and processes that are learnt, developed and sustained as a school's way of 'doing' and 'being'.

This book demonstrates that schools can begin and continue to transform through agentic processes and structures framed and made coherent by the 4C capabilities. Literacy, numeracy, using technology and all the curriculum disciplines are critical to knowledge and education, but what is done with that knowledge is as critical. The potential outcome of knowledge is how it is used to play with possibility (creativity), to solve problems and take action (critical reflection), to generate agency (communication) and advance co-construction and connections (collaboration). Every contributor to this book has demonstrated the courage to lead and to learn how schools can be places of transformation that support well-being, agentic relationships and the development of future-ready education.

The threads of transformation can be found in the patterns created by the patchwork of case studies presented in this book. We hope you the reader are inspired to create your own unique patchwork square of school transformation, innovation or improvement. You will join an ever-increasing number of courageous teachers, leaders and students, who want to expand the true potential of schools as humanizing, empowering and relevant forces for critical hope and social good.

Notes

1 Norman K. Denzin and Yvonna S. Lincoln (eds.), *Strategies of Qualitative Inquiry* (Thousand Oaks, CA: Sage 'Introduction: The Discipline and Practice of Qualitative Research', 2008), 1–44.

2 Maya Angelou quoted in https://www.washingtonpost.com/news/on-leadership/wp/2014/05/28/maya-angelou-on-leadership-courage-and-the-creative-process/.

3 Gary Pisano, *Creative Construction: The DNA of Sustained Innovation* (New York: Public Affairs, 2019).

4　Richard Elmore, "Getting to Scale . . ." It Seemed Like a Good Idea at the Time', *Journal of Educational Change* 17 (2019): 529–37.
5　M. Jefferson and M. Anderson, *Transforming Schools: Creativity, Critical Reflection, Communication, Collaboration* (London: Bloomsbury Publishing, 2017); *Transforming Education: Reimagining Learning, Pedagogy and Curriculum* (Bloomsbury Publishing, 2021).
6　John P. Kotter, *Accelerate: Building Strategic Agility for a Faster-Moving World* (Boston, MA: Harvard Business Review Press, 2014).
7　Pisano, *Creative Construction*.
8　Martha Nussbaum, *Creating Capabilities: The Human Development Approach* (Cambridge, MA: Harvard University Press, 2011); Wulf Gaertner, 'Amartya Sen: capability and well-being', in *The Quality of Life*, ed. Martha Nussbaum and Amartya Sen (New York: Oxford University Press, 1993).
9　OECD (the Organisation for Economic Cooperation and Development) Learning Framework 2030.
10　p. 5, OECD (2015) https://www.oecd.org/education/2030/E2030%20Position%20Paper%20(05.04.2018).pdf.

References

Angelou, M. (as quoted in *The Washington Post*) 2014. *Maya Angelou on Leadership, Courage, and the Creative Process*. https://www.washingtonpost.com/news/on-leadership/wp/2014/05/28/maya-angelou-on-leadership-courage-and-the-creative-process/.
Denzin, N. K. and Y. S. Lincoln (eds.) 2008. *Strategies of Qualitative Inquiry*. Thousand Oaks, CA: Sage. (Chapter: 'Introduction: The Discipline and Practice of Qualitative Research', pp. 1–44).
Elmore, R. 2016. 'Getting to Scale . . . It Seemed Like a Good Idea at the Time'. *Journal of Educational Change* 17: 529–37.
Gaertner, W. 1993. 'Amartya Sen: Capability and Well-being'. In M. Nussbaum and A. Sen (eds.), *The Quality of Life*, 62–66. New York: Oxford University Press.
Jefferson, M. and M. Anderson 2017. *Transforming Schools: Creativity, Critical Reflection, Communication, Collaboration*. Bloomsbury Publishing.
Jefferson, M. and M. Anderson 2021. *Transforming Education: Reimagining Learning, Pedagogy and Curriculum*. Bloomsbury Publishing.
Kotter, J. P. 2014. *Accelerate: Building Strategic Agility for a Faster-Moving World*. Boston, MA: Harvard Business Review Press.
Nussbaum, M. 2011. *Creating Capabilities: The Human Development Approach*. Cambridge, MA: Harvard University Press.
OECD (the Organisation for Economic Cooperation and Development) 2015. *Learning Framework 2030*, 5. https://www.oecd.org/education/2030/E2030%20Position%20Paper%20(05.04.2018).pdf.
Pisano, G. 2019. *Creative Construction: The DNA of Sustained Innovation*. New York: Public Affairs.

Index

3Ps (Pedagogy, Play and Performance) 116
4C coherence makers 11, 17–18, 111, 116–18, 141, 143
4C Transformative Learning (4CTL) 72, 81, 84 n.4, 92, 107, 109
21st Century Skills and Competencies for New Millennium Learners in OECD Countries 140–1

aerosol words 4–5
Akinyemi, Adeola Folasade 96
Alice Springs (Mparntwe) Education Declaration 109
Allen, Jean M Uasike 11
allyship 129
Alvesson, M. 94
Anderson, Michael 11–12, 17–19, 21, 23–4, 33–4, 36, 42, 70–2, 112, 141, 147, 167, 170, 176–8
Aotearoa
  children in material hardship 54
  context of 54–5
  Covid-19 impacts on 54
  family violence 54
  food insecurity, children live with 54
  primary schools in 54
  whole-school mental health education approach in 55–6
  youth suicide rates in 54
Arthur, W. Brian 125, 134
assessment as learning (AaL) 156–60
assessment for learning 10, 12, 140–60
  curiosity and 140–1

Learning Disposition Wheel in 10, 141–2
Oatley Public School (case study) 141–60
autonomy 23, 132

Baldwin, James 37
Before You Were Mine (Boelts) 34
behaviour, students 37
Bell, Alexander Graham 125
Bhasker, Michael 78
Bildung approach to pedagogy 76–80
  characteristics 77
  co-determination 77, 80–2
  for restrained teaching 77
  self-determination 77, 80–2
  for teachers in professional learning 80–2
BLM movement 32–3
Blue Derby Pods 104
blue room 88
Boelts, Maribeth 34
Bourdieu, Pierre 84 n.8
brave 57
Bruner, Jerome 84 n.6
Bruyère, Justine 10, 11, 32

Callega, Gordon 130
Cammarota, J. 63
capabilities 23, 26, 155, 184, 186
  4C 9, 17, 37, 42, 77, 140–6
  individual's 77
  leadership 11, 16
  Prospero's 130

of teachers 25
through simplicity 17
for transforming learning 81
of values and learning 27
capacities in learning
   cognitive 9
   interpersonal 9
   intrapersonal 9
Cart, Oily 125, 133
case studies 2, 181–2
   Fairy Meadow Demonstration School (FMDS) 171–6
   Hurstville Public School 89–100
   Oatley Public School 141–60
   St Eugene College 108–20
   Ulladulla High School 69–83
ChatGPT 134
children with learning disabilities 125–35
class community 63
classroom 34–5, 38–40
   process-drama activities 130
   situated professional learning 24
   and teacher education 166
   vulnerability into 62–4
co-determination 77, 80–2
cognition/enactment, embodied 38, 85 n.21
cognitive skills 9
coherence makers 4–5, 7, 170
   4C 11, 17–18, 111, 116–18, 141, 143
   of collaboration 20–1
   pedagogical change through 24–7
   shared vision and values 18–20
Coleman, K. S. 26
collaboration
   capacity of 25
   cooperation to 91
   definition 97
   environment 38–9
   normal 40–1
   steps in 39
collaboration, communication, critical reflection and creativity (4Cs) 3–5, 7–8, 11, 41
   in curriculum 46–7
   environment 35–48
   in Fairy Meadow Demonstration School (FMDS) 176–7
   in Hurstville Public School (case study) 91–2
   in Miranda North Public School, Sydney 16–28
   for students 32–48
   to teacher education transformation 176–7
Collaboration Circles 20–1, 26, 74, 81, 93, 96–7, 118
collaborative classroom visits (CCV) 24–5, 98, 174
collaborative practices 11, 16–17
collaborative vision making 18–20
collectively noticing, practice of 25–7
communication 25–6, 38, 90–1
community garden 16–17
Community of Practice (CoP) 88–90
   in classrooms 89
   from cooperation to collaboration 91
   definition 89
   at Hurstville Public School (case study) 90–3
      breaking ground 92
      leadership structures, challenging and changing 93–5
      learner agency 95–6
      shared endeavour 97–8
      strategic and regular reflection on practice 98–9
      true collaboration, understanding and recognizing 96–7
   inter-school 98
   qualities 89
   teachers responses to learning continuum 147
competencies 23, 140–1
cooperation
   to collaboration 91
   for establishing CoPs 91
Covid-19 pandemic 131–3
creative disruption 104–20
   challenges 119
   collaborative, festival of 118
   communicative, festival of 118–19
   in education 108–20
   festival of positive 113–18
   Learning Disposition Wheel in classrooms 117–18
   at St Eugene College (case study) 108–20
   teacher feedback on 2020 festival of positive disruption 115–16
   understanding 107–8
creative learning 36
creativity 36–7
   capacity of 25

normal   42–3
for school transformation   106–7
creativity cascade, in school transformation   106–7
critical pedagogy   60
    hope in   62, 169
critical reflection   3–9, 11–12, 15–18, 21–4, 27, 37–8, 59, 77, 79, 81, 143
    as 4C capability   37, 42
    for developing co-agency   82
    environment   36–7
    to identify shared vision and values   18–20
    normal   43–4
    on past practices   108
    students   43–4
C&T   125–35
    and Prospero partnership   127
    as Theatre-in-Education company   126
curiosity   12, 140
    students   140–1
    zone of   158–9
curriculum   3–5, 10, 12, 26–7, 32, 36, 46, 61, 105, 111, 125, 142–3, 185, 187
    4Cs for   46–7
    gaps in   44
    pedagogical knowledge and   73
    political work of   48
    standardized   46
    teachers and   55
    through pedagogical practice   76–80

Dahl, Roald   130
Damasio, Antonio   85 n.21
Dann, Marissa   109
Dann, Ruth   156, 159
Day, Christopher   89
Dean, Max   12, 126–35
Deci, Edward   132
deep learning   19
deep noticing and action (DNA)   98, 174, 183, 186
Denzin, Norman   181
Derby, Tasmania   104–5
    creative disruption model in   105
    mountain biking in   104–5
Derwent Valley Council   104
dialogue   38
Didadtik approach to pedagogy   76–82
discovery scaffolds   73–4

dispositions   23
Dru, Jean Marie   107

educational neuroscience   124
educational transformation   59
Elmore, Richard   145–6, 184–5
embodied cognition/enactment   38
embodiment   11, 32–6
    as learning in action   36
    lessons   36
emerging themes   45
emotion   85 n.21
empathy   10
empowered learners   19
Enabling Praxis (Kemmis and Smith)   168
Engel, Susan   140–1
environment
    collaboration   38–9
    communication   38
    creativity   35–6
    critical reflection   37–8
Equality and Human Rights Commission (EHRC)   128
E scale   147, 150
Eye Gaze technology   124, 126
Eyes that Kiss in the Corner (Ho)   42

Fairy Meadow Demonstration School (FMDS; case study)   171–6
    4Cs approach to transforming learning   176
    4CTL for   174
    about   171–2
    Performance and Development Plans (PDPs) for   173
    process of transformation   173–6
    reimagine professional learning, need to   172–3
    Spiral of Inquiry sessions   174–6
feedback   143–4
feelings   57
    of autonomy/control of own behaviour   132
    of competence   132
festival of collaborative and communicative disruption, 2022   118–19
festival of positive disruption   113–18
Fine, M.   63
Floyd, George   32
focus   10
Fookes, I.   54
formative assessment   144, 159

Fort Royal Community Primary School 125–35
Freebody, Kelly 12
Freire, Paolo 55, 58–61, 169
Fuglestad, T. 124
Future of Learning and the Future of Assessment, The (Elmore) 145

Galderisi, S. 54
Galès-Camus, Le 56
gardeners 16–17
Garner, Rick 124
generative tension 92–3
Gregorzewski, Moema 11
Grice, Christine 11, 89
grit 3, 12, 104, 143, 146–54, 183
Groh, Fabian 133
Grove, N. 125

habitus 84 n.8
Halbert, J. 172–3
Hammond, Linda Darling 106
Hargreaves, Any 96
Harwood, J. 125
Hayhow, Richard 127
Hill, H. I. 158
Ho, Joanna 42
Holt, D. 56
hooks, bell 60, 62
hope 11, 62
Hopmann, Stefan 77–8
hot-seating 42–3
Hsu, Chin-Lung 133
human connections 59–60
Hunter, Debbie 12
Hurstville Public School (case study) 89
 collaboration with 4C Transformative Learning 92
 Collaborative Classroom Visit/Deep Noticing and Action (CCV/DNA) 98
 Community of Practice (CoP) at 90–9
 from cooperation to collaboration 91
 culture 90–1
 learning transformation, strategies for 91–9
  4Cs 91–2
  breaking ground 92
  CoPs 92–3
  leadership structures, challenging and changing 93–5
  learner agency 95–6
 shared endeavour 97–8
 strategic and regular reflection on practice 98–9
 true collaboration, understanding and recognizing 96–7
 staff members 90–3
 whole-school professional learning 91
hydrotherapy pool 130, 134–5

immersive games 130
immersive technology 130
Immordino-Yang, Mary Helen 85 n.21
Indigenous people of Aotearoa 54
inquiry 19, 72–3, 78, 150–8, 169–71, 174–6
interactive water-based adventure story 132
interests of students 18
interpersonal skills 9, 99, 115, 117, 155
intrapersonal skills 9, 99, 115, 117, 155

James and the Giant Peach (Dahl) 130
Jefferson, Miranda 11–12, 17–19, 21, 23–4, 33–4, 36, 42, 70–2, 111–12, 141, 147, 167, 170, 176–8
John-Steiner, Vera 97
Jones, Margaret 12, 126–35

Kahanamokus, Duke 88
kākahu 57
Kapp, Karl 130
Kaser, L. 172–3
Klafki, Wolfgang 77
knowledges 63, 84 n.7
Korthagen, Fred 85 n.20

Lave, J. 92–3
leadership team
 capacities 23–4
 learning 11
 as practice of mobilising others 23
 in transformation 17–20
learning
 authenticity in 19
 needs 18
 values about 19
learning continuum rubrics for LDW 146–9
Learning Disposition Wheel (LDW) 5–10, 95
 and assessment 10, 142
 and curriculum 10

domains   23
in education   5–10
empathy   10
focus   10
learning continuum rubrics for   146–9
and pedagogy   10
in schools   10, 22–4
for St Eugene College (case study)   113–15
teamwork   10
Learning Prism   11, 33–4, 41
on collaboration   38–9
in communion   34, 38
embodied practices   36
as lens   35
planning in   34
shared understanding of   41–2
for students   32–48
students behaviour   37
learning progressions   147
learning reflections   45–6
learning transformation   87–100
for children with special educational needs   123–35
strategies for   91–9
Lincoln, Yvonna   181
LivingNewspaper.net, online documentary drama project   127
Lofts, Denise   11
Lu, His-Peng   133

McAlister, Snowy   88–9
McDonald, Jacquelin   95
McWilliam, E.   173
Mana Model   56
Mana tū   56
Mana ūkaipō   56
Mana whānau   56
Māori   54–5
Mayes, Terry   124
Meader, Jenn   32, 34, 38, 40
Medical Model of Disability   124
Meerkat Strategy   110
mental health   54–7
mentors   47
Mercieca, Bernadette Mary   95
Miranda North Public School, Sydney   12–13
4Cs approach in   16–28
authentic learning experiences at   17
coherence maker for 4Cs approach in   17–18

collaboration, coherence of   20–1
leadership wheel, coherence in   21–4
leading/sustaining transformation as process   27–8
pedagogical transformation   24–7
playground into community garden, transformation of   16–17
shared vision and values, identifying for   18–20
socio-educational advantage   17
teachers   17–19
Mitey   11, 54
arts-based and experiential approaches   57–8
coaches   55
mascot   57
My Kākahu   57
scaffolded modelling approach   62–4
stepped progression of learning   57–8
teachers   63
transformative praxis in   58–9
underpinning pedagogical principles   55
website   55
Wellbeing Review Tool   55
whole-school approach   57–8
mountain biking   104–5
My Kākahu   57

National Lottery Community Fund   128
normal   34
collaboration   40–1
communication   40–1
creativity   42–3
critical reflection   43–4
lesson   39–40
pivot   41–2
worries   44–5
Normal Pig, A (Steele)   34–5, 39–41
Nussbaum, Martha   186

Oatley Public School (case study)   141–60
4C approach in   143–4, 146–9
4C coherence makers in   143–4, 149–50
assessment in learning   145–9
application   158–60
learning continuum rubrics for LDW   145–9
themes for   154–8
views on   145–6
formative assessment   144, 159

Learning Disposition Wheel application in   143–4
   students   142–60
   teacher   142–60
   team's action inquiry   150–8
   themes for learning and assessment   154–8
      LDW learning continuums   156–7
      metalanguage for learning   154–5
      shared teacher dialogue   156
      student self- and peer-assessment   155–6
      student self-regulation   157–8
   transforming pedagogy journey   143
   Wonder Web   143–4, 149–51
O'Connor, Peter   11
Online Distance Learning (ODL) platform   127
online games   133
openness   38
Open Space Technology methods   129
Other Side, The (Woodson)   34

'parents as partners in learning' workshops   26
pedagogical love   60
pedagogy
   Bildung approach to   76–80
   curate   78–9
   Didadtik approach to   76–80
   jump with   83
   of reciprocal vulnerability   62–4
   transformation of   10, 11, 18, 22–4, 69–83
   Ulladulla High School (case study)   71–6
Pedagogy Parachute   70–1
   authentic connections in   72–3, 78
   collaborative inquiry in   72–3, 78
   creative iteration   72–3, 78
   discovery scaffolds   73–4, 78
   dynamic feedback   73–4, 78
   elements in   72–3
   framework   72–3
   as metalanguage for analysing teaching methodology   73–4
   networked schemas   72–3, 78
   reflective experience   72–3, 78
   for teachers to explore pedagogy   71–4
Pellegrino, J. W.   147, 157
Penuel, W. R.   147, 157
Perry, A.   173
persuasive game   133
Pisano, Gary   183, 185–6
praxis approach   58–9, 166–9
   definition   168
   teachers   168–9
principle of coherence   16–17
Professional Learning Communities (PLCs)   110–13
progression   147
'Progress on Disability Rights in the UK' report (EHRC)   128
Prospero   127–35
   interactive water-based adventure story in   132
   online adventure   132

racism   42
reciprocal vulnerability   62–4
reflective practice   22–7
relatedness   23, 132
Robinson, Ken   106
Rourke, Alison   12
Ryan, Richard   132
Ryan, Sheila   2–3

sameness   34
Sardar, Ziaddin   107
scaffolds, Learning   73–4, 84 n.5
schools   2
   Learning Disposition Wheel in   10
   transformation processes   2, 16–28
SDT; *see* self-determination theory (SDT)
Seeing AI (Microsoft)   124
self-concept   23
self-determination theory (SDT)   9, 24, 72–3, 76–82, 132
self-portraits   57
self-reflection   23
self-regulation   12, 72–3
Sen, Amartya   186
SEND (Special Educational Needs and Disabilities)   124, 128–9
Sensory Theatre (Webb)   125
Serengeti plains of Tanzania   80–1
shared vision and values for schooling   18–20
Shepard, L. A.   147, 154–5, 157
Shulman, Lee   84 n.7
Sir John Kirwan Foundation   55–6
skydiving *versus* teaching   69–70
'Skyscrapers and Subways'   129
social interactions   63

Social Model of Disability   125
social relations/connection   59–60
song   57
Spicer, A.   94
Spirals of Inquiry (SoI) approach   169–71, 176–7
Splish Splash   133
staff meetings   25
Steed, Mark   11, 90–1
Steele, K-Fai   34–5
STEGG (St Eugene Guiding Group)   111
Steiner, Vera Jon   91
Sternberg, R. J.   36
St Eugene College (case study)   108–20
   creative disruption at   108–20
   festival of collaborative and communicative disruption, 2022   118–19
   Learning Disposition Wheel at   114–15, 117–18
   making transformation reality at   109–10
   Meerkat Strategy for transformation at   110
   professional learning communities for   110–13
   teacher feedback on 2020 festival of positive disruption   115–16
   transformation, provocation for   109–10
Stormy (Guojing)   34
struggle   11
students   33–4
   4Cs for   32–8
   behaviour   37
   collaboration   40–1
   communication   40–1
   creativity   42–3
   critical reflection   43–4
   curiosity   140
   defeat   38
   emotions with   62–4
   lesson   39–40
   normal worries   44–5
   openness   38
   pivot normal   41–2
   safety   38
   self-determination in   9, 24, 72–3, 76–80
   self-regulation in   72–3
   silence   38
   working in small groups   39

supervision   2
Sutton, Paul   12, 126, 127–35
symbolic control   130

teacher education transformation   165–78
   4Cs approach to   176–7
   and classroom   166
   Fairy Meadow Demonstration School (FMDS; case study)   171–6
   4Cs approach to transforming learning   176–7
   4CTL for   174
   about   171–2
   process of transformation   173–6
   reimagine professional learning, need to   172–3
   Spiral of Inquiry sessions   174–6
   praxis approach to   167–9
   Spirals of Inquiry (SoI) approach to   169–71, 176–7
   status quo, problematizing   166–7
teachers in professional learning   11, 57, 80–2, 85 n.20
   approach for   80–2
   Bildung approach to pedagogy for   76–82
   and case for praxis   167–9
   challenges to change their practice   74–5
   co-determination   82
   collectively noticing, practice of   25–7
   Didadtik approach to pedagogy for   76–82
   how of   82
   Pedagogy Parachute for   70–83
   self-determination   82
   self-efficacy   83
   structuring of   24–7
   what of   82
   why of   82
   'yet-to-be' strength of   24
teaching   32
   collaborative   34–5
   as creative process   60–2
   curriculum, 4Cs in   46–7
   draw outside world inward   47–8
   with love   60
   methodologies   18
   versus skydiving   69–70
   tough   46
teamwork   10
technological innovations   124

Theory of Technology (Arthur)   125
Tiatia-Seath, J.   54
'Time to Be Seen' project   127–9
   art - and science - of combination in   134–5
   Covid-19 pandemic and   131–3
   legacy of   133–4
   origins of   127–9
   structure for   129–31
Timperley, H.   172
transformation   10–11
   4C capabilities to   186–7
   courage to   182–4
   definition of   11
   leadership team in   17
   of learning   87–100
   learning to   184–5
   of pedagogy   10, 18, 22–4, 69–83
   processes to   185–6
   structures to   185–6
   of teacher education   165–78
transformation processes of schools
   4Cs approach   3–5, 7–8, 16–28
   coherence makers   4–5, 18–28
   creativity cascade in   106–7
   how   2, 12
   Hurstville Public School (case study)   89–100
   Miranda North Public School, Sydney   16–28
   playground into community garden   16–17
   purpose   3
   shifting school culture   12
   Ulladulla High School (case study)   69–83
transformative praxis
   approach   58–9, 166–9
   in Mitey   58–9
   nature of   58–9
Transforming Education (Jefferson and Anderson)   147, 178
Transforming Schools (Jefferson and Anderson)   72, 167
Tupou, T.   54

Ulacco, Mitch   12, 116
Ulladulla High School (case study)   71–6
   Bildung approach to pedagogy   76–80
   community   71
   Didadtik approach to pedagogy   76–80
   experience with pedagogy   71–4
   overview   71
   Pedagogy Parachute in   71–4
   vision statement for   78
UN Convention on the Rights of Persons with Disabilities   128
unlearning   12

values
   about learning   19
   of agency in learning   19
   of deep learning   19
Visch, Valentijn   133
vision of education   18–20, 75–6
visual art   57
Visual Impairments (VI) apps   124
vulnerability   62–4
Vygotsky, Lev   84 n.5

Wang, Tingting Windy   124
Ward, Martin   135
Webb, Tim   125
Wegner, Etienne   89
Wellbeing Review Tool   55
Wenger, E.   92–4
WHO; *see* World Health Organization (WHO)
whole-school approach   57–8
whole-school mental health education approach   55–6
wisdom   37
Wonder Web   111–12, 143–4, 149–50
Woodson, Jacqueline   34
Worcester community   128–9
Worcester Play Council   126
World Health Organization (WHO)   54
'yet-to-be' strength of teachers   24

Yoo, Noelle   10, 11, 32–5, 38–9
Youth Music Trailblazer's scheme   134

Zhao, Yong   75–6
zone of anxiety   158–9
zone of curiosity   158–9
zone of relaxation   158–9